THE SECRET OF AN EMPRESS

*Countess Zanardi Landi and her Children
Elisabeth-Marie-Christine and Antony-Francis*

THE SECRET OF AN EMPRESS

BY

THE COUNTESS ZANARDI LANDI

WITH ILLUSTRATIONS

Fredonia Books
Amsterdam, The Netherlands

The Secret of an Empress

by
The Countess Zanardi Landi

ISBN: 1-4101-0439-7

Copyright © 2004 by Fredonia Books

Reprinted from the 1915 edition

Fredonia Books
Amsterdam, The Netherlands
http://www.fredoniabooks.com

All rights reserved, including the right to reproduce this book, or portions thereof, in any form.

In order to make original editions of historical works available to scholars at an economical price, this facsimile of the original edition of 1915 is reproduced from the best available copy and has been digitally enhanced to improve legibility, but the text remains unaltered to retain historical authenticity.

PREFACE

Two questions have often been asked me by people who have known part only of my life-story; and it seems to me that before I begin to tell the whole of that story I should do well to answer them. The first question is, Why did the Empress Elisabeth wish to bring me up as she did, away from the Court? The second is, Why does the Emperor Francis-Joseph refuse me recognition?

Why, then, did the Empress bring me up as she did? It is, I suppose, fairly well known that the Court of Vienna is still under the rule of a code of etiquette which dates from the sixteenth century. But I doubt whether more than a very few outside the Court itself realise how crushing the code is. I shall have occasion later to refer to it in some detail, and shall here speak only of that portion of it which concerns the Empress's position. In Austria the sovereign's wife is a person standing entirely by herself. The Emperor himself is above her, and she is not permitted to go to see him as she wishes. There are always the ceremonies of asking permission before a meeting, and of announcing the approach. All the rest of the Court is below the Empress, and not one of her relatives even may see her without obtaining leave some time beforehand, through the Grand Mistress or her deputy.

This may not be considered a great hardship so far as ordinary relatives are concerned, nor indeed anything out of the way in a high rank of society. But, in so far as the rule applies to the intercourse of mother and child, it becomes tragic in its cruelty. Mere archdukes and archduchesses may associate freely with their children, who are of the same status as themselves. The Emperor and Empress, on the other hand, are hedged round with restrictions. This is not the case, so far as I am aware, in any other country than Austria, other empresses and queens having their children's apartments close to their own and spending hours with them daily.

The Empress of Austria is constantly on a pedestal above the rest of the world, and her children are drilled to look upon her in that way. If she should wish to be present at their lessons, there is no such thing for her as going straight to the schoolroom. Her visit must be announced twenty-four hours in advance, teacher and pupils are dressed for the occasion, questions and answers are prepared, and at the end of the visit her Imperial Majesty graciously expresses her satisfaction to the teacher.

The Empress may not even select the persons who are to be about her children, nor the subjects which they are to be taught. She may never have a simple, informal meal with them nor indulge in a ramble with them out of doors. At all times they must remember that they are in the presence of the almost sacred person of the Empress. The inevitable result is that they are really hardly her children at all; neither has the natural affection of a child for its mother any opportunity for development.

Maternal love being the deepest and most unselfish feeling in the world, the imposition of such restraints as these is a cruel outrage. There are some natures which can seek consolation in a frivolous and trivial life; others to which the mere dignity of rank is a solace; and yet others (as is shown in the history of many a hapless Empress of Austria) which can bow down and accept what appears to be a necessity.

PREFACE

My mother, the Empress Elisabeth, belonged to none of these classes. She had an individuality in the fullest sense of the word. She wished to live her life in perfection. The unnatural was as poison to her, the incomplete like a physical defect. In the artificiality of the existence forced upon her, and the impossibility of her accomplishing what she set her hand to, lay the whole tragedy of her soul.

When she would have surrounded her children with her care and interest, they were torn away from her, one to be made wretched and finally destroyed, the others to be reduced to mediocrity. At last, finding how she had been deceived in her hopes about her fourth-born child, Marie-Valerie, she resolved that for once she would have her own way, and that at any rate one of her family should be as she had wished them all to be.

That is why I was brought up as I was, away from the Court.

There remains the other question: Why does the Emperor Francis-Joseph refuse to recognise me?

All I can say is that I do not believe that it is the Emperor himself who refuses. It is the Court of Vienna which looks upon me as dangerous. Having been brought up by my mother in the free and broad-minded ideas of modern education, I must, I suppose, be regarded as a menace to the traditions of the Imperial House, and therefore recognition must be absolutely denied me.

The Emperor, I must point out, is by no means a free agent; and least of all is he free to give scope to the kindness of heart which by nature he possesses. Since the days of his youth, when he was ruled by his mother, the Archduchess Sophia, he has been compelled to yield to the wishes or, I should rather say, the will of others, and has thereby more than once been robbed of his chances of happiness in life.

To-day the Emperor Francis-Joseph is the saddest and most to be pitied figure in modern history through the tragedies which have befallen him. The hapless Maximilian of Mexico was the first victim, immolated by those who wished him away from his Imperial brother's side. The Crown Prince Rudolf was a second victim, under circumstances I shall relate in the course of this book. My mother the Empress was a third victim, martyred because of the freedom of her ideas and her great love of Hungary. Of the recently murdered Archduke Franz-Ferdinand [1] and his consort, it is too early yet to speak with certainty; but the events connected with their burial are sufficient alone to give rise to suspicion of the most serious kind.

And all the time the most unfortunate victim of all has been the Emperor Francis-Joseph, who has lived while others have died.

Only quite recently I have been told that the Emperor shed tears when he learnt that he was not allowed to meet me and my two children. Of children he is very fond, and this in itself is a proof of a kind heart. As for myself, I can but wonder if it is my fate never to meet him. Who can tell?

So my mother's determination to mould the character of at least one of her children involved that I should be born in obscurity. But that very obscurity was light to me. She taught me to realise the beauty of life, and that

[1] The death of the Archduke Franz-Ferdinand, I may say, has changed the situation somewhat for me as well as for the others. Will those members of the family who are faithfully trying to help me succeed now in their endeavours?

PREFACE

there is in life nothing so sorrowful, nothing so unfortunate that I should not be able to see the beautiful side of it. All such things are but incentives for us to strive toward perfection. The effect of her teaching upon me has been enduring. More and more every day I feel that in the extraordinary existence which has been mine there must be some definite purpose. The experiences through which I have gone, in the comparatively short space of thirty-two years, experiences sufficient for three lives of many people, must have been imposed upon me to enable me to accomplish a mission. And to open the way for my fulfilment of that mission I have now written this book.

C. F. M. Zanardi Landi

CONTENTS

CHAPTER		PAGE
I	My Birth	1
II	Some Early Impressions	6
III	A Home of My Own	12
IV	My Mother Is the Empress	17
V	Elisabeth of Austria	28
VI	Frau von Friese	46
VII	Summer Holidays	61
VIII	I Go to School	70
IX	An Accident; and a Visit to the Riviera	77
X	How a Holiday Was Spoilt	90
XI	Professor Kraus	101
XII	Some Happy Times; and the Professor's Diary	112
XIII	Confidences	132
XIV	Ludwig of Bavaria	140
XV	My "Military Year"; and First Love	156
XVI	Plans for My Future	168
XVII	The Course of Love	178
XVIII	A Tyrolese Holiday	196
XIX	A Thunderbolt	201
XX	Mayerling	207
XXI	After Mayerling	236
XXII	I Go Under Fire	249
XXIII	The End of Love's Young Dream	261
XXIV	Our Last Days Together	273
XXV	The Hand of Fate	281
XXVI	Alone in the World	290
	Epilogue	296

ILLUSTRATIONS

COUNTESS ZANARDI LANDI AND HER CHILDREN, ELISABETH-
MARIE-CHRISTINE AND ANTONY-FRANCIS . . *Frontispiece*
(*From a photograph by Van Dyck, Ltd., London.*)

COUNTESS ZANARDI LANDI WHEN A CHILD 12

HER BIRTHPLACE, CHÂTEAU D'SASSETOT 12

EMPRESS ELISABETH OF AUSTRIA 36

KING LUDWIG II, OF BAVARIA 142

BARONESS MARIE VETSERA 208

CROWN PRINCE RUDOLF 208
(*From a water-color miniature.*)

MAYERLING 208

CROWN PRINCE RUDOLF 230

CROWN PRINCE RUDOLF AND HIS FIANCÉE, PRINCESS STEPH-
ANIE OF BELGIUM 230

EMPEROR FRANCIS-JOSEPH 230
(*From a photograph by Stanley & Co., London.*)

ARCHDUCHESS ISABELLA, ARCHDUCHESS MARIE-JOSEPHA,
ARCHDUCHESS MARIE-VALERIE, AND ARCHDUKE FERDI-
NAND-KARL 244
(*From a photograph by Stanley & Co., London.*)

ARCHDUKE KARL-FRANZ-JOSEPH AND THE ARCHDUCHESS
ZITA 246

ARCHDUKE FRANZ-FERDINAND AND FAMILY 246
(*From a photograph by Stanley & Co., London.*)

THE SECRET OF AN EMPRESS

CHAPTER I

MY BIRTH

I WAS born in 1882, at the château of Sassetot, near Petites-Dalles, in the department of Seine-Inférieure, Normandy. I have never seen the place again since my earliest days, and can give no description of it. With regard to the circumstances of my birth, naturally, the little that I know is learnt from others. I therefore give the details with all reserve, though I have endeavoured as far as possible to test their accuracy by comparison and inquiry.

Semi-officially it was given out that my mother, the Empress of Austria, had met with an accident while out riding. The Emperor Francis-Joseph came secretly to see her, his presence in Normandy at the time being known at the Elysée but concealed carefully in all other quarters. My mother herself had been living at Petites-Dalles under her incognita of the Countess Hohenembs. What passed between her and the Emperor now will never be revealed. A few weeks later, when my mother was restored to health, I had to undertake a long journey — the first of the many long journeys which have been mine in this life. I travelled from Normandy to Vienna.

Foremost in the party was Professor Karl Braun von Fernwald, my mother's physician, a stout friendly man, who had not only assisted to bring me into this world of sorrow, but had also undertaken the responsibility for all arrangements during the opening years of my life. Then there were the Countess Goëss, one of my mother's most intimate women-friends; Aloïs Pirker, who was to be for so many years to come my faithful head-servant; and finally, Theresa Schedivi, my nurse, a Bohemian by race.

The first thing necessary for me in Vienna was a home. As it was my mother's intention to bring me up in perfect secrecy, but not to train me for a life of obscurity when I should be grown up, the task was no easy one. She had particularly expressed her objection to putting me into some aristocratic family in Vienna having a footing at Court, for it would be impossible for such people to keep the secret to themselves. Moreover, the control of the clergy in those circles is complete, and it was her fixed intention that I should not be exposed to undue clerical influence. Prominent Austrian families outside Vienna were also considered unsafe. The instructions given to Professor Braun had been short and unmistakable. I was to be placed with strangers in some well-educated, cultured, and refined family of standing in the place from which they came, but unknown in Vienna.

So it came about that I was taken to the house of Mr. and Mrs. Kaiser, both great friends of Professor Braun, and especially the wife. The Kaisers moved in good circles in Berlin, where the husband had been manager of the Deutsche Bank. But they were not known in Vienna when they arrived, and therefore answered my mother's requirements excellently well. It has occurred to me in later years that the name of Kaiser was in itself a lucky coincidence, for even did I overhear as a child such expressions as "Kaiserliche Mutter, Kaiserliches Kind" (Imperial mother, Imperial child), they were nothing more to

MY BIRTH

me, before I reached years of sufficient discretion to share the secret with her, than plays upon words, and gave no hint of my mother's exalted rank.

It cannot have been an easy task to introduce my infant person into the Kaiser household, and quite a comedy seems to have been played for the purpose. After due preparations, Mrs. Kaiser was suddenly taken ill. Her children had already been sent out with their French *bonne*. The servants were now all hurriedly despatched on various missions — one to fetch the midwife, who lived at a distance, another for Professor Braun, and yet another for Mr. Kaiser, who "very unfortunately" happened to be out at the time. Imagine the amazement of the whole household, when at length they returned, to hear that in the meanwhile poor Mrs. Kaiser had given birth to a little girl, only the nurse, that clever Theresa Schedivi, having been present at the important moment!

In this way was I born a second time.

My earliest recollections of childhood are bright and fair. I lived with my foster-parents in a fine suite of rooms at No. 5, Opernring, near the Imperial Opera House. On the first floor was the business of Frau Caroline Brayer, my mother's dressmaker. The suite above had been expressly taken to enable my mother to come to see me without difficulty or suspicion. It was at the time one of the finest suites of its kind in Vienna. To those unacquainted with the city it may appear strange that fine rooms like these should be located over a dressmaker's establishment, but Vienna is an exceptional place in this respect. It has no particular residential quarter, no particular business centre, no special characteristics in its different parts. One wealthy man, for instance, might live in Section No. 3, and his equally wealthy friend in Section No. 18, at the other end of the city; and a foreigner coming to Vienna on business might have three addresses at which to call, one in the third, another in the sixth, and another in the eleventh section, so that he would have to take half a day over what in London or New York would take him half an hour.

Everybody in the home in the Opernring was kind and good to me, and I was surrounded by all that the heart of a child could desire. Certainly no child living could have had a larger and pleasanter nursery than I had, nor more beautiful dolls and amusing toys. And if I broke my toys or ill-treated my dolls, no one grumbled at me for doing so. Nor yet was I elaborately dressed or annoyed with a multiplicity of frills and ribbons, such as vex the souls and bodies of some little unfortunates and put them in perpetual terror of "spoiling their clothes." There was nothing to be spoilt about my plain little white frocks.

Sometimes, however, I was dressed up in more than usual splendour. Then I always knew that I was going to see that day a beautiful, tall lady. I was very shy in the presence of this lady, although she kissed and caressed me again and again when she paid her visits to us.

Although Mrs. Kaiser was tall and elegant, the visitor appeared even more so, probably because she was slimmer. Her voice was low and melodious, giving to me at least the impression that she could never be cross or angry or unkind. Somehow this only made me the more timid. The lady also seemed rather embarrassed, as though she were at a loss what to say to the child whom she only saw at infrequent intervals. Another thing which contributed to my feeling of awe was the very profound bow with which Mrs. Kaiser always received the lady, for she was

MY BIRTH

not one who usually put herself out, and at all other times was herself the person who received the most respect in the whole household.

All that I have told hitherto concerning my personal recollections is hazy and indefinite in my mind. I move in memory like a traveller making his way through a dark and heavy night. I have to rack my brain to seize upon anything vivid enough to be put into words. But now events begin to grow more distinct. My road lies before me with increasing clearness to the end — to that sad end of another's life, which brought such sorrow upon mine and left me to face the world all alone.

CHAPTER II

SOME EARLY IMPRESSIONS

In the autumn of 1888, when I was six years of age, I lived awhile (for the first time since my birth as far as I know) under the same roof as my mother. Although I was unaware of it at the time, the place in which we stayed was the château of Lainz, originally a hunting-box in the neighbourhood of Vienna, which she had bought from its owner and transformed into a beautiful home for herself. On my arrival here my mother said to me: "Weiberl,[1] now you are going to stay with mother for a time. You will love me very much, won't you, darling?"

I did not understand, for up to then I had always called her *Tante Elly* ("Aunt Elly"), so I looked at her without speaking, my heart beating fast, and began to cry. My childish mind could not grasp the idea of having another mother besides Mrs. Kaiser, to whom I was then very attached, although she spent but little of her time with me or her own children. Perhaps, in a way, this was only an additional reason for my fondness. Anyhow, she often brought home boxes of sweets for us, and that, of course, is a ready road to a child's sympathy.

My real mother, however, as now I learnt her to be, knew so well how to win my heart that I soon lost my shyness, and before many days had passed every other person was put quite in the background. And didn't I have

---

[1] "Little woman." This is an affectionate diminutive used in Austria, and was my mother's most usual form of address to me. I have for that reason kept it untranslated in this book.

a splendid time with her! Just imagine for a moment how delightful it was to sit on her lap every morning, while another lady, dressed in black silk and a white apron, stood for hours brushing and combing her beautiful hair. All the time she would enthral my soul with stories of Cinderella, Little Red Riding-hood, and the like. Still better did I love her singing, and how often would I beg, " Mummy, dear, sing me ' Wenn I komm, wenn I komm ' (' When I come ') ! " And when she had sung that twice or more, she must go on to something else, generally Schubert's " Lindenbaum," every shade and emotion of which was so faultlessly rendered that even I, small child as I was, was deeply moved.

But so quick to change is the mind of children that, I remember, some article upon the dressing-table would suddenly attract my attention and grow infinitely desirable in my eyes — a small crystal bottle, it might be, a little silver box, some exquisite toilet-tray; or perhaps only a flower in one of the ever-filled vases, a few violets or some rare mountain blossom. Then, without the slightest apology or excuse, I would slip off her knees and straightway go towards the object of my desire, sometimes so impatient that I would not wait till the song was finished. But my loving mother had nothing but smiles for this ill behaviour, and would call me back and cover me with kisses. Neither did she become cross when one morning I spilled almost the entire contents of one of her perfume bottles, intending to put some on myself. And it was her favourite scent, too — expressly made up for her — a mixture of roses, violets, and amber.

Every day we went out for a walk in the park. At that time I used to turn in my toes — a habit which was a source of much annoyance to my mother, who was a remarkable walker and famous for her elegant carriage. She would always be saying to me, " Come now; walk like a soldier! One, two; one, two."

During this visit she also tried to teach me dancing, in the learning of which I displayed considerable aptitude, as I had not only a good ear for music but also took delight in exercise. By her special order, when I returned to my foster-parents' home I received regular lessons from a Madame Crombé.

In the winter after this visit an event took place which was the means of turning my growing love for my mother almost to veneration. It was a grey, foggy day in January, 1889, about two o'clock in the afternoon. I had just finished dinner and was in the nursery with the nurse and Laura, my little foster-sister, who was the nearest in age to me of the Kaiser children. Probably we were dressing to go out; I do not remember distinctly. Suddenly Mrs. Kaiser's maid rushed into the room.

"The Crown Prince has been shot . . . killed!" she cried in a terrified voice.

"Not killed," said the nurse incredulously. "You must mean wounded."

The Crown Prince was so extremely popular, so beloved by his subjects, that she could hardly credit the news of his death.

"No, no; dead — quite dead," persisted the maid.

These words impressed me as they would have done any other child. How could I have foreseen what in after years this would mean to me? After this, nothing more was said upon the subject to me for days. Had I not seen the black flags in the streets and the general mourning, I should have forgotten all about it at once.

SOME EARLY IMPRESSIONS

But this was merely the preface to what was to come; and that I recall more clearly than anything else in childhood. Several days afterwards my nurse dressed me in a white frock with a black cashmere sash. This struck me as a strange proceeding. The black sash oppressed and bewildered me, for I had never worn black before. In reply to my question why I must wear this I received the answer, "Don't you know everybody is in mourning for the Crown Prince?"

When all were ready, I drove with my nurse and Pirker in a carriage to a great palace, which I afterwards learnt to be the Hofburg. Here we got out, and my nurse and I passed through a long white vestibule, carpeted with red velvet; then up a big marble staircase, through several large rooms, all richly furnished, coming finally to a drawing-room, where my nurse pushed me gently forward through the door. I thought her behind me still, but on turning my head found that I was alone and that the door had closed. I was dismayed at my loneliness in the strange room, but on recovering from the agitation of the first moments I perceived a dark figure lying on a sofa. How it startled me! Was this my mother, all in black clothes and looking as pale as wax? Her figure seemed shrunken to half its size, a shadow of her former self, almost ghostlike. Never afterwards did I see her looking like that. She did not rise to greet me, as she ordinarily would have done, but held out her arms weakly and feebly to me. I felt that something terrible must have happened, and in spite of my fright ran towards her, clasping my arms around her neck. What followed made an ineffaceable impression upon my mind. My poor mother hid her face upon my little shoulder, while for a moment her whole body quivered with heart-breaking sobs. They pierced my very soul, and caused me to remain perfectly silent, trembling with emotion.

When at last she could control her voice, she begged me not to let anyone know, not to tell even the Kaisers, about her weeping like this. I did my best to comfort her, and she cried, in words that I remember so well, "Oh, you darling little woman, if I could only have you with me, it would be so much easier to bear!"

Could I not come very often to see her? I asked. But she said she must go away again, for she was obliged to travel to Budapest.

I would have loved to say, "Take me with you, mother," but I did not dare.

A few days after this she came to see me at my guardians' home. She was still very pale and sad, but did not cry, and, young as I was, I could feel that her heart would have ached less if she only could have done so.

Still another impression of this period remains in my mind. One night, about twelve o'clock, I was awakened by the sound of horse-hoofs in the street and an unusual stir in our house. I jumped out of bed and rushed to the window, where, spellbound, I watched mounted soldiers filing like phantoms before the house — their long black cloaks shrouding the horses and leaving little of the animals visible but their feet. The gas-lamps in the streets had all had their tops removed, and with their torch-like flames illuminated in a most impressive, and really quite ghostly, way the sombre cavalcade. It was the escort bearing the body of the Crown Prince from Mayerling to Vienna. This apparition passed with extreme rapidity, and but for the vividness with which it was imprinted upon my memory, might have seemed but a dream of the night.

SOME EARLY IMPRESSIONS 11

For a long time after this I could not recover my childish cheerfulness. Although I told no one, at night I remained with wide-open eyes, staring into the darkness, while cold drops of perspiration covered my forehead. These strange events completely confused my mind. The ghastly cavalcade haunted me. Why did mamma wear so much deeper mourning than "Mimeli" (this was the name I now called my foster-mother), who also wore black, like the rest of the people? Why was she so deeply grieved, while "Mimeli" was quite cheerful again? I could not fathom the mystery; yet, strange to say, I was perfectly convinced that my mother's sorrow could spring from no other source than the death of the Crown Prince. Of this I shall have more to say later.

CHAPTER III

A HOME OF MY OWN

IN the year whose early weeks witnessed the events described in the last chapter, a change was made in my surroundings, and my little household (if I may call it by such a name) was increased in size. First came the installation of an English nurse, Miss Ives, who was also entrusted with the care of Laura Kaiser. Soon after the appointment, however, trouble arose. Miss Ives had occasion once to punish Laura for stamping her foot, which she did by striking the offender across the legs with a strap. Upon this Laura rebelled, biting Miss Ives severely on the hand. The English governess at once tendered her resignation. This was not accepted, for she was in possession of my mother's secret, and was, moreover, much trusted by her. Unfortunately for myself, as will be seen, I was of much less warlike a nature than my foster-sister, and so Miss Ives was prevailed upon to continue in charge of me, provided that Laura's nursery and mine were entirely separated. This gave my mother a long-desired opportunity of making an alteration in my place of residence, so as to bring me nearer to her. In the course of a few weeks I was taken away from the Kaisers' house and installed in a home of my own, with me going Miss Ives, a French governess called Mademoiselle Pidon, who had been engaged by Mrs. Kaiser to superintend my education, Aloïs Pirker, and some women-servants.

My new home was at Lainz, not then, as it is now, a

Countess Zanardi Landi when a Child

Her Birthplace, Château d' Sassetot

A HOME OF MY OWN

suburb of Vienna. Here I had been before. But this time it was not in my mother's château that I lived. A house near by had been taken for me, a two-story building in the middle of a fine park, within whose bounds I took my walks. On the ground floor was the hall, a big sitting-room, a dining-room, a study for me, and a small drawing-room for my governess. On the first floor were the bedrooms of my governess, my nurse, and Pirker; and my own bedroom, which, to my great vexation, was called the nursery. This was a huge, bright room, decorated entirely in white, the furniture as well as the walls, while over the floor extended a dark blue carpet. The atmosphere of the whole house was peculiar, arising partly, no doubt, from the absence of an affectionate personal presence in control, and partly from the fact that it was wholly a child's establishment. All provisions for comfort — nay, for luxury — were there; but everything was subordinated to the ideas of discipline and instruction. In fact, it was a superior educational institution, not a home. The actual mistress of all was Miss Ives, in spite of Mademoiselle Pidon, in spite of old Pirker. Mademoiselle willingly let Miss Ives have the reins of the whole household, for it meant to her relief from certain responsibilities and the lessening of a restraint which she was unwilling to endure. Pirker, the valet, on the other hand, gave a grudging consent, being sufficiently philosophical to know that a woman always has the last word.

Under Miss Ives's rule I was forced to arise at 6.30 in the morning, winter or summer. She would come to the bed in which I slept, and, tearing off the coverings, would cry in her abrupt manner, " It 's half-past six — get up! " at the same time shaking me by the arm and giving me no opportunity to go to sleep again. Only half awake, I would creep to my *prie-dieu,* and, kneeling mechanically before it, murmur my morning prayers. Her régime was probably designed for my good, but I certainly did not appreciate it then. Her method of punishment showed to my childish mind a refinement of cruelty. I was compelled to be present at the selection and purchase of the whips which were afterwards to be used on me. I can see now that it was not intentional cruelty, but she had been trained in a school where implicit obedience was exacted, and where the slightest lapse was severely punished. Hence she could never see that a rule might sometimes be relaxed with advantage. So I lived in daily fear. Never did I dare to tell anyone of my sufferings, being afraid of further punishment, and thinking, in my childish foolishness, that my mother both knew and approved of the methods employed. Far from intervening, Mademoiselle frequently seconded Miss Ives. Thus my share of correction was doubled. I was punished not only when Miss Ives found me in fault, but also when Mademoiselle reported to her some childish misdemeanour. In fact, my French governess was by far the more culpable, being lazy as well as deceitful. While in the absence of my mother and foster-parents she had not a kind word for me, in their presence she would show the utmost solicitude for my welfare. This, coupled with the natural deference and reserve of Miss Ives, combined to give those who were primarily interested in my training, and especially my mother, a totally wrong impression of the discipline to which I was subjected. The servants, including Pirker, dared not lift a voice in my favour, Miss Ives being all-powerful.

My mother had expressed the desire that my education should be both comprehensive and systematic. To this end I was placed under the care of Herr Hans Hold, Laura's tutor. As it was considered inadvisable that he should visit me in my own establishment, I drove three times a week in my carriage, accompanied by Pirker, to the home of the Kaisers. Here I was supposed to spend two hours receiving lessons in the elementary subjects. But my actual instruction under this otherwise estimable teacher failed utterly to meet my mother's orders. Herr Hold gave me long exercises without bestowing much attention to their explanation. Many subjects were entirely neglected. For example, he taught me arithmetic for months and months, until suddenly it dawned upon him that grammar had not been touched, when he entirely abandoned arithmetic and devoted his time to grammar. This is typical of his educational methods. Laura Kaiser's presence, too, was a considerable handicap. She often failed to prepare her lessons. On such occasions she would say to her mother, "Oh, mother, do bring in something nice for Herr Hold to-day, so that he will not scold me for not doing my work!" And the indulgent Mrs. Kaiser would always enter the room, soon after the tutor's arrival, with a silver tray of cakes and liqueurs, and would stay chatting with him for a time, so that Laura might escape the penalty of her neglect of work.

In addition to Herr Hold as a tutor, I had Father Lambertus, a Jesuit, for religious instruction, and for the piano Frau Louise Hoffmann, professor at the Vienna Conservatorium.

On the whole, my life at this period was monotonous and lonely. I never met any children besides Laura, except sometimes in the spring, when I went with her and her governess to the Volksgarten and played there for a few hours with other little girls. It happened that we met there several times Julie and Marie, the daughters of Prince Montenuovo,[1] who were about our own age. As soon as my mother heard of this new acquaintance, however, she put an end to it, forbidding all further intercourse for fear of gossip.

My summers still continued, after the setting-up of my establishment at Lainz, to be spent in the company of my foster-parents. My nurse and governess were then away on their holidays, and in consequence life was much pleasanter for me.

[1] Alfred, Prince of Montenuovo, now Chief Grand Chamberlain of the Imperial Court. He is the grandson of the Archduchess Marie-Louise by Adam, Count Neipperg. Their son, William-Adalbert, was created Prince of Montenuovo in 1864 and married a daughter of Count Batthyany. The Neippergs do not recognise the Montenuovos as a branch of their family, not being proud of the connection between Count Adam and Marie-Louise during the life of the Emperor Napoleon.

CHAPTER IV

MY MOTHER IS THE EMPRESS

It was when I was about nine years of age that the strangeness of my position began to impress itself upon me with an insistency that was not far from a pain. The problems that presented themselves to my undeveloped mind were terribly baffling — the fact that I had two mothers and two homes, the long absences of her whom I knew to be my real mother, the secrecy of her comings and goings, the deference shown to her by Mrs. Kaiser, the profound respect of all my household for her, my own secluded life. What did all these things mean?

Again, why must I not tell people that my beautiful, adorable mother was really my mother? Why must I always say that "Mimeli" was my mother? Certainly I was very fond of "Mimeli," but it was with an affection that was being rapidly obscured by the ever-growing love — or rather worship — for the real mother whom now I saw so seldom. These questions haunted my waking hours with increasing persistence, and resulted eventually in a chronic state of mental unrest for me. "Whom can I ask to explain things to me?" I was always demanding of myself. I did not dare to ask any of the members of the little household at Lainz, and besides these, who was there who could inform me? Not Laura, for she knew no more than myself. Not her mother, who would certainly have evaded the question or prevaricated.

There was my beloved mother, my own real mother,

to whom I longed to unburden my heart. She was the one who must be able to set all my doubts at rest. How I thirsted to ask her to explain everything to me — to tell me why I could not always be at her side. But the fear of making her sad tied my tongue whenever I was near her. During her absence I fully made up my mind to question her; as soon as she came back it was always the same — I dared not speak. Even on her return from Egypt, in the latter part of November, 1891, after an unusually prolonged absence, I could not find courage to put questions to her. So the golden opportunity passed once more, and my problems were still unsolved. But now, soon after this, a train of incidents occurred which braced up my resolution and determined me to beg for the truth from my mother, even at the expense of her feelings.

I had always been accustomed to spend my Christmas holidays at the home of my foster-parents, and to receive my presents there. In this year 1891, however, for the first time in my life, mother had a Christmas tree for me in my own home; but on the twenty-third, not on the twenty-fourth, as is customary in Austria. At the lighting up of the tree only Laura and myself were present with my mother. Needless to say, our gifts were very splendid. In spite of this, the celebration troubled my mind and increased my suspicions. Why had our Christmas been celebrated a day in advance instead of on the twenty-fourth, like all other people's? The fact that only Laura and myself were present, instead of the whole household, did not tend to allay my curiosity. My final feeling was one of disappointment.

Of course, it is quite clear, really, why my mother moved the festival forward one day. It would have been impossible for her to absent herself from the Court on this evening of universal celebration, when the kindred of the Emperor, consisting of my sister Marie-Valerie and her husband the Archduke Francis-Salvator, the widow of the Crown Prince and his little daughter Elisabeth, and other members of the Imperial Family assembled at Schönbrunn, the summer castle of the Emperor. Moreover, it was my mother's own birthday, which naturally made her the central figure of the festivities.

Mother's long-continued absence after the Christmas tree at Lainz, coupled with my intense desire to speak to her, made me keep asking the time of her return. I knew she was in Vienna, for otherwise she would not have failed to bid me good-bye. My unceasing requests finally led Mademoiselle to tell me that she was ill, and could not come to see me. Then, of course, I wanted to go to her. Upon this Mademoiselle only scolded, telling me not to make such a silly and impossible request. On my demanding to know why it was impossible, she ordered me not to worry her. Naturally I was desperate, but through fear of punishment I kept silence thereafter. I learned in later years that what had happened was this. First, mother herself was ill and was confined to her bed for nearly a month. Then my sister Marie-Valerie, almost immediately after the birth of her first child, had a bad attack of pneumonia. As soon as mother was able to go out again she came to see me, but owing to her anxiety about my sister her visits were very short ones. What little time she had to spare was not, as usually before, spent alone with me but in the presence of my nurse and governess, so that private conversation was impossible. The whole month of February passed in this unsatisfactory fashion. On March 1st mother set out in her yacht for Corfu; and I, none the wiser, was again left alone.

For a while my mind was more than ever in a state of confusion and perplexity. Then the unexpected happened. The thoughtless words of a couple of servants, overheard by accident, revealed the mystery to me with startling clearness. Does chance actually help us sometimes when we are in distress, or is it we who seek chance? The latter is more probable, for we take notice of incidents which before escaped our observation. Perhaps rather by instinct than of set intention, I listened more to what was spoken around me. Now it happened that my photograph had been taken a short time previously, and a copy of it stood on my governess's writing-table, in the drawing-room adjoining my study. I was sitting as usual one morning, when a few words from the other room caught my ear — and all of a sudden my attention was enchained. The voices were those of my nurse, Miss Ives, and of an old servant Pepi, who was sweeping out the room. As the door was ajar, I could hear every word distinctly.

"Oh, miss, isn't it a nice photo of our little Princess?"

"Princess! What Princess? What do you mean by using such a title?"

"Now, miss," replied the old servant's slow, drawling voice, "do you take me for a fool? Do you think I don't know that she has a right to it? She is a 'Kaiserliches Kind' (Imperial child), and I consider it a cruel shame to keep anyone's rights away from them."

It really must have been a great effort for Miss Ives to refrain from raising her voice to the pitch customary with her in moments of extreme agitation or excitement. But she simply said: "Sh — sh! stop that nonsense! It is none of your business. You will bring trouble and disgrace upon us all."

The old woman, however, was obstinate and garrulous. She would not hold her tongue. She was neither a fool, she protested, nor one of those interested people who were always in terror of losing a good job. But she had too much love and veneration for the good Empress to wish to bring harm upon her.

"Be quiet — I insist upon it!" cried Miss Ives suddenly; and, without giving the other a chance of further words, she hurried out of the room.

My brain was in a perfect whirl. There was a roaring in my ears like the pounding of the surf upon the shore. Incredulity, amazement, and a realisation of the truth succeeded one another in my mind in great waves, as the full force of what I had overheard burst upon me. Then came a feeling of pure, intense joy, such as I have never experienced before or since. Now I understood everything — or, at least, at that moment I thought I understood everything. A thousand impressions passed through my mind. So then, really, my beloved mother was the Empress, and I was her child. And, of course, if my mother was the Empress, my father must be the Emperor. Why had I never seen him? What was the meaning of all this secrecy? If my parents were the Emperor and the Empress, I must be a princess. How funny — I a princess! I had imagined a princess to be a very different kind of a person from what I was.

Day after day passed after this without my being able to answer satisfactorily the accumulating questions. I always returned finally to the same conclusion: that to my mother, and to her alone, must I talk about this. But she was still in Corfu, and I was obliged to wait patiently for her return. But, as everything comes to one who waits, so at last the long-looked-for day arrived in May, 1892.

She seemed to me, if possible, even lovelier than before. I did what I had never ventured to do hitherto, and threw both my arms spontaneously about her neck, as if to assure myself that I really had the right to this privilege. On her side it seemed to make her happy that I had at last overcome all my shyness in her presence. After our first tender greetings, she seated herself in an armchair in the large drawing-room, while I took a footstool at her feet. Full of anxious questioning, I looked deep into her eyes, while my heart beat so hard that it seemed almost to suffocate me. I did not know how to begin. At last, with a great effort, I forced out a few words — something like, "Oh, mamma dear, I do love you so much!"

She did not fail to notice my extraordinary embarrassment, and grew alarmed. "Weiberl, darling," she asked, "what is the matter? Why are you trembling like this?"

The excitement was too much for me. I forgot all the resolutions I had made to keep calm, and burst into tears, though I could have given no reason for those tears. In a few moments I regained my self-control and raised my head. Only then did I notice how deathly pale my mother was, and how vainly she tried to conceal her agitation with a smile. She urged me that she, my mother, was the last person in the world of whom I ought to feel afraid; and as she spoke her sweet voice had a magical effect upon me. Slowly I began to tell her how I had been tortured by doubts for months past, and how, as my perplexity increased, I became more and more convinced that the only way was to talk to her.

Here, I suppose, I hesitated; but my mother divined

the rest. She knew that I had found out who she was. So without further difficulty I was able to tell her how unexpectedly the truth had been revealed. But unfortunately her time was so limited that all too soon she rose to go. Bidding me an even more affectionate good-bye than usual, she departed, promising to come again to see me the following week.

As she went out, it is probable that she rebuked my governess and nurse for having failed to gain my confidence; for about half an hour after her departure both rushed into the study. "Ah! petite misérable!" screamed Mademoiselle, stepping towards me, "we will teach you to listen at the doors and gossip afterwards!"

Too much astonished to move, I stood staring at them, knowing myself innocent of having done them any harm. But before I could recover from my amazement, both women threw themselves on me like two furies, and punished me unmercifully. They were two grown-ups against one child, and for the time being I could do nothing but submit.

To the great surprise of myself and the household, on the following day mother came again quite unexpectedly. This had been made possible by the postponement for a week of a proposed visit from my sister Gisela, with her two daughters from Munich. Immediately upon her arrival she rushed into my study, instead of waiting, as had hitherto been her custom, for me to come to her in the drawing-room. The result of my punishment on the previous day was that I certainly could not walk with the ordinary ease and activity of a child. She noticed at once, and cried in alarm, "Whatever is the matter with you?"

My answer was to kiss her hands, and seeing now that I was going to be avenged on my tormentors, I smiled, in spite of my pain. I told her of the cruelties which my nurse and governess had inflicted upon me, and how I foolishly had thought until now that she would not be angry with them about it. She listened indignantly, saying that now she understood why I had always been so reserved and nervous in her presence. She made me describe to her everything, and as she heard the details of my misery, physical and mental, during the past years, she hid her face in her hands. "Oh, what did I intend to do," she moaned, "and what have I succeeded in doing up to now?"

Of the conversation which followed I cannot, of course, assert that I am able to give the exact words. But it was the longest and most impressive conversation which up to this time I had ever had with my mother, and much of it seems even now fixed in my memory. It gave a direction to my steps, a mould to my character, so that I have indeed reason to remember it. With the infinite gentleness and sweetness that were all her own, my mother gave me to understand that from now onwards she wished us to work hand in hand. Her desire was to make a capable woman of me, a person who could accomplish something, not a mere useless doll. She aroused, as she spoke, the thoughts which up to then had only hazily crossed and recrossed my brain. Suddenly I realised why I had felt so much pleasure in learning that I was the daughter of an Empress: that it was not out of idle vanity, but because I saw that my exalted position would help me to do good in the world. The offer to work hand in hand with me made me truly proud and happy. The melancholy life which I had been forced to lead had matured my mind out of due season. Thus the words with which I answered were perfectly sincere, which is doubtless the

reason why they have not faded from my recollection.
"You will lead me, mamma, won't you? I will follow you, as if blindfolded, every step of the way. If sometimes I fail, spur me on by reminding me of the promise which I have given you to-day."

At these words my mother's face lighted up with joy. "You have given me to-day," she said, "the first real pleasure I have felt for many years, and now I believe that some Power above must have suggested my course of action to me."

I did not understand, and my eyes looked a mute inquiry.

"Are you not curious to know why I keep you here all alone?" she asked.

I was to learn so much that I wanted to learn, and the thought gave me courage indeed. I broke out into eager questionings. Why was there all this secrecy? Had I any brothers and sisters? Why was I not with them? Why was I brought up in this solitary fashion?

At this flood of queries my mother grew first red and then pale. She answered somewhat sadly: "That, darling, is a sad story which at present you are almost too young to hear. But I will tell you as much of it as I can now." And then she explained to me for the first time why she had kept me hidden away from nearly all the world. She had married when she was very young — only a little more than sixteen years old. When her first little baby was born they had taken it away from her, saying that she was not old enough to take care of it herself. This was my eldest sister, Sophie, who died when she was only two years old. Another little girl, Gisela, was born, and then a little boy. These two children they also took away from her.

Many years passed, and then there came yet another girl, Valerie. This time, perhaps because she was now older, they had given her permission to take the child's education into her own hands, and she felt very happy. Valerie was a dear, intelligent little creature, and she conceived great hopes about her. But gradually the realisation dawned upon her that her independence in the matter of even this child's education was only a pretended one. She had not really the right of choosing those whom she wished to have about Valerie, but was restricted to a selection from among the names on a list submitted to her.

Even this might have been endured, had she not been forced to come to the conclusion that any girl brought up in the uniform, systematic manner of the archduchesses of the Imperial family could never become any other than a common, everyday princess, with no experience of real life, no breadth of views, no deep feelings, and with a more or less selfish heart. Once more she was bitterly disappointed. " Then other years passed," she said, " and you came."

She remained silent for some moments. Then in the quick, impatient manner so characteristic of her, she continued: " This time I did not intend to be made their dupe! " She drew me towards her and whispered eagerly: " You were to be my vengeance for all the wrongs which they had inflicted upon me. I wanted you entirely for my own, not with a selfish mother's love, but that I might preserve you from the useless and dangerous life of Courts, because I did not wish you to be an empty-headed, empty-hearted princess. Never forget this, that I want one day to show the world through you that to be born a princess does not only bring with it the privilege of being flattered by a vain crowd of courtiers, but brings, too, the necessity of carrying a heavy burden and the ability to carry it."

With these words she rose from her seat, and so did I. Putting her arm around my shoulders, she made me take a few turns up and down the room. Suddenly she stopped, and in a very serious voice begged me to keep all that we had discussed together a secret between ourselves alone. And whatever we might talk of together in the future I must always remember to keep to myself, unless I had special permission from her to mention it to others. If I forgot this, I might inflict upon her the most cruel sufferings.

Our conversation had lasted for a long time, during which I had entirely forgotten my surroundings. My mother called me back to the world by saying: —

"Now we must finish the business here. You are a clever girl, so you can drive alone with Pirker to the Kaisers. And you will tell Mrs. Kaiser that Mademoiselle and your nurse beat you so cruelly last night that you are still suffering from the effects. Tell her that yesterday we had talked together longer than usual, and that they suspected you had at last told me all about their ill-treatment of you; that to-day my unexpected visit was the real cause of my learning all about it. Tell her that they are to keep you until further orders from me. Neither Mademoiselle nor Miss Ives are to be admitted to their house. I will send them full instructions, at latest by to-morrow night."

As soon as my mother had left me — which was almost immediately — the maid put a few things in a valise for me, and together with Pirker we drove to my guardians' house. What happened to my two tormentors I do not know. I never saw either of them again.

CHAPTER V

ELISABETH OF AUSTRIA

AT this point in my story it seems a fitting opportunity to turn aside from the direct narrative and devote a few pages to that sweet and gracious woman to whom I owe my birth, my upbringing, and most of the happiest memories of my life. Much has been written about the Empress Elisabeth of Austria since the fatal day in September, 1898, when the assassin's hand struck her down — much that is foolish, much that is malicious, and more still that is false. For the most part the inventions of the various writers have gone without challenge; or if they have been challenged the world has been as careless as it usually is in such matters, and falsehood has continued to spread its poison nevertheless. I wish in this book, to the best of my poor ability, to vindicate my mother's name from the charges which malice or ignorance, or the two combined, have brought against her. If I can do so, I shall, I know, discharge but a minute portion of the debt which I owe her. But even that small payment will be a satisfaction to me.

Elisabeth-Amalia-Eugénie was the second daughter and third child of Maximilian, Duke of Bavaria, and the Princess Ludovica, second daughter of King Maximilian (Joseph) I of Bavaria.[1] By this marriage, the Royal and ducal lines of the Wittelsbachs in Bavaria were reunited, having separated in the seventeenth century — the

[1] The children of Duke Maximilian and his wife Ludovica were eight in

ELISABETH OF AUSTRIA 29

Royal house springing from Christian II, Count Palatine, and the ducal house from his younger brother, Johann-Karl, Count Palatine. As is probably well known, the Wittelsbachs are a noble family of great antiquity. They trace themselves back to an ancestor in the tenth century, though the royalty of their senior branch dates only from the time of Napoleon, who rewarded his ally Duke Maximilian-Joseph by making him King Maximilian I of Bavaria.

Much has been written about the Wittelsbach family, their degeneracy and eccentricity, and the story of their later representatives has been used to point a moral as to the evil of consanguineous marriages. But it seems to me that the talk about " inbreeding " is a very great exaggeration; for a study of the family tree does not bear it out in the Royal House, and the ducal line, which shows a certain amount of inbreeding (if we include a reunion of blood after two centuries), is not that which is open to the charge of insanity. As for the madness upon the throne, what warrant at all is there for the statement that Maximilian II, father of Ludwig and Otto, and uncle of the present King, showed symptoms of a mental breakdown at the end of his life? On the contrary, he died in full possession of his faculties, and left behind the reputation of a good and kind ruler. Concerning Ludwig II my

number: (1) Ludwig (born 1831), who renounced his rights to the succession in March, 1859, and two months later married morganatically the actress Henrietta Mendel, created Baroness Wallersee, by whom he was the father of the present Countess Marie Larisch; (2) Hélène (born 1834), who married the Prince of Thurn and Taxis; (3) Elisabeth (1837); (4) Karl-Theodor (1839), who married the Infanta Marie-José of Portugal, and was succeeded on his death in 1909 by his son Ludwig-Wilhelm, the present head of the ducal line in Bavaria; (5) Marie-Sophia (1841), who married Francis, Duke of Calabria, later King Francis II of Naples and Sicily; (6) Mathilde (1843), who married Louis, Prince of Bourbon-Sicily, Count of Trani; (7) Sophie-Charlotte (1847), who married the Duke of Alençon; and (8) Maximilian-Emmanuel (1849), who married the Princess Amélie of Saxe-Coburg-Gotha and left at his death in 1893 three sons, all still living.

readers will hear in a later chapter my mother's firm conviction of his sanity, so that I will say no more here. There remains the unhappy Otto, whose nominal reign was brought to an end last year, but who still drags on a hopeless existence at Schloss Fürstenried, near Munich. About him there is something that must be said, however painful it may be to say it.

Queen Marie, the wife of Maximilian II, was brother's daughter to King Friedrich-Wilhelm III of Prussia. She was therefore a Hohenzollern. Now it cannot be denied that there was a taint of madness in the Hohenzollern family. Friedrich-Wilhelm himself, husband of the celebrated Queen Louisa, was more than merely weak-minded, as the charitable have represented him to be. One of his sons, Friedrich-Wilhelm IV, elder brother of the old Emperor William I, was undoubtedly mad. If insanity were transmitted to either of the offspring of Maximilian II and Marie, it came through the mother — not the father. Moreover, though the former Princess of Prussia figures in history as a Queen of Sorrows, she cannot be exonerated from being the cause of many of the sorrows, both to herself and to others. Her treatment of her sons was not good. In the case of Otto, born prematurely at a time of great anxiety in Bavaria as elsewhere in Europe and for long not expected to live, brutality is not too strong a word to use of her conduct. She would punish him by striking him on the head, and it is said that one of the doctors who examined him later stated that he bore traces of a serious injury to his head in childhood. Be this as it may, she was not at all the kind of mother to look after such nervous, highly strung boys as her sons were.

It was not on the Wittelsbach side of the family that

insanity came, I affirm. Among all the Royal houses of Europe the Wittelsbachs were pre-eminent for charm, kindliness of heart, and simplicity. They were affable and friendly to the humblest of their subjects. Now this is a trait which in rulers seems always to be regarded as a sign of weak-mindedness — by envious courtiers who see others of far inferior rank preferred to themselves. Talk is always spread of a taste for low society, and the virtue of simplicity is degraded into a vice. No better example of this can be found than in the history of the Wittelsbachs. The few voices which have been uplifted in their defence have, I fear, failed to reach far, drowned by the chorus of those whom self-interest, servility, or mere malice has inspired to slander and belittle them.

My mother would often talk to me about my grandparents on her side. The Duke Maximilian was a good-looking, easy-going, and broad-minded man. He was not deficient in artistic tastes, for he loved music, and could play the zither well. But perhaps it may be said of him, without injustice, that he was somewhat lacking in refinement. To a greater extent than his Royal kinsmen, he liked the society of peasants better than that of courts. He was devoted to horses and dogs, and was a tremendous walker, a trait which my mother inherited from him to the full. His wife has been misrepresented as *bourgeoise,* which she most certainly was not. The adjective might far more reasonably be applied to her husband. The Duchess Ludovica was compelled by circumstances — that is to say, by lack of money — to live a rather *bourgeois* life, but it was very much against her wishes. Like her sister, the masterful Archduchess Sophia, so many years the real ruler of the Austro-Hungarian Empire, Ludovica was a strict, narrow, and ambitious woman. But though she might scheme like Sophia, unlike her she had no scope for her scheming. Her husband's home in Bavaria was a humble place compared with the Imperial palace in Vienna.

My mother was the pet of my grandfather, but did not find so much favour with my grandmother, whose idol was her eldest daughter Hélène. Hélène received all the training necessary for rank in life, while her junior was neglected, the Duke not troubling himself with such matters as the education of his girls. It was a great grief to my mother as a child that she had no sister near to herself in age; Hélène was nearly four years older than she was. It was her brother, Karl-Theodor, two years younger, who, among all the family, was her greatest comrade and playmate. In his company — herself more like a boy than a girl then — they wandered through the woods of their summer home at Possenhofen, on the banks of the Lake of Starnberg, and paid visits to their friends among the peasantry. Curiously enough, in childhood she was not very good-looking, and as she had been a pretty baby, my grandfather used to repeat to her an old proverb, which admirably suited her case: "Schöne Wiegen Kinder, grobe Gassen Kinder, schöne Leute"— literally, "Fine cradle-children, rough street-children, fine (grown-up) people."

Karl-Theodor was also my mother's comforter and her only companion when she was obliged to remain upstairs in her room while guests were being entertained below. If the opportunity offered, he would steal down to the kitchen or the pantry and forage for forbidden delicacies; or perhaps one of the servants might bring ice-cream or some other dainty up to them that they might enjoy it together.

The story of the romantic courtship of Elisabeth by the Emperor Francis-Joseph has often been told. I must say, however, that what my mother herself told me does not entirely bear out the ordinary version. Francis-Joseph, it is true, went to Possenhofen in 1853 to see his cousin Hélène, being entirely under the influence of his mother, who had no doubt concerted a scheme with her sister for the marriage of their children. I know nothing of a meeting between him and my mother then, or of a formal proposal by him for her hand. It would rather seem that they met at Ischl in the summer of that year, when the ducal family went on a visit to their Imperial relatives, stopping at a hotel not far from the residence of the Emperor and his mother. A dance was given at the grand villa, to which Francis-Joseph insisted that Elisabeth should come as well as her elder sister. Here Elisabeth happened to please her aunt better than Hélène did, and so, for once in a way, the Archduchess Sophia yielded to her son's wishes. Doubtless the Archduchess was influenced by another motive besides a preference for the younger girl's looks. She thought that her youth would make her easier to manage than Hélène, who, like the majority of her sisters, was of a very determined character, and had reached an age when she made the fact plain.

Mother often talked to me about her wedding, and how, in spite of her pleasure in making herself beautiful and being the centre of attraction, she still dreaded her newly found greatness. Up to now she had always been kept in the background at home. Suddenly, at the age of only fifteen and a half, she found herself, as it were, in the full glare of the footlights. She had seen the Emperor but a few times before her engagement to him, and his passion quite carried her away. Her happiness on the day of her betrothal was something which she could not forget. And how proud she was when she had to attend with him the church at Ischl! — and even the mother of her fiancé, until that day the first lady in the land, was obliged to yield precedence to her. The engagement was announced in the *Wiener Zeitung* the same day.

Yet with it this sudden greatness brought many trials for her. From the time of her betrothal in August to that of her marriage in April, 1854, was only eight months. In that short period she was called upon to perfect herself in the knowledge of those social conventions which up to now she had so neglected. "I did not like it at all," she would say to me. "Up to this time I had worn short dresses and run about with the boys, just like one of themselves; and now, all of a sudden, I had to be a great lady!"

The difficulty of her position was increased by the fact that my grandmother had wished Hélène to occupy it, and had educated her with that end in view. Hélène had overawed my mother with her knowledge; she was versed in many matters of which, as my mother said, she herself knew only enough to disgrace her. The only things which she knew much about were walking, dancing, and riding. Because of the many deficiencies in her education, she was obliged to shelter herself behind a mask of dignified solemnity and coldness, which at first won her much admiration in Imperial circles. Unfortunately, according to her own account, this was the only Imperial quality she had. The prevalent opinion was that she was beside herself with joy over her new-found magnificence — an opinion which was of equal perspicacity with the common estimate of her intellectual qualities. As a matter of fact, she was well able to appreciate the difficulties of her position. She confessed that her splendour was indeed a source of great pleasure to her, but this was never sufficient to counteract her constant anxiety.

The actual day of her wedding, however, remained for my mother one of the happiest days of her life. The coronation ceremony in Hungary was more magnificent, but the wedding brought more happiness. It was one of the few occasions in her life when she could not deny that vanity mastered her. The more admiration her appearance caused, the greater was her joy. The train of her dress, borne by ladies of the Court, was so heavy that she could scarcely walk, yet that did not trouble her. Her toilet took hours; but instead of this making her impatient, each additional article was the occasion of a new outburst of ecstasy. And the more those about her exclaimed, the prouder she felt. She really must have looked most enchanting. I begged her once to give me a description of her wedding-dress, which she did. "My dress," she said, " was made of heavy white brocade, embroidered with gold and silver, as also was my court train. This train was fastened on my shoulders with diamond clasps. I wore on my head a wreath of myrtle and orange blossoms — flowers which also formed the trimming of my dress; and a diadem of diamonds, a gift from the Emperor's mother, which she herself had worn as a bride."

She must, I repeat, have looked enchanting. Countless brides are called beautiful upon their wedding-day; but my mother was not one of those who owe much to their dress. She was beyond dispute a beautiful woman. Her features were regular; her eyes of a curious, indefinite shade, which at some distance might be mistaken for dark blue, but at times showed a yellow, even golden, light; her hair chestnut, in youth almost inclined to auburn, later in life growing darker. In stature she was tall, with a charming figure. I always had the feeling with her that she was on horseback — such was the grace of her carriage. Also, to put it another way, she was more really " swan-like " than anyone else whom it has been my lot to meet.

In spite of her girlish slenderness, she had a slight tendency, perhaps, to grow stout. There are two strains of the Wittelsbach blood, the stout and the exceedingly meagre. My mother had a morbid fear of belonging to the former class. I would not deny that she might have become stout, had she not trained herself to keep thin. She certainly never was of the " skin-and-bones " figure like her brother Karl-Theodor, for instance, or my sister Valerie. She walked a great deal, which was beneficial to her general health. Other items in her system of training were no doubt too severe to be good for her — though she never really used to sleep, as has been alleged, with wet compresses round her waist to lessen its girth — and she maintained her slimness at some expense to her strength. Whenever her weight exceeded one hundred and twenty-five English pounds, she would deny herself for days any food except oranges. During these voluntary fasts, she drank nothing but an occasional glass of port wine when she felt weak or faint. As all the time she was keeping up her regular gymnastic exercises on the rings and parallel bars, it will readily be understood that she laid a very severe tax upon herself.

Yet in spite of this, it could not be said that she was exactly vain. If she would spend much time thus in training her body, on the other hand she was never one of those women who waste a whole morning seeking for the precise shade or colour which suits them best, and who must

Empress Elisabeth of Austria

be up-to-date in dress or die. She did not run after fashions. Although she was always well dressed, she cared nothing for new gowns, and disliked especially to get herself up for State occasions. She bought clothes largely to benefit the tradespeople and her own servants. Her special abomination was new shoes. She purchased these in quantities, but wore the same pairs for months at a time, while the new ones were either given away or else sold by the servants without her knowledge or consent — a fact which sometimes led to amusing *contretemps*. On one occasion she asked that a new pair of shoes, which had very recently been ordered, should be brought to her. She waited some minutes, and still they did not come. Finally, turning to her woman of the bed-chamber, who had just returned after making inquiries into the cause of the delay, she broke into a laugh and exclaimed: " I should like to bet that I know what the matter is. My new shoes have gone where hundreds of other pairs of mine go. Never mind, bring the old ones, and order another new pair at once; but tell the maker to be quick, as I want them as soon as possible."

Mother, in fact, while appreciating her natural loveliness, disdained artificial means of heightening it. Even her hair, which was famous for its beauty, was arranged very plainly, without attention to the fashion of the day. The French word *soignée* conveys better than any other the impression which she gave to the beholder. Her chief vanity, I should say, was the desire to be individual, just herself, unlike anybody else; and in this she succeeded most admirably.

To return to the position of affairs after the Imperial wedding. The Archduchess Sophia, it has been said, probably reconciled herself to the idea of having Elisabeth, rather than Hélène, for her daughter-in-law on account of her youth. She felt at first considerable sympathy for one upon whom she looked as a mere child. Soon, however, she began to find her a troublesome child, and to hate her for that youth which, expected to be an advantage, proved in reality to be a disadvantage from her point of view. My mother herself admitted afterwards (I mean to say that she admitted in talking to me) that her extreme youth at the time of her marriage made her more stubborn and unreasonable than she would have been had she been older — say twenty, like her sister Hélène, for example. Yet she saw a certain justification for her conduct then in the fact that the Archduchess Sophia was utterly heartless and treated her very badly. As an example of her tyranny I may mention the following story. My mother, with whom charity was a very genuine feeling, would have liked to visit regularly, but unofficially, the hospitals and other benevolent institutions, and as Empress she began to carry out her wishes.

One day, as she returned from a hospital, she was met by the Archduchess, who asked her where she had been. On being told, she remonstrated strongly. Mother answered that she should go where she pleased, whereon the Archduchess went at once to the Emperor and complained of her behaviour. The upshot was that it was laid down that in future she must always get her husband's permission previous to going anywhere but certain prescribed places. For one who always took the unpleasant things in life so tragically as she did this was a cruel blow.

The Archduchess set herself to alienate her son's heart from her daughter-in-law. This was particularly the case after the birth of the first two children, the short-lived

Sophia, and Gisela. She told Francis-Joseph then that if he did not wish his wife to be his master, he must prevent her interfering in his affairs at all; and he took the advice, with the result that an estrangement grew rapidly. I should say here, however, that my mother spoke to me very little about the Emperor. I did not understand why at the time, but I do now.

Mother, it must be admitted, did not play her rôle at Court at all well. The stiffness, which at first won her praise there, was not an attitude which she could maintain without a great strain upon herself. In reality she was far too cheerful and natural for the grey old Court. Her timidity in such surroundings made her appear stiff, especially on public occasions. The commonly held opinion that she was of a serious, indeed too serious, disposition my mother denounced as an absolute falsehood. At the time when she became Empress she was the most high-spirited being imaginable, and as fond of fun as she could be. But of course she could not give way to her inclinations in public. The pose of seriousness was forced upon her by the necessity of avoiding the appearance of childishness. Nor yet in private life, hedged round about as she was by the terrible etiquette of Imperial Vienna, was she allowed to be gay. If she tried to be so, she was compelled to listen to lectures upon her conduct. Yet even reproaches did not spoil her natural good humour; she was too young to be bad-tempered for long.

As time passed, however, and the novelty of her position wore off, she grew very tired of the monotony of her life. In particular, she resented the ordeal of being constantly stared at, to which she was subjected in Vienna. The Viennese, in her opinion, were frightfully inquisitive and unrefined.

I remember that I once asked her if the same was not the case all the world over where sovereigns and their subjects were concerned, and that she answered that she did not think so, for in other places people seemed to have more to do, and less time to devote to prying into the affairs of their neighbours. She compared the Hungarians very favourably with the Viennese. At Budapest she always felt that she was among friends. To illustrate the difference in the atmosphere she said to me: "As you know, I was always passionately fond of riding. In consequence, the loyal Hungarians gave me the title of 'Queen of the Amazons.' With the Viennese, on the other hand, my nickname was 'The Circus Rider'!" I was silent, for I liked Vienna and its people — as I do still — and was sorry that they should make her feel like this about them.

As is well known, my mother became a great student after her marriage. The Duke Maximilian, I have said, troubled little about her education before. But afterwards she discovered that she liked study, and devoted herself to it. She became a remarkable linguist. History and poetry both attracted her strongly. It was a curious trait in her that, especially with regard to the poets, she preferred always reading the same authors and did not seek after new books. "I can always find something new in the old ones," she would say. Her favourite poets were Heine and Shakespeare, for both of whom she had a sincere esteem. Of Shakespeare's works she loved *Hamlet* and *King Lear* the most.

Among the teachers whom she kept at different times to instruct her, especially in Greek, two, both of them Greeks, have written books in which they have borne testimony to her abilities as a pupil. With regard to one of

these, Christomanos, however, I feel it incumbent upon
me to make a most emphatic protest against an insinuation which he has made. From his book one might gather
that he was in love with the Empress who employed him,
and that she reciprocated. Nothing could be further
from the truth than the last suggestion. Dr. Christomanos was an intelligent and interesting man, and she
undoubtedly liked him for this. But, as for any stronger
feeling, shall I be considered uncharitable if I ask how
any man could be so vain as to imagine that she, with her
passionate adoration for physical beauty, could be attracted by one who was almost a hunchback? I must
confess to a feeling of great indignation that it should be
necessary for me to write thus.

Mother was very fond of music and played the piano
well. She was a great admirer of Wagner, and on one
occasion helped him with a present of twenty thousand
florins. She paid a visit to Bayreuth, I can remember on
one occasion, with the express purpose of hearing *Parsifal;*
and Bayreuth then was not the goal of pilgrimages to such
an extent as it has since become.

She was naturally liberal-minded, and, as will have been
gathered, anti-clerical. She has been accused of revolutionary, even anarchistic, sympathies. But in reality she
was only very "modern." If she was revolutionary, it
was in theory, not in practice. Although she rebelled
against the restrictions of Court life, I very much doubt,
whether, had she had the power, she would have swept
them away. She was, indeed, too impatient to carry out
such a reform.

She was, it hardly need be said, of an extremely romantic nature. Of her sisters, the Countess of Trani and
the Duchess of Alençon were most like her in this; but out

of her whole family she was the least gifted with common sense. She thought herself, indeed, as is often the case with people of such character, very common-sense and logical, but she was far too much under the dominion of caprice to be the latter. Capriciousness, and not logic, is the mark of the romantic soul. And, of course, her surroundings conduced to the encouragement of her caprices. She was, if I may say so without appearing undaughterly, like a beautiful actress spoilt by the attentions showered upon her — though it is not the English word " spoilt," nor the French *gâtée,* which conveys my meaning so well as the German *verzogen.*

Nothing is more unjust or untrue, however, than the accusation which some people (including more than one who ought to know better) have dared to bring against the Empress, that she allowed the attentions paid to her to turn her head to the extent of making her — shall I say indiscreet? Mother was of a very solitary nature, and liked few people, men or women, very much. She showed no preference for the companionship of one sex rather than the other. She might take an interest in a man, but it would not be as a man, but as a human character that he would be interesting to her. The man might misinterpret this interest, it is true; as, seemingly, in the case to which allusion has been made a few paragraphs earlier. That was not her fault.

Toward people of unsympathetic disposition she was almost careless in her behaviour. This, I suppose, is what some have called her arrogance. As for her alleged cynicism, I can only conceive that it is her manner of speech which is alluded to. She had an original way of speaking, which was very humorous as coming from her, and perhaps could not be understood by the undiscerning.

The eccentricity of behaviour which is imputed to her towards the end of her life is also a figment due to lack of understanding. Her impatience increased in later life, but then she was very worried. I have no doubt that the one great cause of worry was the uncertainty of my own future. Her mother's heart foreboded the misfortunes which actually befell me after her death. But, anxious as she was, it is not true that she lost all her good spirits as she grew older. Nor is it true that the effect of the tragedy of Mayerling was that, in the conventional phrase, she never smiled again. I can remember that during our visit to the Riviera she went over to Monte Carlo and risked some money on the tables. She did not cease to take pleasure in going about incognita, and talking to people who never suspected who she was. She was, indeed, the very reverse of the gloomy being, with suicidal tendencies, which some biographers have made her out. The famous detective Paoli, for instance, though in his Memoirs he has spoken of her with high admiration and esteem, totally misrepresents her in this respect. But then how could a man in his position, however eminent in his own particular line, be sufficiently intimate in his acquaintance with her to be able to read her heart?

Evidences of her eccentricity have been found in her passions for building and for travel, of which much has been written that has little relation to fact. One would suppose, if one believed all one read, that she spent a great deal of her life out of Austria-Hungary. Really she went abroad only from December to March each year; and before the death of the Crown Prince only from January to March. After the Mayerling tragedy, it was but natural that she should wish to avoid the gaieties of the first half of the Vienna season, and especially the Christmas festivities of the family which would never see him again. It is true that she always travelled about a good deal within the limits of Austria and Hungary, though why that should be considered a mania I do not understand.

With regard to her building extravagances there has been gross exaggeration. Lainz was not a magnificent palace. The Achilleion, her villa at Corfu (now the property of the German Emperor, who has made of the temple attached to it a memorial chapel to my mother), may truly be called an extravagance. But it was her Italian architect, Rafael Carito, the husband of a former lady-in-waiting to the Queen of Naples, who was responsible for the vast expenditure of money upon it. Mother had intended to have a small villa at Corfu, with beautiful gardens attached to it. The cost was not meant to exceed a million pounds in English money. Under Carito's direction it reached more than three times that sum, and the villa became a miniature palace of the most splendid description. The first time that the Empress set foot in it she exclaimed: "I shall never be happy in such a place as this!"

As a matter of fact, my mother knew nothing about the value of money, though it was a foible of hers to think that she did. She spent it, not because she loved spending, but because she never knew what she was spending. And, while she was being the most lavish, she might often at the same time make some small economy; which proved better than anything else could her ignorance of values.

I hope that I may have succeeded in giving of my mother some picture which does more justice to her as a woman — though the very word "woman" itself seems to misrepresent one who had so much of the spiritual, so little of the bodily — than the accounts of many who have taken upon themselves to write about her. What I am conscious that I have failed to convey is the unique charm which she had in her. But my pen could not accomplish that task, and it is wiser therefore to leave it unattempted. It was my privilege to live with her, if only at intervals, in an intimacy which she allowed to no one else in the world; and for that very reason I cannot trust myself to speak. Out of the fulness of the heart the mouth is sometimes silent. We cannot adequately express that which we feel the most.

CHAPTER VI

FRAU VON FRIESE

AFTER the events narrated in the fourth chapter, ending in the summary dismissal of Miss Ives and Mademoiselle Pidon, my mother spent much time and trouble searching for someone to whom she could safely entrust my education. During the months that she remained in Vienna before going to Carlsbad, she made many attempts to find a suitable governess for me. The task proved the more difficult because she wanted somebody who would stay with her for years and supervise my training through girlhood, a person of good social status as well as of high intelligence. Such a lady, if chosen from among Viennese residents, would be certain to be the cause of gossip and of awkward questions. The problem was the same that had existed when a home had to be found for me in infancy. The difficulty had been met by the choice of the Kaisers, on the recommendation of Professor Braun. Now the summer passed without bringing the required governess.

During the summer months I stayed with Mr. and Mrs. Kaiser and their children at Vöslau, where they were spending the holidays. One day in the autumn — to be precise, on October 26, 1892 — my mother's private carriage called for me at my foster-parents' house, which was now in the Kantgasse, and in it I was driven to the Strohgasse in the neighbouring third section of Vienna. We stopped at the door of a small but elegant mansion, where I got down. On entering the house I found myself in a marble hall, the floor covered with a soft, thick carpet. Passing through this and an antechamber, I was led into the drawing-room, where sat my mother and another lady.

Mother greeted me with a kiss upon the forehead, as was her usual custom, and taking my hand in hers said: "Come and say How-do-you-do to this lady. She is a very kind and good friend of mine, and from now onward she is to be the third in our league."

I looked shyly at the lady, of whom my first impression was that she was rather imposing in appearance, so that I felt inclined to be afraid. While I was taking stock of her, my mother went on. I knew, she said, that she herself travelled about a great deal, and that it was impossible for her always to have me with her. So Frau von Friese — the lady whom I saw — was going to do her the great kindness of taking me under her special care. She had just come to live in Vienna. She had no children of her own and felt very lonely, so she would look upon me almost as her own daughter. But I must know that it had taken some time to persuade Frau von Friese to accept the responsibility, for she was afraid that a child of my age might have already become too independent for her to manage.

At these last words my heart sank, and I hung my head. But now Frau von Friese spoke. "I am afraid your mother wishes to give you a better opinion of me than I deserve," she said with a silvery laugh, which seemed to come straight from the heart. At the sound of it I was at once impressed in her favour and all my fears vanished.

"What your mother has told you of my ideas is quite true," she continued. "But what she perhaps does not know is that I have one corner in my heart that is kept specially for little girls, and where there is no room for anything else. All the same, I have some special peculiarities which may not be entirely to the liking of the little girls. When once I have come to the decision to educate one of them, I centre in her ambitions which I do not wish to see disappointed. This means, in a few words, that I expect strict obedience. If one is to get this one must begin early, or else the result is painful to both sides. But I am not one who likes to give pain, especially not to my little pupil, whose love I am anxious to win. I should give up my task at once if my care of her were only to result in grief to her."

I besought my mother to tell Frau von Friese how I had been accustomed to show obedience, even to people who were not at all kind to me. She answered that Frau von Friese had already been told all about my late nurse and governess, and that it was what she had heard that decided her to undertake my education. She and my mother had so much the same views on such matters that they were sure to work together successfully. "And you, darling, I know, will do your best," concluded my mother.

Frau von Friese, with whom I was destined to spend so much of my time for years to come, was a Danish lady. At a first glance one could not fail to notice in her the peculiar characteristics of this race, which combines so admirably French grace and vivacity with German simplicity and reserve. She was a real daughter of Copenhagen, tall and slim, with a typical Northern head, a long oval face, grey eyes, and dark hair. Every word and every movement showed the *grande dame*.

Six years after her marriage, Frau von Friese's husband died, leaving her childless, but with a fortune sufficient for her needs. She had a charming and well-cultivated voice, and as a girl her ambition had been to become a professional singer; but her family had opposed the idea so strongly that she was obliged to give it up. To fill the void left by her frustrated ambition, she had read very widely. To this she added the culture inseparable from a life of travel, to which her inquiring nature impelled her. Withal she was most womanly and sweet.

It was while she was abroad that Frau von Friese met my mother, at Arcachon, in the summer of 1890. My mother was staying at Arcachon under the very unpretentious name of Madame Folna, from Corfu, and she remained unrecognised during her sojourn of a week, taking the sea-baths. The two women were mutually attracted at their first meeting on the beach and forthwith entered into conversation, which informal acquaintance resulted in their spending most of the remainder of the week together. Though parting firm friends, they lost trace of each other until they met again unexpectedly at Carlsbad during the summer of 1892. Mother was there, this time quite officially — if one could ever use the word officially in connection with my mother — as the Empress of Austria, and while walking alone in the woods was so fortunate as to meet Frau von Friese, who though she had recognised in the streets of Carlsbad her friend from Arcachon, had not dared to call upon her. My mother, on the contrary, was quite in ignorance of the other's presence at the baths, and was delighted as well as surprised at the meeting.

"Dear Frau von Friese, are you here? This is a real pleasure! I have often wondered what had become of you," she exclaimed, stretching out both her hands. Frau von Friese, now that she was acquainted with the exalted rank of her friend, felt very much embarrassed. But my mother soon put her again at her ease; and as Frau von Friese had not a trace of servility in her composition she remained as friendly and intimate in her manner as before.

My mother had been in a state of great anxiety at her failure to obtain a suitable guardian for me, and looked upon the second meeting with the Danish lady as almost a special intervention of Providence. She did not make up her mind at once, however, and almost a whole month elapsed while she made minute inquiries about Frau von Friese. I was told later how one day, as they were out walking in the neighbourhood of Carlsbad, chance brought them to an understanding. Frau von Friese had been speaking about her sorrows and her loneliness, and how much happier life would have been for her if she had had a child of her own to watch over and to care for; particularly a daughter, to whom she could have consecrated her life. This outpouring of confidences gave my mother the desired opportunity, and revealing her secret to Frau von Friese, she asked the latter if she would take charge of me.

The question may be asked, why did not my mother leave me in the care of Mr. and Mrs. Kaiser? The great obstacle to such a course was Mrs. Kaiser herself. She was that kind of woman who, even towards her own children, showed her love by many kisses and caresses, seeming to forget them when they were not about her. She did not concern herself about them for days, but left them to the care of governesses and tutors, paying little or no attention at all to the development of their characters and abilities. Moreover, she had one other marked defect which prejudiced my mother against her; a quick, abrupt manner and a tactlessness of speech which made every visit of my mother (who was extremely sensitive) more or less of an ordeal to her.

Naturally Mrs. Kaiser was much offended at my being quite withdrawn from her charge; but as she was a woman of no depth of character, her annoyance soon passed. Mr. Kaiser, on the other hand, understood my mother's reasons perfectly; for, could he have followed his inclinations, he would not have committed his own children to his wife's care. In fact, his position was little altered by my removal, as he had never paid much personal attention to me; and he remained my mother's financial adviser and the executor of her wishes concerning me.

On the day following the interview recorded at the beginning of this chapter, I left the house of the Kaisers to settle permanently in my new home in the Strohgasse. This had been purchased for me by my mother in the name of one of Mr. Kaiser's friends, and it was peculiarly suitable for allowing her to visit me in secret. I still continued, three times a week, to spend two hours with Laura and her tutor, Herr Hold, although the time was almost thrown away; but this had to be arranged so that I might keep up the appearance of being the daughter of Mr. and Mrs. Kaiser. On these days I usually lunched at the house, and sometimes after this I went for a walk with Laura and her governess. With the exception of these few hours my time was spent at my own home. Besides these lessons with Herr Hold, Frau von Friese made me study a great deal, being not at all an indulgent teacher. She seemed very well satisfied with me, however, and one day expressed her approval in the following words: " They may have ill-treated you, but nevertheless they have done justice to your education." And I was as proud of this commendation as if I had educated myself!

My life should now have been perfectly happy, for Frau von Friese treated me with the utmost kindness. The only cloud upon my happiness was my religious teacher, Father Lambertus. Although Frau von Friese felt that the Jesuit was not at all well suited to his task, she did not wish to bring about a change after so many years, fearing to make an enemy of him. Father Lambertus was a man of medium build, with jet black hair tinged with grey. His cadaverous face was of a dyspeptic yellow, and it really made one feel ill just to look at him. He was the regular type of the Jesuit whom one meets in Austria, narrow-minded and bigoted; and his personal manner was ill-tempered and harsh. Poor Frau von Friese did everything in her power to make us tolerate each other, but the old priest would not give way an inch, and I was impertinent as well as obstinate, I must confess. However, she had great influence over me, and through her kind insistence brought me at least to the point of promising not to answer him rudely nor to revolt openly against the arrogance and dogmatism which made his teaching repulsive to me. Every lesson, notwithstanding, was the occasion for a new quarrel, and I constantly forgot my good resolutions and committed some grave indiscretion. At last, naturally enough, my governess lost patience and punished me.

With this exception my days passed away quickly and peacefully. I often look back upon them with regret as having been, perhaps, the happiest of my life.

A month after I had settled down in my new home, mother again left Vienna for a cruise in the Mediterranean. The regularity of my life was no longer interrupted by the agreeable excitement of her visits. On November 27th she had come to say good-bye to me, and had great pleasure on hearing that Frau von Friese was well satisfied with me.

With the exception of Laura, I no longer saw any other children, for my mother had given very strict orders upon this point, and they certainly were never disobeyed. Of course, I was very lonely, for I did not even come in contact with very many grown-ups. Besides Frau von Friese I had a lady as a companion, a Fräulein Hain, who had been a school teacher, and who was now given the post with me in order that Frau von Friese should not be too much tied down. This arrangement gave my "Aya"[1] an opportunity of indulging her taste for the opera, and allowed her some leisure to meet her friends in their homes. On such occasions I used to remain with Fräulein, doing needlework or playing the piano. It was strictly forbidden that I should talk to the servants, for, like most young girls, I was fond of encouraging their chatter. I am afraid that the fact that I was forbidden to talk only gave me the more pleasure in doing so. When Frau von Friese was away from home I never could refrain from addressing a few words to Pirker while he was waiting on us at supper in a vain endeavour to make him lose countenance. It would have amused me immensely; but he always remained perfectly grave. I also tried repeatedly to enter into conversation with my maid while she brushed my hair for half an hour every evening. Sitting in front of my dressing-table, I could see in the looking-glass the embarrassment on her face; and the more confused her answers were, the greater was my pleasure.

[1] The word "Aya," in its best Continental sense, means "an instructor" who is especially gifted and cultured, in charge of a pupil of high rank. It is not really to be represented by the English word "governess."

It was perfectly useless for Fräulein to say to me, as she did, " Stop your talking, or I shall tell the gnädige Frau."

A great delight to me was to go to the kitchen to pay a visit to Agnes, the cook, a stout old woman with an expression of doglike faithfulness on her face. It pleased me, too, to see the two smart kitchen-maids in their uniforms of blue or pink, making a pretty picture against the white enamelled tiles on the walls. Agnes loved me dearly, and when, once in a way, I could escape to her domain for a few minutes, her face lit up with pleasure, particularly when I said a few words to her in her own language (Hungarian). For example, I would say, " Edes jo Agnes, nagion ches vagyok " (" My darling Agnes, I am very hungry "). Then she knew she was to treat me to something nice, but often before she had time to do so one of the servants would come in, calling, " Euer Gnaden, Fräulein is coming." [2]

Most of the servants in the house, I am sure, had their suspicions as to my rank, but all were too well provided for to risk losing their places through injudicious gossip. Those who were fully informed were Sophie, Frau von Friese's maid, a quiet, elderly person who talked very little; my own maid, Mina Etlinger, a woman of thirty, who was so haughty towards the other servants and almost everyone else with whom she came in contact that she never would have honoured anyone by taking them into her confidence; and Pirker, the major-domo. The last-named, of course, knew more even than myself, but was as dumb as an oyster. I believe he was so accustomed to being silent that, as with Grimaud in " The Three Mus-

---

[2] Although literally the words " Euer Gnaden " mean " Your Grace," they have not the same significance as in English, being addressed only by servants to persons of rank when they do not know the proper title. They are not usual as an address to a child.

keteers," it was an effort for him to talk! He could sit for hours and hours in a large armchair before the fireplace in the hall, never uttering a word. He thought it his duty to rise like a soldier every time I passed. And I, like the mischievous child that I was, used to take a perverse pleasure in disturbing his doze by entering and leaving the hall unnecessarily. He was the only person in the house, perhaps, who dared to be independent towards Frau von Friese; and nothing would have induced him to give up certain of his ways — such, for instance, as being the first to read the newspapers when they arrived. Although he was extremely respectful towards her, he sometimes tried her patience severely with his laconic answers. For instance, she hated to sit at the evening meal with the curtains undrawn. To see to this was the task of the footman, Leopold, but it was Pirker's duty to make certain that it was done. It so happened once that this had been forgotten. To the remark of Frau von Friese that she did not want the neighbours watching us at our meals, Pirker answered coldly, and with a face devoid of all expression, " The people will only see a well-appointed table, with well-behaved people seated at it."

He never allowed a table-cloth to be used twice. If a dish had the slightest crack he destroyed it at once. If he were told that it could still be used in the kitchen, he answered, " Oh, there are too many plates and dishes — they get in the way." Then he would relieve his mind by scolding the kitchen-maids for their carelessness in breaking everything. We had fresh flowers on the table-centre every day. At the suggestion that pot-plants might be used instead of flowers to reduce the expense, he remarked: " It is all the same to me. It is not my household. Only, suppose Her Majesty should come here unexpectedly!" Needless to say, the suggestion was never repeated.

Pirker did not like to hear the other servants scolded or even complained about. In fact, he always shielded them in our presence, as he did in the matter of the undrawn curtains, although we could be sure that Leopold got his lecture afterwards. This Leopold was really intolerable —a regular *parvenu*, if a footman can be a *parvenu*. To his superiors he was servile, to his inferiors rude and arrogant; not at all like Pirker, who was courteous to everyone. Leopold's greatest grievance was that he had to wear a green livery while the older man wore black. And he grew perfectly indignant when, after five months' residence with us, upon my mother's return from Corfu he was finally obliged to wear a braided coat, knee-breeches, and white silk stockings whenever he was required to wait at table during her visits. Pirker, on the contrary, would not for anything in the world have waited except in his black silk stockings and black silk knee-breeches. He seriously approved of this ceremonial attire, and nothing would have induced him to serve even a cup of tea in any other dress. When mother arrived unexpectedly, as was often the case, he ushered her into the sitting-room and vanished immediately, to re-enter a little later in changed attire. She was secretly rather amused at this singular homage, and once, in a moment of very good humour, could not refrain from making a remark to him about it. But, in spite of her mirth, he retained his gravity and replied: "May it please your Majesty, I never forget what is due to my position, both as the servant of your Majesty and as the major-domo of this household. I must be careful in all circumstances to set the right example to the other servants."

FRAU VON FRIESE

Ever after this, at Christmastide, Pirker received the same gift from my mother, a pair of silk knee-breeches, with a gold coin sewn in a piece of paper in place of every button — of which there were in all about twenty-two.

I have mentioned already that the cloud upon my happiness at this period of my life was the presence of my religious instructor, Father Lambertus. As time went on the situation grew worse, and at last it reached a climax. I cannot help thinking that the right kind of priest would have had a great opportunity with me. It is true that I was of a rather obstinate nature, but my mind was very inquiring, and I thirsted for information as to the purpose of life. I was forced to build up a religion of my own, for the Jesuit father had nothing to tell me. The traditions of the Church and the glories of the saints, which, with the simplest Bible stories, were all that he thought fit to impart to me, interested me not at all. Any questions which I might venture to ask were treated by him as mere impertinences. One day matters came to a head. He had been more than usually dull and prosy that morning over the visit of Jesus Christ to the Pharisee, and I suddenly broke out with an attempt to discuss the subject of the remission of sins! I had, of course, at that time no idea of what the Magdalene's sins were, but I boldly asked whether the washing of the feet and the drying of them with her hair were not a very small service in comparison with the wrongs she had done before. Father Lambertus rose in his wrath. His complexion was no longer yellow; in his excitement it turned to olive-green. I continued foolishly to argue, when he banged upon the table with his fist and shouted that these ideas were none of my own — that I was prompted by someone else, and that he had had enough of it. I would be made to repent of it.

Totally unprepared for the outburst, I shook like a leaf. He raved on, and the sound of his voice reached Frau von Friese in the next room. She rushed in to find out what had happened, and, taking in the situation, simply pointed to the door, saying to me, "Go to your own room!" What followed I did not hear, though I learnt, long after, that the Father directly accused my governess of perverting my mind and setting me against religion. I have no doubt now that he had long cherished ideas of having me placed in some convent, and that he had been trying all the while to lead my ideas in this direction. Frau von Friese being a Protestant — a Lutheran — and over him in the control of my education, Father Lambertus considered her his arch-enemy. Of course, this was not true. She was much too fervent a Christian to allow me to speak disrespectfully as I had done. Indeed, my mother was much more liberal in her views than she was, being inclined to the religion which, for want of a better name, we call Pantheism; and it was doubtless from her that I inherited my ideas. But this the priest did not wish to recognise. His main object was to make the quarrel so complete as to force Frau von Friese's resignation or dismissal. She on her part strove in vain to pacify him. They parted open enemies.

The immediate result was to render Frau von Friese terribly angry, and entering my room she chastised me severely — for the only time in all our connection. She then wrote at once to my mother, who had arrived in Vienna ten days previously from Corfu, telling her everything. In the letter, which Pirker took immediately to Lainz, she begged mother to choose between herself and the priest, saying that one or the other must go, and concluded by asking her to come as soon as possible. Mother could not come at once, and wrote the following letter: —

10th *May*, 1893.

MY DEAR FRIESE,

I cannot come at the moment. It is too late now, for at three o'clock the Crown Princess and Erzsie are dining with me. But do not worry yourself, my dear Friese; you know which of the two has to go. As for Caroline, tell her, please, that I am very indignant with her. There is no punishment too great for her, and I personally order her to be shut up by herself for a whole week. Please arrange a special room for the purpose. I don't want to see her when I come to-morrow. She must understand by that how deeply she has hurt my feelings. It is disgraceful in a girl of her age.

With my kindest greetings to you,
My dear Friese,
Yours very sincerely,
ELISABETH.

My whole body quivered as this message was read to me, and I sobbed long through the night. But how much sorer was my grief the next day when I heard under the porch the rolling of my mother's carriage wheels. Would she come to the little room in which I was a prisoner, I wondered? For nearly an hour and a half I waited, until I heard again the rolling of the carriage wheels underneath. Then I knew that she had insisted upon the strict carrying out of my sentence. I might have known it before, for she never wavered in her resolutions. For the moment I thought my heart would break, as I sat alone in my prison with no companion but despair.

For the whole of the week mother remained inexorable. Then on the eighth day she came back. Timidly I entered the drawing-room, but she took me in her arms at once and said, "Come, little sinner; I do not want to hear anything more about this story."

The rule of Father Lambertus was over and done with.

CHAPTER VII

SUMMER HOLIDAYS

SUMMER had now come again, and brought with it another change for me. It was arranged that my house should be left in the care of the servants. Frau von Friese desired to pay a visit to Denmark, while I was to spend part of the summer, as usual, with the Kaisers. I was sorry to go, because I had grown very attached to my home and my kind if strict Aya. And, worse still, the holiday involved another separation from my mother. The weeks immediately preceding my departure were spent as much as possible in her company. On the fine days we went out for long walks together in the neighbourhood of Vienna. When it rained she would come to the Strohgasse and pass all her spare time there. I have no doubt that the " eccentricity " of her conduct, about which so much has been said and written, was particularly noticed now. How little did people understand her motives!

I remember that at the time she was suffering from a family bereavement. Her youngest brother, the Duke Max-Emmanuel, the pet of the whole family in childhood and known to them all as " Mapperl," after the name invented by himself originally, had just died in Bavaria.

On June 29, 1893, mother went to Gastein, and I to St. Gilgen, close to Ischl, where the Kaisers had hired a house for the holidays. St. Gilgen was at that time a nice quiet little place; in fact, hardly a regular summer resort as yet. It was still quite in its infancy and for just that reason was attractive. Its general scenery had the aspect typical of all the Salzkammergut district — a beautiful little emerald-green lake, old forests of fir and pine, interspersed with oaks, a small village, a few picturesque châlets, and the whole enclosed by high mountains. Probably on account of its simplicity, and because it was not known to the crowd, society here was especially select. Really one would have had to go far to find more interesting people gathered together in one small place than just then at St. Gilgen. Among others spending the summer there were Theodore Billroth, with his guests, Johannes Brahms and Karl Goldmark; the sculptor, Karl Kundman, with his four daughters; and the Baroness Ebner von Eschenbach, the poetess, who came bringing in her train a select party of literary aristocrats. Although sixty-three, the baroness was extremely vivacious. She was very fond of children, with whom her obvious sympathy made her a great favourite, in spite of her great plainness. We spent many happy hours listening to her charming talk.

The weeks spent at St. Gilgen would have been very pleasant indeed to me, had it not been for my longing to return to the peacefulness of my home life — a longing intensified by the uncomfortable relations existing between Mr. and Mrs. Kaiser. Really they never did get on well together, but just at this time I noticed it more than ever. He was kind-hearted but very quick-tempered, and his outbursts were dreaded by the whole household.

One day toward the middle of July, news came that the Emperor was to pass through St. Gilgen and that he would stop for a few minutes at the station. The whole place was *en fête*. Everyone was excited. My own feelings were mingled curiosity and shame. I longed to see my father, whom I had never seen in my life, yet I felt that it was scarcely right that my first sight of him should be obtained from the ranks of the crowd. As the hour of his arrival drew near, I felt that I wanted to remain indoors, but I did not dare to say so.

At half-past eleven in the morning a telegram came. Wandering in the grounds, I had chanced to meet the messenger, and as if in unconscious expectation of deliverance from my anxiety followed him into the house. I stood behind Mr. Kaiser as he read the message, and I saw the words, " Make excursion to-day." Instantly Mr. Kaiser turned round and seeing me said angrily, " What a piece of impertinence! " But I did not mind. I was too glad, for I knew I should not see my father.

I went out for the day, with Mr. Kaiser only, as the rest of the household wished to witness the Emperor's arrival. I think that my foster-father was secretly pleased at the turn of events, appreciating that it was not really fitting that I should see the Emperor in this manner. His wife, over whom in such matters he had not the slightest influence, had seen no inappropriateness in the meeting. Fortunately my beloved mother, with her usual thoughtfulness, had foreseen all and sent orders accordingly.

Several weeks after this incident, Frau von Friese, having returned from Denmark, came to St. Gilgen for a few days. Words fail me to express how glad I was to see her. I had felt lost without her amongst so many strangers.

Soon after her arrival, she received the following letter from mother, written at Ischl: —

My dear Friese,

I have long been proposing to spend some time quite undisturbed with my child. As it is not possible for me to be very much with her, I wish all the more to devote every minute I can spare to her. How else are my duties as a mother to be fulfilled? You know I have told you that I did not wish to be the average mother, who believes she has done her duty in kissing her child on the forehead a few times in the course of the day. I want to be her best friend, and as I am often unable to be with her for months together, my only remedy is to live, for a time at least, constantly at her side. In God's free world I will walk with her and make myself mistress of her child-soul.

On the 19th of the month precisely, I go to Langbath Lakes accompanied only by one of my ladies, and you must come on the 19th and bring my baby to me.

I wonder what they will say about me this time? Not that I care!

Yours very sincerely,
Elisabeth.

In obedience to this command, on the morning of the 19th, Frau von Friese with myself and my maid set out for Langbath Lakes, where we arrived the same afternoon. My mother was there to receive us.

Langbath Lakes is an Imperial hunting lodge, on the shore of the lakes of that name. Here we spent a week. How happy I was to be under the same roof with my mother. My bedroom was next hers. For a whole week we were scarcely separated for a minute. I always went to bed at eight o'clock, and then she sat beside me, so that it was with her beloved face before me that I went to sleep. Waking up once in the middle of the night, I was astonished to perceive her still there. Sleep had not come to her — as so often was the case — and she had probably sat by my bed for hours. With a smile she kissed me now, telling me to go to sleep again; and I, with a child's wonderful feeling of confidence in the presence of a protector, drowsily obeyed.

My mother was justified in her expectations. From this time forward I lost the last remnant of diffidence caused by our frequent separations. The ties which bound us grew stronger and stronger; death alone could sever them now.

Those were golden days. The sun seemed brighter than usual, the wind softer, the very air sweeter. Hours and hours we spent wandering through the woods together. Often long intervals of time would pass in silent enjoyment, then at some unexpected beauty of the forest — the peculiar shape of an old, gnarled oak-trunk peering through the undergrowth, the dewdrops on the moss sparkling in the sun, or some charming vista revealed by a sudden turn in the road — mother would burst into exclamations of pleasure.

Sometimes we did not leave the neighbourhood of the hunting-box, preferring a short ramble to a longer and more tiring excursion. On these occasions mother would put her arm through mine, and as we walked along slowly we would discuss all kinds of subjects. I felt very proud that she found me already worthy to have serious conversations with her. She sought for the topics which might interest me most, social and philosophical questions as they are sometimes called. She must have been amused occasionally at my original ideas, but she never ridiculed them, listening on the contrary quite gravely, agreeing or disagreeing as the case might be, and enlightening me on a variety of points which were very important in the formation of my character.

Although it was our custom to choose lonely paths, we frequently met wayfaring peasants, who bowed very respectfully. Sometimes we stopped to chat with those we knew. Occasionally we met tourists, who, although not recognising mother, never passed without turning round to look at her. Then I always felt very proud at having such a beautiful mother. But she was also very particular about my appearance, making me dress in white, and pay great attention to my hair. I was a big girl for my age, and my white cloth costume made a strong contrast with her black one, so that it was quite natural that tourists should stop to look at us as we passed.

We rose early, and as the mornings were usually too cool to take breakfast out of doors, it was served in mother's boudoir. She herself ate, like a bird, very little indeed, while my appetite was always so good that it amused her greatly. She used laughingly to say, "Oh, Weiberl, Weiberl, if you go on like this you will become a regular giantess, and they won't need the statue of Bavaria in Munich, they will take you instead!"

In the end she seriously asked Frau von Friese to take care not to let me grow too stout.

This anxiety concerning my rapid growth led one day to a chance remark, which really opened to me a new page in my life. Mother had been saying, while we were out for a walk, that I looked more like a girl of fifteen than a child of twelve. "You have inherited this from the Wittelsbachs," she continued. "Ludwig was also a giant."

"Which Ludwig do you mean, mother?" I asked.

"Which Ludwig? Why, Ludwig the Second, of course."

She brought the words out in the quick, impatient manner so characteristic of her, and began to walk faster. But she must have noticed my air of utter bewilderment, for she spoke again in a much calmer tone.

"My poor Weiberl," she said, "of course you can't remember him. You were only three years old."

She stopped and put her arm through mine. Then, after we had proceeded a few steps, she suddenly stopped again, and drawing me towards her, kissed me feverishly.

After this we both remained silent until we reached home; my mother wrapped up in her own thoughts and I trying to recall some faint, distant memories. Some place in the country came back to my mind, and there was a gentleman in my mother's company, someone very tall. It was all rather like the shadow of a dream to me, but I seemed to remember that he took me on his knees and played with me. I remembered, too, a rose-filled garden. But what I remembered most distinctly was a cornflower-blue sash on my white embroidered frock. Only in later years did it occur to me that these were the Bavarian colours, that the place must have been the Isle of Roses, and my costume a homage to the tall gentleman — King Ludwig II of Bavaria.

Unfortunately this sojourn at Langbath Lakes passed all too quickly. It was necessary for mother and me to part again, though only for a short time. I went direct to Venice with Frau von Friese, while mother went back to Ischl, following us about a week later. This Italian visit was quite different from that to Langbath Lakes. We were obliged to be more careful about our meetings, though we lived in the same hotel — the Hôtel de l'Europe. Mother, travelling under the name of the Countess Hohenembs, was accompanied by the Countess Festetics, her lady-in-waiting, by Baron Nopsca, and by her private secretary, von Feifalik. Moreover, we were in a big city and not in an out-of-the-way country place. Notwithstanding this, life in Venice had charms of its own. We bathed in the Lido waters, and in the evenings drifted in gondolas down the Grand Canal, enjoying the softness of the air and dreaming of the vanished glories of the old Republic, the silence broken only by some whispered question of mine or my mother's answer in the same low tone.

I recall particularly one of these evenings in Venice, when mother was very quiet and melancholy, and the silence seemed to weigh us down. We were sitting in our gondola, and instead of remaining as usual on my cushions I crept up nearer and nearer to her. Finally I plucked up courage to express the sympathy which I was feeling in my heart, and whispered softly in French, " Maman, chérie, qu'astu? "

She answered, with a caress of the hand: " Nothing serious, only memories of my youth which make me rather sad."

At once I guessed that she must have paid a visit to the Palazzo Reale, to which she had long been wishing to go, while at the same time shrinking from the ordeal.

" Something drew me thither that I could not resist," she said. " The first impression was not too painful — but when I went into poor Ferdinand's room . . ." She broke off abruptly, leaving her sentence unfinished.

On her first visit to Venice, in 1854, when the city still formed part of the Austro-Hungarian Empire, she had stayed at the Palazzo Reale. It was soon after her marriage, and the young sovereigns were accompanied on their tour by the Archduke Ferdinand-Max, afterwards

SUMMER HOLIDAYS

the tragic Emperor Maximilian of Mexico. The remembrance of Queretaro overwhelmed her as she entered the room that her brother-in-law had occupied.

The weeks of our holiday slipped by rapidly, and at last the time came for us to part again. Mother left at the end of September for Gödöllö, the Hungarian Royal château not far from Budapest,[1] and I returned to my home in Vienna, and to the care of Frau von Friese.

[1] Gödöllö has been spoken of by some writers as if it had been my mother's own property. This was not the case. The château belonged to the Emperor as King of Hungary.

CHAPTER VIII

I GO TO SCHOOL

FRAU VON FRIESE now proceeded to carry out a scheme which she had been maturing since her return from Denmark, when she found me unhappy about being amongst so many strangers at St. Gilgen. Her profound experience of life had taught her that a knowledge of books, however wide it might be, was no substitute for the culture imparted by social intercourse. Also she felt that casual meetings with strangers like those in the past summer had little value in the formation of character. It was by systematic and regular association with others, and especially with girls of my own age, that I must learn self-possession and the right bearing in the world. Employing all her habitual tact, she urged my mother to send me to school instead of continuing my lessons with Laura under Herr Hold.

Mother had been displeased that the Kaisers had allowed me to meet so many people at St. Gilgen, but when she spoke of this, Frau von Friese observed that, so far from this seeming to have done me any harm, on the contrary, I appeared the better able to appreciate what I had in life. Mother could not argue that I had received any harm, and began to weaken. She hated and detested the very idea of sending me to school, however, for fear of what might happen to me there, and protested that she could never feel safe if I were under any care except Frau von Friese's own. But my governess still fought on, and her steady persistence won the day in the end. She was

I GO TO SCHOOL

perhaps the only one of my mother's friends who could persuade her to alter her decisions.

The school to which she wanted me sent, explained Frau von Friese, was a private one, quite the best in Vienna, to which only the daughters of high families, official and military, were wont to go. "Or should I suggest the Convent of the Sacred Heart?" she added with a smile.

"A convent? Never!" cried my mother. But she agreed now that I should go to the suggested school, if it were arranged that one of the teachers should have me under her special supervision. Accordingly preparations were made for my admission to the institution of Fräulein Alma von Gunesch. Miss Bartholme, the teacher of English, was to pay particular attention to me, and in order that this would not be too obvious she was appointed mistress over the whole class in which I was placed.

And now I felt very happy. For years it had been my great ambition to go to school, and nothing gave me greater pleasure than starting off in the morning with my books under my arm. I went three days a week, for five hours each day.

On the opening day of the school term, October 1, 1893, I was directed to a form in the second row, with room for three pupils. During the first hour, from nine o'clock till ten, the seats beside me remained empty, although the other rows were almost all full. At ten o'clock a young girl came in and looked about timidly for a place. I made signs for her to come and sit by me, when Miss Bartholme at once ordered her to another seat, and told me not to take things upon myself, for I was at school now, and it was not my business to say where the pupils were to sit.

For the moment there was nothing more for me to say; but I could be very persistent when I wanted a thing very much, and in three days' time that girl was sitting next to me.

There was really no reason for my request not being granted, as Elsa von Thyr belonged to one of the very first families in Austria. Her father had been a field-marshal who had died only one year ago. Like me, she had never been to school before, as she soon told me. I did not feel particularly drawn towards her in the beginning, and it was only my obstinacy which made me wish especially to have her beside me. But afterwards we became fast friends, and for years she was the only girl to whose home I was allowed to go.

My first visit to her mother's house came about in the following way. One morning, after we had been acquainted for some months, Elsa very gravely told me that she had written me a letter.

I had not received it, as it had been addressed to the home of my foster-parents, and so I answered with some astonishment: "A letter to me? Where did you address it? Can't you tell me what was in it?"

"Oh, the letter was just for form's sake, for your parents to see, my mother said."

"But what was it about? Please tell me."

Elsa was timid in many ways, and she hesitated before replying. Finally she said: "I sent you an invitation to come to see me next Sunday afternoon. I told mother that your parents seemed to make a great fuss about you. So she said it was better to write a letter."

My first emotion was one of great pleasure. Then a cloud came over my thoughts. Should I be allowed to

I GO TO SCHOOL

go? Elsa noticed the change in my expression, and asked me what was the matter. Did n't I want to accept?

But now Miss Bartholme had come up, attracted by the sound of our voices, and inquired what we were talking about. "I think it was very kind of Her Excellency to invite Lily," she said, speaking of me by the name under which I passed in the Kaiser family and at the school. "But she goes out so seldom that she must first get permission from her parents."

Elsa's face showed some annoyance, and she asked sarcastically if my mother and father thought I was made of sugar.

"No," I answered awkwardly, "but, don't you see, my mother does not know yours."

Elsa burst out with the remark that she would have thought that "ihre Excellenz von Thyr" ought to be good enough for my mother to know. She was very cross, and spoke as haughtily to me now as she usually did to the rest of the school. I on my side was raging, but I controlled my temper with a great effort, smiling disdainfully and saying nothing. "If you only knew!" was what I thought to myself.

But I quickly repented of my behaviour. After all, was she not perfectly justified? Frau von Thyr was certainly just as good as Mrs. Kaiser, and Elsa, not being a clairvoyant, could not guess who my mother really was. I determined that I would do all I could to obtain permission to accept the invitation, and I made up the quarrel with Elsa at once.

It was only after much persuasion that I got leave to go to the von Thyrs' house. Mother was not in Vienna at the time, but was away cruising in the Mediterranean;

so that Frau von Friese had to take the responsibility in the matter upon herself. I coaxed and coaxed her, until finally she decided to confer with Mr. and Mrs. Kaiser. My foster-father had to make inquiries about the family, and after he found out that everything was satisfactory, they told me that I might go, but that Mrs. Kaiser, as my supposed mother, must accompany me on my first visit.

My new friends resided in the district of Vienna which is called "The Cottage," where they had a mansion in the middle of a beautiful park, several acres in extent. Elsa's mother lived a very retired life, seeing only her intimate friends, all of them distinguished people. Really it seemed that, had one searched all over Vienna, a more suitable girl friend could not have been found for me.

On her return from the Riviera, toward the end of April, mother found me greatly changed for the better, and was very glad that she had consented to send me to school. I was no longer so childish and unformed, but had begun to be more womanly in manner.

"You are always right, and I am always wrong, my dear Friese," she said to my faithful Aya. "From this time on I shall never veto anything that you may decide on Lintchi's behalf.[1] I can see clearly now that I understand nothing about the ways of the world. But there you are — our education unfits us for real life! You are bringing up my girl as I have always intended to have her brought up. I see now that I personally should never have had the energy necessary for success. With all my good intentions, I should probably have made out of her

[1] My mother never called me Lily, but usually Lintchi — or Linka, which is the Hungarian form of the diminutive of Caroline.

I GO TO SCHOOL

nothing but a commonplace, everyday princess, after all. You really are my guardian angel, sent to help me in my time of need!"

Frau von Friese was very pleased with this expression of approval. But, as I have said before, there was not a trace of servility in her nature — which was the chief reason why my mother loved her so much — and she answered: "As your Majesty is so kind as to praise what I have done, I will be frank and admit that you have sometimes made matters a little difficult for me. That renders your Majesty's approval all the more valuable now, and you can give me no greater proof of your confidence than by allowing me to carry out my plans for Lily in the future."

"You shall, my dear Friese. It is time that we should show the world that our class knows its duty to be to educate our children to help their fellowmen. These children must not be conceited because of their rank, but must realize that if fate has given them a leading place it is in order that they should set an example by their character and conduct."

She pulled me toward her and whispered in my ear, "Now life really has an object for me!"

There are occasions, not very remarkable in themselves, which nevertheless greatly impress the mind of a child. My mother's remarks were the last link in a chain of influences which helped to mould my character. My regular life, and freedom from the fear of punishment; the good rule of Frau von Friese; the greater intimacy with my mother; and last, but by no means least, my intercourse with other children of my own age — these were the other links. From this time forward I began to observe myself more closely, and to think, quite without conceit, with regard to every action of mine, " Is this worthy of an archduchess?"

At the end of May my mother and I went to Munich for three days. We lived in the "Vier Jahreszeiten" Hotel. The first two days my mother was in rare good spirits such as were seldom hers. On the third we went together to the sepulchre of Ludwig II. She was entirely changed — bowed down with grief, deathly pale, feeble, and languid. We both knelt down at the foot of the tomb, when, taking my two hands, she placed them upon it, with her hands resting on mine. So we remained some little time. On rising we stood still for a moment; and then finally she spoke, with so mournful a solemnity that I was perplexed and oppressed.

"My child, remember that if ever at any time you come again to Munich you must come here. This is a sacred duty which your mother lays upon you."

Then she took my arm, and without another word we walked out.

CHAPTER IX

AN ACCIDENT; AND A VISIT TO THE RIVIERA

THE first summer after I went to school I had no desire for the holidays. The chief reason for this was that I knew that I should not be with my mother. She went this year to Madonna di Campiglio in the Tyrol. It had been her intention that I should follow her there, but at the last moment it was decided that she should be accompanied by a large suite, and that the Emperor should join her shortly afterwards. It was therefore out of the question for me to be with her there. My disappointment was very great, and the question tormented me, "What was to become of me?" I secretly hoped that I should not have to spend the summer with the Kaisers. I had forgotten the necessity of keeping up appearances. When Frau von Friese told me that it had been arranged that the Kaisers should take me with them again, I was plunged in despair.

"I know that it is hard for you, my dear," she said, "but it is just for that reason that I wish you to go. If you had really enjoyed the irregular life of last summer and had wanted to go, it would have been my duty to forbid it. You must learn, you know, to bow to the inevitable."

This was her system, for the good of my character. So I went away with the Kaisers once more. Good luck, however, befel us — if it is not hard-hearted of me to say so — for toward the end of July Mrs. Kaiser had such trouble with her eyes that she was obliged to go to a sanatorium at Salzburg. At first it was thought that this would be only for a short time, and I was left with Laura under the care of her governess. But as weeks passed by with little or no improvement in Mrs. Kaiser's condition, Frau von Friese, who had only just returned from another visit to her own country, thought it unwise to leave me any longer without a special guardian to take charge of me, and so came to fetch me away. The rest of the summer we spent together at Gmunden, which is quite near to Ischl, so that we were able to see my mother as often as she could manage to get away from her suite.

At the beginning of September mother proposed to take me with her on a visit to Corfu. Again fate intervened to keep us apart. At the last moment my sister Valerie and her husband, Francis-Salvator, announced to my mother their intention of spending September with her. This was a great disappointment to us both.

In October I returned to school. I was glad to meet Elsa again, with whom I had kept up a regular correspondence during the summer. Everything seemed to go on just the same as before the holidays. In the meanwhile, mother, who had gone from Corfu to Gödöllö, returned to Vienna on November 3rd, so as to be able to spend the 4th (which is the name-day of my patron, St. Charles) as usual with me. This time I received my first present of any value except the unset six-carat diamond, which was always purchased for me on that day as for all the archduchesses of the Austrian Imperial family. My new present was a pretty string of pearls, each the size of a pea.

A few days after, on November 7th, I was alone in my study with Frau von Friese when Pirker announced a

A VISIT TO THE RIVIERA

visitor to see her. This visit was quite unexpected, and it left me, as very rarely happened, alone in my room, Fräulein Hain being out for the day. Now, like most girls, I loved to arrange things to suit my own taste. There was a picture on the wall which was not hung to my fancy, and I determined to use this moment of freedom to change its position myself. I called Leopold to bring me a ladder; but, as he was busy or probably too lazy to obey, he sent it to me by one of the maids. Mina, who had seen the girl with the ladder, followed her into the room, and begged me to wait for Frau von Friese's permission. But I laughed, and ordered her to stand near the door and give me warning if footsteps should be heard approaching. The ladder was one of those double ones, and in my hurry I forgot to put the crutch in. I had climbed up, and was leaning over to lift the picture when Mina sounded her note of warning, "Die Gnädige kommt" (Madame is coming). I tried to get down quickly, and in my haste caused the ladder to slip, throwing me heavily to the floor. I tried to rise, but in vain. Somehow, I had hurt my back. At this very moment Frau von Friese entered the room. She stared at me terrified. Then, growing angry, she exclaimed: "Get up, you careless girl. What were you doing with that ladder?"

"I can't get up," I answered.

My governess was naturally pale, but at my words she became as white as chalk. Mina had now hurried to my side, and cried reproachfully: "What did I say? But, of course, no one ever listens to me!" The remark, no doubt, was meant not so much to cast the blame upon me as to exonerate herself from the charge of allowing me to use the ladder in the absence of Frau von Friese.

They put me to bed with considerable difficulty, every movement causing me great pain. Then Frau von Friese got Mr. Kaiser to summon Professor Lorenz, the famous surgeon. The Professor declared that my back had been severely strained, and that I must be put into plaster at once — a proceeding which was so excruciating that I had to clench my teeth to prevent myself from crying out.

After the Professor's departure Frau von Friese said despairingly: "Now I must inform Her Majesty. What *will* she say?" This was probably more for the benefit of Fräulein, who had just returned, than for mine.

"Oh, don't tell mother that it is serious," I exclaimed, in spite of my pain. "I don't want her to know how badly I am hurt. Besides, I will tell her that it was all my fault."

"No, my dear, I cannot deceive your mother," answered Frau von Friese. "I must tell her every word that the Professor has said. And it *is* my fault. I should have given orders to say that I was not at home to anyone when I knew that Fräulein was not with you."

The same evening mother arrived, pale but outwardly quite composed. As she bent over and kissed me, her touch seemed to relieve the pain, as though she really possessed the gift of kings. With Frau von Friese she was as gentle as only she could be, and embracing her said she never could be convinced that it was her fault. Was I not, after all, no longer a small child, but a girl quite old enough to take care of myself?

She spoke so unconcernedly, and her whole manner was so cheerful and natural, that none of us realised what agony she suffered inwardly, thinking that I should be lame for life. She remained with me all night. My suffering was so great that for some time I could not sleep.

A VISIT TO THE RIVIERA

But mother took one of my hands in hers and held it. Then there stole over me that feeling of calm confidence, which her presence and her touch always inspired, and I fell asleep. How long I remained so I do not know. The rustling of her skirts awakened me. We were alone. She, thinking me asleep, had knelt down by my bedside. Opening my eyes I saw that hers were red with weeping. Poor, poor mother! What must have been her anxiety to cause her to cry like this? When she saw that I was awake, she rose and bending over me pressed her cheek against my face, so that I felt her burning tears running over my temples. I put my two arms about her neck, and strained her to my heart as tightly as I could.

Her presence at my bedside was the cause of some trouble. On leaving the Hofburg, as she intended to return almost immediately she had omitted to confide in any of her ladies-in-waiting where she was going, or to say that she might remain away all night. When they discovered her absence they kept silence at first. However, as time passed and she still did not return, they thought it best to inform Baron Nopsca, the Master of her Household. In ordinary circumstances he would have reported this immediately to the Emperor, but supposing it only some small matter which detained her, he too kept silence. As hour after hour passed by and she did not come back, the anxiety of her attendants grew acute. They dared not now inform the Emperor, for the result would be a severe reprimand, perhaps even dismissal. Still less did they dare to institute a search for Her Majesty, lest worse should follow. So the night came to an end, leaving them all in a terrible state of mind. Events justified their conduct. My mother, after having forgotten them all in her trouble about me, returned to the Hofburg at six o'clock in the morning. Then the storm broke. Baron Nopsca, who was wrought up to fever-heat by his anxiety, accused her of trying his patience too far, and informed her that if such a thing should occur again, he could not take on himself the responsibility of keeping silent. Mother was nervous and unstrung with all that she had undergone, and, bitterly realising that she was never free to do as she wished, lost her temper suddenly and struck him in the face. After this, of course, Baron Nopsca could not remain longer in her household, and demanded to be allowed to resign.

My mother, needless to say, afterwards repented of her hastiness on this occasion, and seized every opportunity of showing Baron Nopsca marked attention. Once, I know myself, on the occasion of a dinner given by her in honour of my sister Gisela and her husband at Budapest, she sent to him in Vienna a present of fruit.

For three weeks after my accident I was obliged to lie on my back. At first, regardless of everything else, mother came every day to see me. Then, when my recovery was assured, arrangements having been made previously for a trip to the Mediterranean, she left Vienna on December 1st, after commanding Frau von Friese to inform her every day by letter and telegram of my condition.

My convalescence was so rapid that before Christmas I was able to be up and walking, and finally even to go back to school. According to her regular custom, mother passed this winter in the south. This was for me usually the longest period of separation from her; but this year my accident came to my assistance. About the beginning of January Professor Lorenz decided that it was advisable for me to have a change of air. Frau von Friese

A VISIT TO THE RIVIERA

made no reply at the time, so that my surprise and pleasure were very great indeed when, a little later, she informed me that I was to spend some time with mother on the Riviera. I was so overjoyed that I danced from one end of the room to the other. "Oh! You *are* good!" I cried. "Am I really to see mother so soon and so unexpectedly?"

"Of course," she replied. "We shall all live at the same hotel. No one will be any the wiser. Your mother has known me for years, and can talk with me as often as she wishes without its being remarked upon by any one. So we shall be perfectly free."

My joy speedily gave place to doubt. The news was surely too good to be true. Many things might happen to prevent our departure. The doctor might alter his mind. Mother might countermand the order. I magnified my groundless fears until school-work became impossible to me, and at nights I would lie awake until thoroughly exhausted. So things continued until the date of our departure arrived. That day I was in a worse fever of impatience than ever. Only when we had reached the train and entered our compartment, and I stood at the window watching the last preparations, could I breathe a little easier. Then the guard blew his whistle, the train gave a jerk, and we rolled out of the station on the way to Nice. There was no turning back now. I lay back in my seat, feeling supremely happy. At last I was really on my way to the Riviera, the earthly Paradise, with my darling mother as the guardian angel of it.

A disappointment was awaiting me on my arrival. For I was greeted by a bleak north wind, a wintry, dust-covered landscape, and a dull sky. Was this, then, the Riviera? But I was soon reassured. On the following day a soft southerly breeze was blowing, sky and sea were a perfect blue, and the landscape was bathed in the golden light of the southern sun. Suddenly an overwhelming love for this beautiful country sprang up in my heart and possessed it. It possesses it still, and will do so until my heart shall cease to beat.

On the first day after my arrival mother took me to see the famous gardens of Mortola. As we wandered through them I could not repress my enthusiasm. My first exclamation, I have since been told, was: "Mother dear, how lovely it would be to die here! I feel happy beyond all wishes, with all this beauty and with you. The only thing to make me sad is when I think that it cannot last."

For hours and hours, covering miles and miles, we wandered about together each day. Mother always left the hotel unaccompanied, and we met at some appointed place. How glorious were these times! However far we might walk, no distance ever seemed to tire us. She was very solicitous about me, however, constantly asking, "Weiberl, does your leg hurt you, or do I go too quickly for you?" And all the while, without any visible sign, mother herself was suffering tortures from sciatica.

Never before did I realise how much happiness my presence gave her. Often in the course of our walks she would draw me to her and kiss me; or else she would take my hand in hers, and so we would go along hand in hand.

Occasionally during our walks we had rather amusing experiences. One day, I remember, we lost ourselves, or at least went a lot out of our way, in an olive-grove in the neighbourhood of Rochebrune. As usual mother was afraid of tiring me, and so we had sat down on a fallen tree, the only seat which we could see about us. We had only been there a few minutes when a stout lady, accompanied by a girl of about twenty, came along and in broken French asked permission to sit on the tree-trunk beside us. As we did not intend to move at once, mother, of course, not wishing to be rude, immediately answered, "Yes." Then turning to me she half-whispered a few words which the elder lady recognised to be German.

"Oh, the ladies are German," she began at once in her own language, her face radiant with that patriotism which is so strong in the heart of every German, and which they manifest so plainly when they meet with one of their fellow-countrymen.

Mother explained that we were Austrians, and entered into conversation with the zest which she was wont to show upon such occasions. She dearly loved to be incognita, and was only cold and distant with people who knew her rank and with whom she had to be, as she expressed it, "on parade." The German lady proved to be very talkative, and had soon told us where she came from and how she liked the Riviera, but found Monte Carlo too noisy, and a difficult place to recognise celebrities on account of the crowds. She catalogued the royalties in the Riviera for the season, or likely to arrive soon — the Empress Eugénie, Queen Victoria, the Prince of Wales, and the Emperor and Empress of Austria. I could scarcely restrain my laughter, but mother gave no sign. In spite of the unhappiness of her life she still kept a spirit of mischief in her. She encouraged the German lady to talk of the Emperor and Empress, and then, as the other remarked what an interesting person the Empress was, she broke in with, "Oh, she's a crazy woman; I would not go a yard to see her, with her fan spread out in front of her face the moment she thinks you are looking at her. I would just as soon look at my own fan "—at the same time striking it against her knee and rising to go.

The friendly German expressed her pleasure at having met us, hoped to see us again, and gave the address of her villa, as though inviting an exchange of confidences. Mother hurried me away, scolding me mildly for the mirth I was now making violent efforts to control. Our inquisitive friend would soon enough find out to whom she had been talking, she said. She was quite right. Very shortly after the adventure in the olive-grove, mother told me that as she was taking a walk with the Countess Festetics and General von Berceviczy, she again came across the lady, who stepped on one side with a deep curtsey and a smile which showed that she had recognised her.

But the incident did not close here. A few days later, when I was out walking with Frau von Friese, we met the two ladies again. Now, however, instead of stepping aside, they crossed our path to speak to us, and after a low curtsey, the old lady haltingly began: "Your Imperial Highness, please excuse me if I take the liberty of stopping you. I only wish to beg of you to convey my deep apology to Her Majesty, if we have perhaps behaved in a way we ought not to have."

If the good lady was embarrassed, I was still more so, but Frau von Friese came to my rescue and answered for me: "There is nothing to apologise for, my dear ladies, since nothing unpleasant occurred. Nevertheless we will convey your message."

The Germans were not yet quite reassured, and the younger one took up the tale. I felt very sorry for them;

A VISIT TO THE RIVIERA

and, embarrassed myself at their very embarrassment, I suddenly blurted out: " I will explain to mother —"

I stopped abruptly. What a fearful blunder I had made! We rushed away immediately. Frau von Friese had turned quite pale, and for once was deprived even of the power to scold me.

During this visit to the Riviera, not a day passed without my seeing mother. She seemed so happy about it, and indeed quite as happy as I was myself. Even if we could not see each other in the daytime I would creep into her bedroom for an hour after she had retired. To do this, I had to descend from my own room on the first floor to the main hall of the hotel on the ground floor. Then, taking great care that no one should see me, I slipped into the corridor leading to my mother's apartments. Hurrying down this, I passed through the room reserved for the ladies of the bedchamber into my mother's own room. She was always in bed before I arrived, and I would sit on the edge of it, or else would lie down near her, often in her arms, with my head on her shoulder. We were both silent and both content at being in each other's company.

It must not be thought that it was easy for me to escape observation. My mother's attendants, though few in number, were always on the alert, and might easily have caught me had they wished. There were General von Berceviczy; Feifalik, her private secretary; Pali, her Greek reader at that time; and the Countess Festetics, besides her other ladies and the servants. But at my approach they all vanished. I was so naïve as to believe then that their disappearances were accidental and that none of them knew what I was doing!

"My poor Weiberl," mother said to me on one of the first evenings of our stay, after I had crept tremblingly to her room, "you are a brave little girl. Now I want you to tell me the real truth. When you have to humble yourself like this for my sake, don't you feel vexed with me?"

"Oh, mother dear!" I cried, "have I ever given the slightest sign of vexation? Are you dissatisfied with me that you should speak like that?"

She saw that I was upset, and hastened to comfort me. She explained that she had only been afraid I might think it was owing to a caprice on her part that I had to live as I did, in such secrecy always, and that I might feel that I was being deprived through her of the rights and privileges which should be mine. I was an Archduchess, and did it not seem wrong for me to go through the streets unrecognised, instead of receiving the salutes of the soldiers and the homage of the crowd?

But I assured her that such things as these were nothing to me, when I was really so much better off than the other Archduchesses, living under her care, as Gisela and Valerie had never been allowed to live. I know that I was perfectly sincere in talking like this. I did not consider myself in the slightest degree lowered, but, on the contrary, raised to a height by my manner of life, in such intimacy with her. Nothing else could have brought me such happiness. Moreover, the comedy of concealment which we played together was too amusing and, above all, too romantic not to please me. With the Wittelsbach blood in my veins I could not escape the heritage of a romantic nature.

What my mother said on another occasion comes back to me in connection with this question of an Archduchess's

A VISIT TO THE RIVIERA

position. "You know, Weiberl," she told me once, " it is the excessive honours they receive which spoil the characters of those who are too young to understand that such honours are paid not to them personally, but to the family they come from. It is only natural that children should have their heads turned in this way and come to consider themselves of a superior clay. If I had had anything to say in the matter, I should have forbidden them to ride in the golden Imperial carriages or to receive military salutes before their sixteenth or eighteenth year. But, of course, if I had even hinted such views I should have been declared a lunatic, and so I never interfered. For my own part, I do not care for such extravagances. I should like to see them abolished. But the public loves them. Drums and trumpets amuse it!"

Like everything else in life, my enjoyable time on the Riviera came to an end. In February, after several weeks' holiday, I returned to Vienna with Frau von Friese. Mother left at the beginning of the following month for Ajaccio, whence she sailed for Naples. And here she went on board her yacht the Miramar, and paid a visit to her villa at Corfu, which she had built a few years earlier.

CHAPTER X

HOW A HOLIDAY WAS SPOILT

IT was on May 1st of this year, 1895, that my mother returned to Vienna, and she came to visit me at once. As the Emperor went to Pola for some days on the 7th and Valerie had gone home, she was perfectly free for a time to spend every moment with me. When the weather was fine we made excursions; and when it was wet we passed the day at my home at Lainz. I kept a diary then, from which I take a few extracts.

May 4*th*. To the Hinterbruhl with mother.

8*th*. With mother to Klosterneuburg, over the Leopoldsberg and the Kahlenberg, where we took tea. We went down by the funicular railway to Nussdorf, and from there home in a carriage.

9*th*. To Hernals to see a poor family named Sperl. Mother wanted to find out what they needed. [She afterwards set them up in a small grocery business, without letting them know who she was.]

10*th*. Mother with me in the afternoon. Mr. Kaiser's birthday. Lunched there. It rained all day.

11*th*. Rain again.

14*th*. A long walk to the Augarten with mother. Weather still bad.

15*th*. Mother only with me for an hour.

May 16*th*. Over the Aninger to Baden with mother and Frau von Friese.

HOW A HOLIDAY WAS SPOILT

19*th*. Mother could not come to-day. There is a big dinner-party at Lainz. Father back from Pola. Count Kalnocky, Prince Liechtenstein, and Count Paar were at the dinner.

20*th*. Examination at school. Mother again could not come to see me. Another dinner-party at Lainz. Father, mother, Stephanie, and Erzsie.

21*st*. Mother came to see me and told me she could not come again for several days, because Valerie was coming. She stayed with me all the afternoon.

22*nd*. Franz [the Archduke Franz-Ferdinand] came to Vienna alone. Valerie ill, and two of her children with chicken-pox. So mother will be able to come and see me. How lucky!

23*rd*. With mother to Förstel's in the Kohlmarkt. Bought a very nice handbag for Elsa's birthday. The first time in my life with mother in town. No one recognised her.

27*th*. Franz has gone back to Wels. He was waiting for Valerie all the time, but she could not come.

28*th*. Mrs. Kaiser has very bad eyes. Mother went with me to see her. Laura is so silly.

31*st*. Elsa's birthday. A girls' party there. Princess Jeanne Ghika, Alica von Matacziz, Laura, and myself.

June 1*st*. End of school term. Most of the girls cried. Some of them wrote their names in my album. Among them were Sera Vlassak, Mizza von Voinovicz, Marianne von Pittreich, and Wilma Röll.

2*nd*. Gisela came from Munich with her two boys. She will remain a whole week, so I shan't be able to see mother. I am so disappointed. She would have been free, as father has gone away to Graz.

On June 10th my mother left Vienna for her annual pilgrimage to the tomb of King Ludwig at Munich. She stopped on the way to visit Valerie at Lichtenegg. She had originally intended that I should meet her at Wels, whence Lichtenegg can be reached by carriage. By this arrangement we should have travelled together, as we did in the previous year; the time of her departure from Lichtenegg being undecided, however, this was impossible. It was usual, when we went on a railway journey together, for mother to have a private carriage attached to the train while I took a separate compartment in the other part of the train. Then, after we had started, I would make my way to her carriage, so that, while officially she was alone, actually I travelled with her. On this occasion, according to her instructions, I left on the 11th for Munich, accompanied by Frau von Friese. Our separation was really fortunate; for Gisela met mother on her arrival at the station, and had we been together, even if as usual we had left the train separately, it might easily have been very awkward for us.

Our week at the Hôtel Continental in Munich was really delightful, though we were depressed by our visit on the 13th to the tomb of the king. In token of her never-failing remembrance, mother left a wreath of jasmine and roses, his favourite flowers.

On June 18th mother returned to Vienna, while on the 20th I went to spend the summer at Gmunden. This time I was not separated from my dear Frau von Friese, and we lived together in the same villa as in the previous year. It was very charming, this little villa with its groves of walnut trees and pines at the back and both sides. In front was a lawn with a fountain in the centre, bordered by two rows of ancient trees interspersed with

HOW A HOLIDAY WAS SPOILT

sweet-smelling jasmine and lilac. Gmunden itself is one of the finest spots in the Salzkammergut, and as it is less than an hour from the Imperial summer residence of Ischl, it is much patronised by fashionable people.

A summer morning in this place is most lovely. How enjoyable it was to breakfast on the terrace, with the whole scene sparkling in the sun, the mountains only wrapped in a light veil of fog; the air fresh with dew, a perfect blue sky overhead, suggestive of unending peace and quiet, and in the distance the mirror-like dark green lake, where now and then the creaking of the oars of a rowing-boat and the following splash were the sole sounds to break the silence! How glorious it all was, and how *blasé* must be the people who can look upon such beauty with indifference, as if it were merely something else which they can purchase with their gold!

Mr. and Mrs. Kaiser had also leased a summer villa here, and so I spent some of my time at my own home and some at theirs, especially at the beginning of the visit; for mother stayed over three weeks at Bartfeld, in Hungary, for the waters. She wanted at first to take me there too, but she decided not to. She was afraid that, owing to her great popularity in Hungary, she was more likely to be recognised there than elsewhere when she had me with her. Besides, she was accompanied by a big suite, including the Countess Festetics, the Countess Kornis, the Countess Mikes, her lady reader Fräulein Ida von Ferenczi, and her Greek reader Pali. Her fear on this occasion was no exaggeration, for she wrote me that she could not go for a walk, even in the least frequented parts of the forest, without seeing someone apparently bent on meeting her. She also spoke in one of her letters of the thoughtfulness shown by the Hungarians in furnishing and decorating her private apartments, and expressed particular pleasure at the delicate perception which caused busts of her beloved Heine, as well as of her two favourite Hungarians, Deak and Jokai, to be placed in her sitting-room.

On July 24th she arrived at Ischl. After this we met several times at Rimbach, a little place at the end of the Lake of Gmunden, called also the Lake of Traun.

The first time we were alone together, my mother said to me: "Babe, we have become indispensable to each other. We spoil one another, and are too happy. You will see that Fate has some trick to play upon us."

Prophetic words!

At the beginning of August the King and Queen of Roumania arrived at Ischl, so that mother was unable to come over to see me. Thinking to occupy the time, which hung heavily on my hands, I begged to be allowed to visit and nurse Laura, who was ill with bronchitis, following upon an attack of measles. Frau von Friese and the doctor at first opposed my idea, but ultimately gave way, the doctor saying that Laura's illness was not contagious. Frau von Friese probably consented the more readily because she desired to make her annual visit to Denmark. Besides, she strongly approved of my affection for my foster-sister. So it came about that I was installed as a nurse, but not for long. On the sixth day I felt unwell myself. I kept silence regarding my feelings, but the next day I was so ill that I was compelled to remain in bed. My attack, however, was slighter than Laura's, since I was confined to bed four days only. During this time Mrs. Kaiser nursed me. I must acknowledge her great goodness in taking entire charge of me on this occasion. She even went to the extent of putting me in her

HOW A HOLIDAY WAS SPOILT

own room, leaving her own daughter to the care of others. The malady must have been really very catching, for on the day I rose from my bed Mrs. Kaiser was obliged to take to hers.

My governess's absence, coupled with the illness in the Kaiser household, prevented mother from being informed at once of what had happened to me. In fact, she only learned of it on the same day that I got up. She came over instantly to see me. Poor mother! At the sight of me she could not keep back her tears, so anxious did she feel about me. She herself had not been well, and it made my heart heavy when I saw the tears rolling down her cheeks. Had those who called her cold and lacking in heart seen her then, they never again would have dared to speak a word against her.

Though the illness proved so catching, mother insisted on seeing Mrs. Kaiser to thank her personally for the great care she had taken of me. " You go first into Mrs. Kaiser's room," she said to me, " and tell her that I want to see her. But for goodness' sake let there be no fuss. Tell her she *must* remain in bed. If she tries to get up, say to her it is on account of the servants that she must stay where she is."

I carried this message word for word to Mrs. Kaiser, who smiled and consented to remain in bed. Then mother went to her, and was really wonderfully gracious.

" Mrs. Kaiser," she said, " you have made yourself ill through nursing my girl. Now it will be her turn to take care of you."

Mother had arrived at the house quite alone, and, like an ordinary stranger, had asked Mrs. Kaiser's maid (who happened, unfortunately, to be a comparatively new one) if she could see her mistress. How great was her embarrassment when, instead of being admitted at once, she received the answer that Mrs. Kaiser was ill and could see no one! Timidly mother asked for Miss Lily or Miss Laura. All this took place at the entrance to the villa. How degrading it was for her, the Empress, to have to beg for admittance at the hands of a maid, who, not knowing whether she was really a friend of the family, was undecided as to the advisability of letting her inside the house! I wonder that she did not become angry before Laura, whom the servant finally fetched, came to her rescue.

During the whole of Mrs. Kaiser's illness my mother sent every day to inquire after her and showed many proofs of her especial regard. Among other presents came several bottles of the priceless Imperial Tokay. Her gratitude for Mrs. Kaiser's kindness to me was deep. But then gratitude was one of the most marked of mother's good qualities.

Mrs. Kaiser's illness took a dangerous turn. After a few days she became delirious, and she remained in this state for weeks, so that the worst was almost expected. She had two nuns to nurse her in turn, day and night. In her delirium she tried to send them away, not recognising the moving black objects.

Although Laura was not far removed from me in age, her character was much less mature than mine. Besides, she was too impatient to be able to nurse her mother, so that I felt it my duty to be near her. Frau von Friese by this time was back again from Denmark, and, highminded woman that she was, was quite convinced that it would do me no harm to see this side of life.

Mother, who was leaving for Aix-les-Bains on the last day of August, had arranged that I should follow her there, and on this account had leased Dr. Vidal's garden, so that we might the more easily meet each other. In order not to run the risk of disappointing me at the last moment, as had happened before when something unexpected caused a change in her plans, she had told me nothing about this. After her first visit to Gmunden during my illness, she came to see me several times again at my own villa, where Frau von Friese now was, and it was only on the last day that she spoke of her plan of taking me with her. Unfortunately, just on the impulse of the moment, I cried: " But can I go? Suppose, while I am away, Mrs. Kaiser —"

I stopped short. But my mother drew me towards her, and feverishly pressed kisses upon my eyes. She fought a silent battle within herself, and finally she said in a voice that was no more than a whisper: " You are quite right, Weiberl. You cannot go away now. You are a good, dutiful girl."

I was too young and inexperienced to understand then what it cost her mother's heart to make this sacrifice. All the summer, probably, she had been looking forward eagerly to this time. She had planned everything so carefully, and had not breathed a word of it before the proper day. Even at the time I had an intuition of her grief, although I could not realise how deep it was. I tried to take back what I had said, and to argue that events might take quite a favourable turn after all. I must confess that I too was heartbroken now, when I thought of all the lovely times of which I had deprived myself. But it was in vain. Mother shook her head and said: " Weiberl, darling, did you not hear me? I have decided that you have to remain."

Then I knew that not a syllable more must be uttered,

if I did not wish to make her angry. I could guess that those firm words were meant more, perhaps, for herself than for me. And so I stayed behind.

The succeeding weeks slipped swiftly by until the end of September arrived. Laura had gone back to Vienna with her father, and had been placed in a boarding-school under the management of Fräulein Hanauseck. Mrs. Kaiser was now quite out of danger, but the doctors ordered a complete rest for her. As I never returned to Vienna so early in the autumn, and as mother was in Hungary, where she had gone from Aix-les-Bains, I remained with Frau von Friese at Gmunden and spent much of my time by the bedside of the patient. The autumn was beautiful, and I enjoyed to the fullest extent my walks in the neighbourhood.

I remember several curious occurrences at this time. I was known to everyone in the place, and there was plenty of gossip about me. I noticed that I was even treated with more or less deference, as befitted my real rank. I was known by the title of " Princess," and was supposed to be staying at Gmunden incognita. As I was walking on the esplanade, it frequently happened that gentlemen stopped to bow deeply to me, and that young girls made curtseys. When I went to the bathing-place everyone stared at me. It was probably considered remarkable that I was always accompanied by Frau von Friese and a maid; especially as the former never took the baths herself and the latter was manifestly waiting upon me. Perhaps some people had already seen me in my mother's company. Although the society at Gmunden was very select, the place was a regular nest of gossip — probably because the aristocratic quality of the visitors furnished the local *bourgeoisie* with the more food for discussion.

HOW A HOLIDAY WAS SPOILT

One day early in my visit I was standing by chance at the gate of the Kaisers' villa in the dress which is called the Dearndl — the costume of the upper Austrian peasantry, very fashionable at that time for ladies also. This suited me well, as I was rather big. I did not notice that, as I stood at the gate, a man with a camera took up his position opposite me. I was therefore much astonished when he came up to me and said: " I have taken the liberty of taking a snapshot of you, mademoiselle. I could not resist so charming a subject."

I only smiled bashfully, not knowing what to reply, and he did not wait for an answer but passed on. How great was my amazement when, as I was walking out one day in the autumn with one of Mrs. Kaiser's two nuns, I met the same man, who halted before me and with a low bow said: " Your Imperial Highness, I owe you an apology. Your Highness will remember that this summer I took the liberty of taking a photograph of you, but I did not then know who the charming young lady was. Your Imperial Highness may rest assured that no one shall ever see the photograph."

For a moment I did not know what to answer, but I did not lose countenance. With a smile that helped to hide my embarrassment, I answered: " Keep it as a remembrance of me, but please do not show it to anyone else."

And then, inclining my head slightly, as I had seen my mother do, I passed on. What did the man mean? I wondered. Who had been talking to him?

A second little adventure happened soon after this. It was on a Sunday afternoon, very grey and dull. Sister Elizabeth, one of the nuns, noticing that I seemed rather lonely and bored, said to Mrs. Kaiser, " Would not the young lady like to go to the entertainment which the parishioners have got up to-day for the curé of our church, in honour of his seventieth birthday? It will not be a very grand affair, but it will serve to pass the time."

Of course I was eager to go, and as Frau von Friese and Mrs. Kaiser raised no objection, a servant was sent to the town to see if seats could be obtained. He returned with two tickets. As Frau von Friese was not at all interested in such things, I went accompanied by my maid. We were shown by a young priest to some seats in the third row. Just as we were about to take our places another young priest hastened up, whispered something to our conductor, looked hard at me for an instant, and hurried away.

"Euer Gnaden, please have patience a moment," said the first priest. And now in front of the very centre of the first row, where the old curé himself, Father Mayer,[1] was seated, we saw them place two large armchairs. Then, with a low bow, the young priest motioned to me to take these seats.

During the performance the actors, too, made most respectful bows to me — to my great confusion. But the climax came when the performance was over. The curé rose to thank those present for their attendance, but first of all he turned to me and expressed his gratitude for the great honour shown him by my presence. To make matters worse for me, I had forgotten to put on a belt when I dressed to come out, and so was obliged all the time to keep my coat on, lest the watchful eyes of the audience should notice this defect in my costume!

[1] Father Mayer is still living, I believe. I noticed in a Vienna paper last year, or the year before, a mention of another entertainment at Gmunden in honour of his birthday.

CHAPTER XI

PROFESSOR KRAUS

MRS. KAISER being almost restored to health, and the end of October having arrived, we all returned from Gmunden to Vienna. Although I had regular lessons from Frau von Friese even when I was in the country, my studies there were nothing like those in town, and this winter saw a great increase of work compared with what had gone before. For certain afternoons in every week I attended classes at the school where Laura was boarding, Fräulein Hanauseck's. Then, in addition, I had a number of private tutors at home, who taught me Greek, Latin, mathematics, history, geography, literature, music, et cetera. It was not intended by my mother or Frau von Friese that I should be idle.

Among my teachers I had a special preference for the one who instructed me in general history, in the history of art, and in psychology; and he merits some attention here. Professor Kraus, in spite of his forty years, looked, with his eye-glasses and his clean-shaven face, more like a student than a professor. It was with great reluctance that he had agreed to give lessons to a girl — a thing he had never done before in his life. In this instance he consented for the sake of Frau von Friese, with whom he was very good friends. But he told me afterwards that he was glad he had consented. The hours spent with him were not given over strictly to lectures from him, but rather to an agreeable interchange of ideas on the matter under discussion. My observations appeared to amuse and interest him very much. I remember that once, having been allowed to choose my own subject, I wrote an essay outlining a new law to help the unemployed. Upon reading the title he looked at me and smiled, but when he had finished the essay he said: "You should keep this. You may have use for it some time. There are some Utopian ideas which you will discard, but the rest is very good. Unfortunately, I myself am not an expert in political economy, so that I am unable to advise you. But you seem to have a natural talent in this direction, and will not need much instruction."

We spoke of many subjects together, and after I had related to him the miserable experiences I had had with Father Lambertus, I thanked him for being the first to teach me to think in a logical way.

By chance the Professor came to know my secret. The discovery was made one afternoon soon after my return from Gmunden. It had been arranged that he should sometimes give me my lessons in the library instead of in my study, especially when I was engaged upon the history of art; for then we examined illustrated works on the subject, which were too large to be carried easily into the study. Now on the library table stood a framed photograph of my mother. On the first day, immediately he entered the room, he noticed it and remarked quite casually, "Ah, the Empress!"

"M — mm!" was all I could mutter in reply. I really did not know what to say. He stared at me for a moment, but said nothing more at the time.

Another afternoon, not long afterwards, Frau von Friese was not at home, and Fräulein Hain was with us in the library, when suddenly mother arrived, quite unexpectedly. She was told that I was having a lesson, and that Frau von Friese was out. Now the servant had not noticed that I was in the library, and it was this very room that my mother entered to wait until I should come to her. It happened that just at that moment we were silently examining a book, so that not even our voices gave her warning of our presence. She opened the door — and imagine her stupefaction! I can still almost hear her little cry of dismay as she shrank back from the room. But it was too late. Quickly as she had retired, Professor Kraus had seen her first. Fräulein Hain rushed out of the room. The Professor looked at me and smiled, while I, I should imagine, was wearing the most imbecile expression that a human being could wear. The Professor, however, was quite equal to the occasion. Taking up my mother's photo, he said: "Please do not be troubled, Princess." He sometimes already jestingly addressed me thus. "On the day that you answered 'M — mm,' I felt that I had not made any mistake when I instinctively gave you the title of Princess; and to-day I am doubly proud. It is none of my business to inquire how you are connected with the Empress. But," he continued smilingly, "if it will reassure you, Princess, I can promise you, upon my honour, that I can keep silence, and I hope you will place at least as much confidence in me as you do in your servant."

For answer I gave my hand. I was rather touched and could only say, after a pause: "I will ask 'the authorities' for permission to tell you my secret. I hope it will be granted, and then if it is, I shall be giving you the greatest proof of my confidence."

The Professor now took his departure immediately. Mother, when I entered the room where she was waiting for me, did not know whether to laugh or not. Of course, she was somewhat vexed at what had happened, but she was not disposed to take the affair too seriously. Poor mother! She had been through too much real tragedy to be much upset by such a trifle. When I saw a smile on her face, I could not contain my pleasure. And then I told her how very considerate the Professor had been, and concluded by asking if I could not tell him our secret. Frau von Friese, who had returned while this was going on, assured mother that he was really a trustworthy person, and so mother gave a gracious consent.

"I propose, dear," she said, "that we give this story a pleasant ending. When does the Professor come again?"

"The day after to-morrow, in the afternoon."

"Very well, then, I will come too. But before I see him, Babe, you must tell him who you are, and say that after the lesson your mother wishes to make his acquaintance, so that he is to come into the library."

I was so happy that I threw myself upon her to kiss her, and put my two arms tightly round her neck, a thing I never used to do; for my respect for her would not allow me to do so. Usually, when my feelings were stirred, I would kiss her hand passionately, and then she would take me to her and cover my face with kisses. But this time I was quite beside myself with joy at the granting of my prayer concerning the Professor. Mother gave the constrained little laugh peculiar to her in moments of nervous tension, and said to me, "Babe, Babe, soon I shall be unable to call you by that name. You seem to be so grown up already that you put yourself quite on a level with your mother."

I hid my face abashed on her shoulder; for, gentle as

PROFESSOR KRAUS

her words had been, I understood that they conveyed a rebuke. She had her own peculiar way, not only with me, but, I believe, with her other children also. In her eyes I had committed a great error. A child should not be so familiar with her mother. And she was right, for a mother does lower herself in the eyes of her child if she does not insist on due respect.

However, there was the excitement of preparing the revelation for Professor Kraus to help me for the moment to forget my deserved rebuff. Two days after the incident in the library I had another lesson from him, and, of course, immediately confided to him my secret. When I told him that I was the daughter of the Empress, he was overwhelmed with astonishment. "I was eager to know who you really were, but I did not expect that!" he exclaimed. "I racked my wits to solve the problem, but in vain."

As mother had ordered me, when the lesson was over, I asked him to permit me to present him to her in the library. He appeared quite embarrassed at my request. Not being a courtier, he did not know what to say, and so endeavoured to escape. "I shall be most honoured," he stammered. "But I am not suitably dressed. And, besides, what shall I say on the spur of the moment, all unprepared?"

I could not help laughing, and tried to encourage him, assuring him that mother was far more unassuming than any woman he could possibly know; and as for his costume a frock coat would put a stop to all friendliness.

He scratched his head in trepidation still, then quickly passed his hand over his hair to make it smooth again, and we went into the library. His embarrassment did not last long, for mother, when she wished, could be more winning than anyone else I ever met, and now she was at her best. She gave him her hand, and in a moment put him entirely at his ease.

They talked together for nearly half an hour. Mother told him how she had heard, through me, several of his ideas, both literary and psychological — ideas which interested her very much and which she wished to talk over with him personally. If it were possible, she would like to be present at my next few lessons from him.

And indeed she did come several times, and to me it was really a pleasure to listen to them discussing.

"Do you know, Professor," mother said to him the last day on which she came, "I would like to spend some time in the country with you, where, unhampered by convention and inspired by Nature, we could freely exchange our views."

She spoke in her impulsive, charming way, which really was far indeed removed from flirting, though no doubt, especially when she was younger, it might easily deceive a man with a good opinion of himself.

One had but to know my mother to realise that with her to say a thing was to do it. Once an idea entered her mind, she proceeded at once to carry it out. So now, before she left for Mentone, she said to me: "Now, Weiberl, try to be very clever! I am going away for some time. While I am away, you must think of some plan by which we can spend this summer together without being disturbed."

Once again I was on the point of throwing my arms around her neck. But, guessing my impulse, she came towards me and put her arms about my shoulders. I was so happy I almost cried.

Might I talk with Frau von Friese about the plan? I

asked. Of course I might, mother answered; and we would invite little Professor Kraus to help us spend the time.

And now I vainly cudgelled my brains, day and night, for a suitable scheme for our summer holidays. Frau von Friese would teasingly ask me how far I had got in my undertaking, which made me feel desperate. Somewhere in a quiet corner of the world, where nobody would come to disturb us, in some remote little country place we must meet. This was not so difficult. No one in the house would dream who mother really was. But how to get rid of her attendants quite baffled me. So time passed on, and my despair increased, for I naïvely imagined that mother had really relied on my ingenuity to find a plan. I asked Frau von Friese how mother had managed in other years when I had to spend weeks and weeks with her.

Then I had been a little girl, Frau von Friese replied, and my mother might have been supposed to have taken me with her out of charity and to amuse herself. But now I was too big; and, besides, I had grown too like her in appearance for anyone to miss the resemblance and believe the story of my being a motherless child upon whom the Empress had taken pity.

How relieved I was when mother came back at last and I found that it did not really depend upon me to invent the plan! She soon put me out of my suspense. As she smilingly asked how I had progressed with my scheme, I understood all, and was all impatience to hear what she had arranged. She had discovered, she said, a charming little place, quite near Ischl. It was so close to the Imperial villa that she could easily visit me for a short time at least every day. As she was in the habit of making long excursions from Ischl into the mountains, it was very much to the satisfaction of her suite when she suggested that she should leave them at home. The worst that could happen was that she might have to take some of her more intimate attendants with her now and then. Once or twice a week she would be able to remain away overnight, and if at any time she did not feel like walking she would stay with me in my home. The suite would only say that the wandering instinct was stronger in her than ever before, but no one would attempt to hinder her. So this would be the nicest time we had ever spent together.

I was so happy that I could have danced for joy as she unfolded her plan. And she, too, seemed to be in such good spirits over it as were unhappily not too common with her now.

When she had left me last I still felt some little shame over my too impulsive conduct on the day when she had granted my request concerning Professor Kraus, and her mild rebuke still dwelt in my mind. But the remembrance only made me the more feverishly anxious to see her again. She had gone from Vienna to Mentone and from there for a cruise in the Mediterranean. Toward the end of March she had written to me from Corfu and sent me a marble statuette after her statue of Achilles. By doctor's orders she had remained at Corfu nearly the whole of April. But the enforced rest and quiet did not relieve her nervous trouble so much as the doctor had anticipated. She wrote to me that this was probably on account of her intense longing to have me with her. She was so forgetful and abstracted at the time that her attendants would often stare at her in wonder. Poor mother!

On the last day of April she arrived in Budapest to be present at the opening of the exhibition in connection with the Hungarian millennium, and there she was detained nearly two weeks. My diary shows me that it was on May 13, 1896, that she came at last to see me again in Vienna.

On the day that I knew that she was coming to me my excitement was so great I could not sit still. Every few minutes I went to the window to see if her carriage was in sight. The more impatient I became the more time seemed to creep. I kept looking at the clock to see if it had not stopped. Then I tried to read, but in vain. A carriage would pass through my quiet street, and again I would rush to the window, but still she did not come. I crept into the library and finally into Frau von Friese's room, like a fretful child. And then, at last, a soft rumbling was heard from afar, there was a rolling of the carriage under the porch, and my heart brimmed over with joy and happiness; and, laughing and shouting at the same time, I sped out of the room — and into mother's arms. How can I describe such a moment? Words fail me; but I can recall still the quiet happiness in her incomparable eyes, the perfect silence of the first moments, and then the outburst of speech. What a lot we had to talk about!

How well she made me understand the intensity of her longing for our meeting. She repeated to me what she had so often written already about the days of torture and the nights without peace. All remedies were vain — all except one, at least, and that she knew she must not take. If she had sent for me she would have been cured. But I must be left to my studies, and so she conquered her heart.

Now that we were together again she seemed to be trying to fathom the uttermost depths of my soul. On my part, I felt bound to confess to her every thought of mine, however insignificant. She looked at me so searchingly that I could keep nothing from her, much less tell her an untruth. These moments were to me far more sacred than an actual confession to a priest has ever been. Kneeling at her feet, I could have prayed to her as to a saint. And the more she questioned me, the more I loved her, for I was the better able to realise how great was her care for me.

After we had unburdened our hearts like this, mother would ask Frau von Friese to come to the drawing-room with us, and the time would pass very pleasantly, for their enjoyment of each other's society never grew less. Even now, sometimes, I live these scenes over again. On evenings when the silence of my room is undisturbed save by the ticking of the clock or the whirl of some passing motor-car, time is no more, and I am at one with the past. Again I see my beloved mother sitting in the large, pale-blue armchair, her small white hands resting on its arms, her soft smile expressing the happiness of the moment. Again I hear her low, sweet voice mingling with Frau von Friese's cheerful conversation, which always seemed to refresh her so. And then comes Pirker, wearing his most solemn expression, and almost noiselessly he opens the folding doors leading into the dining-room. Mechanically all three of us rise. Mother takes my arm, and we go slowly into the next room. The conversation is continued while Pirker serves the tea, and with it usually mother's favourite dish, cold game-pie. In the midst of the talk, mother takes, it may be, a little flask out of her pocket. It is of crystal, beautifully cut, and has a golden stopper. On its sides is a representation of the dance of the Nine Muses in relief. On the top is an enamel face, wearing a black mask, the eyes being little diamonds. Frau von Friese admires the flask, but with some restraint, for she knows what is coming.

"Do you like it, my dear Friese? I bought it in Paris. It is really most artistic."

And now Frau von Friese is bound to acknowledge its delicate beauty, whereon immediately mother says: "Would you care to have it, dear Friese? Please do me the favour of accepting it. It is none the worse for the few weeks' use I have given it. Perhaps it will remind you sometimes of your loving friend."

Slightly embarrassed, Frau von Friese accepts the gift. I cannot remember that mother ever made her a present as if she were saying, "Here is something for you." She always knew how to manage it so that my governess seemed to be conferring a favour upon her in accepting it.

At the end of the tea, just before rising, mother slips something surreptitiously under her serviette. But Pirker knows very well what it is.

CHAPTER XII

SOME HAPPY TIMES; AND THE PROFESSOR'S DIARY

It was my mother's custom to remain for a considerable part of each spring in Vienna; that is to say, at her own palace of Lainz. This year, 1896, I saw more of her than ever before. A restless eagerness for my society seemed to possess her. She usually came over to my home early in the morning, and we either took long walks together or else she remained with me in the house. She took an interest in the smallest matters which concerned me, and supervised everything. For instance, because I did not hold myself well, she ordered me to sleep without a pillow on my bed. As I did not place my feet correctly when walking, she directed that I should wear iron supports for my boots. She thought I was growing too stout, and so I was put on a special diet, which deprived me of my favourite dishes. Every day saw some new command intended for my good. She seemed to find great happiness in being thus able to watch over me; and I, for my part, was both happy and proud that I absorbed so much of her thought and attention. The little discomforts of my daily programme mattered not at all to me. I felt with delight her guiding hand in all the details of my life.

At the end of May the Emperor Francis-Joseph went to Budapest, and mother was quite free to do as she wished. Her health had grown very much better during the past few weeks, and she was often in quite good spirits. On the afternoon of the day the Emperor left Vienna she came to see me. We were in the sitting-room after our five o'clock tea, and I was expecting her to depart within the next quarter of an hour. But I noticed a playful smile about the corners of her mouth, like that on the face of a card-player about to put on the trump card that will win the game. Leaning back in her armchair, she looked first at me and then at Frau von Friese. Neither of us had the slightest idea of what was to come. Suddenly she turned to me and said, "Do you think, Babe, that you could find room enough in your bed for me to-night?"

I was so amazed that at first I could not realise the meaning of her words. This seemed to amuse her greatly, for she laughed as heartily as if she were making up for years of restraint. The next moment I was out of my chair, dancing and clapping my hands as I shouted: "Mammi, Mammi, Jeckus! Mammi, ist's möglich Du bleibst da?" (If I had been a little American girl I might have said, "Oh, Gee! Mamma, do you mean to say you're stopping right here?")

"It is quite true," mother answered. "I did not tell you of my intention before because I wanted to enjoy your surprise more thoroughly."

Frau von Friese now suggested that it was not necessary for mother to sleep in the same bed with me. But she answered that it was just here that the pleasure of the whole escapade lay, and that she did not wish it otherwise.

Mother had sometimes lunched at my home, and regularly took tea with me; but this was the first time she had ever had supper with me in Vienna, in fact her first evening spent with me except on the occasion of my accident. She did not wish us, she said, to add anything to our menu on her account, except some Frankfurter würstl and horse-radish. (This liking for Frankfurt sausage, by the way, has been imputed to her, if not as a crime, at least as a serious error of taste!) I see from my diary that we had for supper also herring salad, veal cutlets done with bread-crumbs, green peas, and cakes and fruit. It is curious how children love recording such details! The greatest fun came, however, when we were going to bed. I was so big that she could wear my night-gown, and I shrieked with laughter when I saw her attired in it. We slept together, and she had to stop me talking, or else I should not have gone to sleep at all that night. I remember well the pleasing impression I had upon first waking the next day. Mother was already awake, and greeted me with a bright smile. That morning there were no lessons. Mina had a difficult task in brushing and combing mother's hair, and it was Frau von Friese who had finally to arrange it to the best of her ability. I have often wondered how mother, with her quick, impatient nature, could show herself so particular and so patient over the dressing of her hair.

The same afternoon my mother left us and she purposely kept away on the following day so as to prevent too much comment on her conduct. Further to lull suspicion, she went for a long excursion with the Countess Festetics and Christomanos, whom she had recently engaged for the second time as her Greek reader. They visited the Kahlenberg on June 1st, my diary records. On June 2nd, however, she took me with her over the Helenenthal to the Eisenes-Thor (the Iron Gate), the greatest height in the neighbourhood of Vienna. She parted with me at Baden station, and from there I went the same day to stop with the Kaisers, who were on their summer holiday

THE PROFESSOR'S DIARY 115

at Vöslau. On June 1st Mr. and Mrs. Kaiser had celebrated their silver wedding. Among other presents that Mrs. Kaiser received was a pair of beautiful grey pearl earrings, set in diamonds, from mother.

It was arranged that I should go to Vöslau, because mother was obliged to pay a second visit this year to Budapest in honour of the millennium of Hungary's existence as a nation. There was a great assembly on this occasion in the House of Magnates, at which both Emperor and Empress (or King and Queen, as I should say) were present. President von Szilghy in his speech paid special homage to mother; so touchingly, indeed, that it was noticed that she could not answer, and that her eyes filled with tears.

On the 10th mother returned from Budapest, and during the remainder of the month we met frequently and made many excursions together around Vienna. On July 1st I went with Frau von Friese to Ischl, where mother had taken a place for me. It was more like a hunting-box than a villa, but was none the less cosy for that. It stood in the middle of a park, surrounded by old trees; adjacent to it were farm-buildings and stables, which gave the whole a very rustic appearance. It was quite an ideal place for the simple life.

Mother did not arrive until two weeks later. She first went to Bavaria, to spend some days at Tegernsee with her brother, the Duke Karl-Theodor. With him she went to Hohenschwangau, where also they were joined by my sister Gisela, wife since 1873 to Leopold, second son of the Prince Regent of Bavaria. On July 4th, only three days after my arrival at Ischl, a note from her came unexpectedly to Frau von Friese. She wrote very briefly, and quite in her own characteristic style: —

"Bring my Babe over to Hohenschwangau on Friday. Am making an excursion on foot, and want to take her with me."

This idea had occurred to her quite suddenly, and she herself posted the little note. The knowledge that she was only a few hours away from me made it impossible for her to resist the temptation to have me with her. With one guide we made the journey round the Plansee to Linderhof, and remained there overnight. For this one among King Ludwig's palaces I have never cared. It might impress simple minds as being magnificent, but to the more sophisticated it can but appear as lacking in refinement. The king was not a practical architect, and his builders had ample opportunities of tricking him. At the end of two days I returned to Ischl; but mother went to Munich, on her visit to the grave of King Ludwig. On June 15th she arrived in Ischl.

Of the pleasant summer idyll this year at Ischl I have a description written by an abler pen than mine — an extract from the diary kept by Professor Kraus. I must give a few words of explanation as to how this diary came into my hands.

One rainy afternoon, after my mother's departure from Ischl, Professor Kraus was sitting in the writing-room, with a manuscript book spread out on the table before him. As I went up to the table, just by chance my eyes caught the word, "Princess." Of course, I immediately concluded that he was writing about myself.

"Professor," I cried, "that is something about me! You must let me read it. Please, please!"

I was curious, I must confess, to see what he had written — not so much about me as about mother. But that I should ever use his notes one day in a book of mine was about the last thing I should have dreamt of then. Professor Kraus now smiled at me mischievously through his glasses, and told me that it was impossible I could see his manuscript. Still I persisted; and still he refused. I tried all ways to persuade him. He must have said something bad about me, I remarked at last. He accused me of vanity in thinking he had written only of me. Thereupon I became offended and haughty, which had the desired effect. He protested that he had not meant to be rude, and that the few memoranda which he had made for himself alone about his pleasant visit were not worth my reading, and would only make me laugh. I made no answer and pretended to be unmollified — until he handed me the book. He did so not altogether unwillingly, it occurred to me after, for he could not really be displeased that we should see the complimentary things he had said about us.

I myself was so delighted with what Professor Kraus wrote and his manner of writing that I copied the whole of it into my own diary before I returned him his book. Here is what he said: —

"*July* 11*th,* 1896. Frau von Friese and the Princess invited me, some time ago, to pass a few weeks at their little summer-place near Ischl. Her Majesty also took it into her head that she wanted to know what I would be like in the country. All three ladies promised me that my time would be well spent. Now that is just where it was. My time, my precious time — should I risk its loss in this Court atmosphere? But they all guaranteed that no courtly taint should be allowed to reach me; and finally I accepted. Very many, no doubt, would be astonished at my reluctance, would eagerly grasp at such an opportunity and look upon it as a great honour. But this is how I am built. I am an untamed creature, and a little bit of a revolutionary. I don't care a fig for these honours. Why then have I accepted? I had no plan for the summer, and, to make it worse, all my friends kept asking me the same dull questions —'What are you going to do with yourself this year?' 'Where are you spending your holidays?' 'You are up to something extraordinary again, of course?' So I really had to think what I could do. With six months ahead of me and a comfortable balance at the bank, I should have been all right. But I had only two months, and funds were low! Should I go to some place for the waters? Such a plan never appealed to me. Should I make a walking tour in the mountains? I should be a dwarf amongst the giants, and I never envied the pygmies. Besides, it would mean toiling up the mountains, and I am too lazy for that sort of thing. What about the seaside? I was there during the whole of last summer, so I have had quite enough of that. Then there was the simple life in a country village. What amusement could I find in that? Certainly I do not care a snap of my fingers for society. But total isolation — no reasonable man could stand that for more than two days at a stretch. I speak from experience!

"I see nothing else left except to try the little fairy castle. I do not expect very much, but perhaps, after all, there may be some surprise in store for me. It is true there will only be women there — yet not ordinary women. I have a rooted aversion to the word 'superior,' and only use it sorely against my will. So here I make a vow that I will not allow myself to be imposed upon by the 'superiority' of their birth.

"Thus it came about that early in the morning of July 9th, my one-horse cab, which I had ordered the day before, stood at my door. In spite of the early hour, the air was very sultry. *Bon voyage!* The omens are good. In such weather one might be tempted to feel sorry for the poor people who have to remain in this oven of a city, but then I am not so kind-hearted as all that. The thought only made me feel the more comfortable, and it was with a cruel and malicious joy that I stepped into the cab. My trunk was already on the box beside the driver. At a crack of the whip Rosinante sets herself in motion. But the pace is not very great, for at every second corner building operations are in progress, filling the air with an atrocious dust. Again we have to stop in front of reeking cauldrons of liquid tar, belching forth their poisonous fumes; or are held up by a whole file of rattling and whistling street-cars, blocked on the line. Finally the station comes in view. On the platform there is a tremendous bustle. Every compartment is overcrowded, and each passenger wants one to himself. But everything has an end — or, rather, a beginning — and so we begin to move. I won't describe the journey; journeys are all very similar. There are the mothers with their families, hunting in the racks for packets of provisions; the children quarrelling over a magazine; the men grumbling because they are in the wrong carriage and cannot smoke; the old maids shivering and complaining about the draught; and so on and so forth.

"At Ischl station an elegant two-horse equipage is waiting for me. Adolph, I say to myself, from now on you must play the *grand seigneur;* and with this I lie back in the carriage as if I had never known what it was to walk. The drive is a fairly long one. We pass several farmhouses, where the dogs bark after us, and barefooted children bow humbly — to the elegant carriage rather than to its occupant, I am sure. We roll past woods and meadows, and finally turn into a shady chestnut avenue. We go more and more slowly, and just as I am beginning to realise how dusty and dirty I look and am pulling out my handkerchief, we stop at a small flight of steps. It is too late. Pirker, the Princess's major-domo, comes to meet me. I am ushered into a fairly large but very cosy hall, with bamboo chairs and numerous palms and ferns. All is perfectly silent; quiet and rest seem to smile out of every corner. Pirker leads me up one flight of stairs. On the landing stands a footman, who opens the door. For a moment I hesitate. I cannot possibly present myself before the ladies in such an untidy state. But Pirker is evidently a thought-reader, for he says immediately, 'This is the Professor's apartment.'

"Reassured, I step in. My room is a big one. There are two windows, in deep recesses; on their sills stand flower-pots. Between the windows is a gigantic desk, and beside it a book-shelf full of books. In the middle of the room are placed a large sofa and two heavy leather chairs. Against the back wall is an old oak wardrobe, and the bed stands in an alcove. A Persian carpet spreads over the whole floor and gives the finishing touch.

"So far all goes very well, I think to myself. I could not be better lodged; and if they make it as comfortable for me in everything else, they will not get rid of me quickly. Pirker was standing behind me. 'If the Professor needs anything,' he said, 'will he please just ring the bell? The footman is at his service.'

"I nodded a dignified assent and asked, When may I pay my respects to the ladies?'

"'The ladies are out driving. They will meet the Professor downstairs in the hall a little before seven.' With this Pirker bowed low and retired.

"More than an hour and a half still remained to me before the *rendezvous*. I proceeded to make myself comfortable and ordered a bath. I lingered over one thing and another, so that, before I realised it, it was already a quarter to seven. Slowly and quietly I went downstairs, step by step. Half-way down I heard already the cheerful noise of mingling voices. Scarcely was I on the last step when the Princess rushed toward me crying: 'At last you are here, my little Professor!'

"Except for her and Frau von Friese, I did not know anybody. I was presented to a lady with exquisite manners, the Marquise de Pourtalès; to an old clergyman from Denmark, Herr von Jordans; and to a young man, who, as I afterwards learned, was a painter, Raday by name.

"The whole party was exceedingly amiable to me, probably because I was a distraction to them. We conversed for a few minutes, and then Pirker came to announce with a deep bow that dinner was served. He was the only thing in the place to remind us that we were not in the presence of ordinary mortals!

"Dinner was not laid in the dining-room; we stepped out upon a great terrace. One could not imagine anything more delightful than the view. All around were the dark green woods, separated from the house only by a lawn, dotted here and there with blossoming rose-bushes. On the terrace itself stood groups of orange trees in tubs, with their golden fruit shimmering amid their green leaves. The air was impregnated with the scent of roses and oranges, pleasantly mingled with a faint odour of the coming meal, which reminded one of matters less poetical, but nevertheless very welcome to anyone as hungry as I was at that moment. The dinner was really excellent. I do not know why, I had an envious feeling that I must find something wrong, something to criticise. I could not resign myself to an admission that, for once in my life, everything was exactly to my taste.

"We remained on the terrace, after drinking our coffee, until half-past eleven. A lovely summer night, with myriads of stars. Princess retired about nine o'clock.

"*July 12th.* One can have breakfast between seven and ten. At half-past eight I was on the little veranda of the breakfast-room, as it is called. This room is a fine example of the old German *stube* [living-room]; time-blackened panels on the walls; a big heavy table in the middle, with high carved wooden chairs around it; along the walls the typical pewter-ware; in the windows leaded glass. All that was missing to complete the picture was some old character of the right period, Hans Sachs, Albert Dürer, or the like. The veranda itself looked more like a summer-house, all overgrown with vines.

"At the table Frau von Friese was already seated, and at her side the clergyman. Just as I arrived Princess also came in, with the Marquise de Pourtalès. Everyone greeted the others; a few words were exchanged, but soon silence reigned, for each of us was satisfying his or her hunger. The breakfast was an ideal one, to my mind. Our tea was brought round to us; but everything else stood on the table, and we helped ourselves as we liked — to pale-pink, home-cured ham, fresh crawfish, pâté de foie gras, caviare, eggs, honey, cherries, strawberries, apricots, and cakes. The first to talk again was the old clergyman, who had been earlier at the table than the others, but gradually the conversation became more animated.

"'Please do not take any notice of me,' said Frau von Friese. 'You must excuse me while I make my daily notes in this book.'

"We were still sitting when Pirker brought the morning post to us. Frau von Friese said to Princess in a most matter-of-fact way, 'A letter from your mother.' Princess's face lighted up with joy. But Frau von Friese read the letter herself and put it on one side, as if this was the natural thing to do. I stared in amazement. Why did she not pass her the letter? Frau von Friese did not seem to notice my surprised glances. But Princess did, for she looked at me, and I imagined that I could read in her eyes the words, 'You see what I have to put up with!' I cannot tell why, but suddenly a great feeling of pity for her came over me.

"*July* 14*th*. Never could I have believed that I should feel so much at home as I do. Everyone does as one likes here. I only wish life could go on like this always!

"Princess has an admirable character. It cannot be easy to be uniformly patient when one has to do just the contrary of what one would like to do.[1] . . .

"*July* 15*th*. For the last few days I have been taking a walk every morning with Princess at seven o'clock. It is a lesson in psychology that I am supposed to give her; but while we call it psychology, we talk about everything under the sun.

"She loves her mother fanatically, and in turn, it seems to me, is completely dominated even to the extent of

---

[1] I realise acutely that I must ask the reader's indulgence when I reproduce these compliments to myself. I have, indeed, cut out some sentences here and elsewhere, in which the Professor passes a judgment upon me which I feel to be unduly favourable.

tyranny by her mother's love for her. Everything the child thinks, she must try to remember so as to be able to repeat it to her mother. I asked her what obliged her to reveal her thoughts thus; whereupon she answered me: 'For nothing in this world would I hurt my mother by refusing her anything.'

"'Princess, there is no question of that,' I said. 'What the eye does not see the heart does not grieve for.'

"'Well, I shall never try to hide any of my thoughts from mother. And, besides, it is a great pleasure to me to tell them to her.'

"'Now, if I were in your place,' I said, 'I should tell what pleased me and keep the rest to myself.'

"'Dear Professor, if you were sitting in front of an angel like my mother, a person in whom you could never find the slightest fault, who was purer than all the world, could you then have the heart not to tell her all that she wanted to know — especially if you understood that she only expected this in order to be able to protect you the better?'

"'Then, Princess, not one single idea belongs to you alone?'

"'No, not one.'

"A question came into my mind, but I did not know how to put it. Forgetting that, in spite of her grown-up ways, she was still but half a child — and my pupil to boot — I determined to ask it.

"'Princess,' I began, 'as we are studying psychology, there is a problem which I should like to ask you to solve.'

"'Ask it, Professor; I hope I shall be able to give you a satisfactory answer.'

"'I am very bold, Princess, for I am going to ask you a question which even Her Majesty has never asked.'

"I paused for a moment. Princess was walking a step ahead of me, and although I bent down to pull a blade of grass to induce her to stop, she did not do so. I put my question therefore.

"'Princess, did you never lie awake in bed?' I asked.

"On this she did stop for a moment, and she fixed a pair of astonished eyes on me, as if she now would ask me for the solution of an enigma. Did she understand me, or did she not? Still she said nothing, and I was forced to continue: —

"'I remember you told me that you were once ill for a long time, and you had to remain in bed. . . . Princess, about what used you to think then?'

"'Oh, about all sorts of beautiful things — things that one can never really experience in this world.'

"The absolute candour of her reply was such as could only come from perfect purity of mind.

"'And you have shared all those dreams with your mother?'

"'Mother once questioned me, Professor, in the same way as you; but with this difference — that she wanted also to know all the details. At first I hesitated and — I will be frank, Professor — I even cried a little when I was forced to confess these thoughts of mine. But mother made me understand *why* I should confess everything.'

"'And you have never the slightest doubt, Princess?'

"'A doubt about my mother?'

"I looked at her for a long time. She is a strange creature — so intelligent, and so independent, so quick-witted for her age, and yet, in spite of all this, her self-denial is so great. Again I had that peculiar impression I have so often had of her, that she really likes this life of self-denial and effacement.

"*July* 18*th*. The Empress is here now. The charm of our little society, strange to say, has only increased since she came. I imagined that everything would become stiff and uncomfortable, and am astonished. Of course she decidedly dominates all, but she would dominate just the same if she was not the Empress of Austria. She has a kind of triumphant grace about her; and what is so peculiar is that one can never for a moment think of her as an elderly lady. She is not in as good health as usual, and cannot gratify so much as she would wish her passion for mountain climbing. We have a great deal of music. Frau von Friese has a glorious voice, and Princess accompanies her. The painter also sings very well. . . .

"*July* 26*th*. To-day I had a walk with the Empress alone. After discussing all sorts of subjects, she said something which led to a long conversation: —

"'People do not understand the way in which I treat my daughter. The day will come when they will understand my intentions. My method is obscure to you, too, Professor, is it not?'

"This brusque question took me by surprise, and I answered in some embarrassment: 'I admit, your Majesty, that I don't entirely understand it.'

"'For instance, Professor, I allow my child so little freedom of thought.'

"I could see that the topic had not come up merely by chance.

"'But it is really awful,' I blurted out, letting my tongue run away with me.

"'Awful?' repeated the Empress. 'Awful for whom?'

THE PROFESSOR'S DIARY 127

"'Why, the Princess, your Majesty. This imprisonment of the thoughts, just at the age when the fantasy is beginning to develop so rapidly. . . .'

"'Yes, and to bring with it mischief upon mischief. Is it wrong, then, if I talk over everything with my daughter and enlighten her in my own way, and keep from her the wrong impressions which she might get from others? You call this imprisoning her thoughts, Professor?' She gave a low laugh, and continued banteringly: 'Professor, do not look so gloomy. I am not in the least annoyed with you. On the contrary, I thoroughly understand you because you have the common point of view. But think, Professor, of the gnawing worm which eats into the heart of the child brought up according to the current ideas. Let us be logical. If a child does an exercise badly or answers in a way it should not, we are allowed to scold, to punish, yes, even to whip it — are we not? Or if a child reads a forbidden book, we take away the book and we blame the poor child. But the Book of the Soul, which we read every night when we lie in our beds, which in our youth excites us so much sometimes that a cold perspiration runs down our foreheads; this book we must leave open for the child, with its restless imagination, to read. This is your view, is it not, Professor, that we should not interfere? So that, in fact, all we must do for the moral education of the child is to give the outer surface-polish. We all forget our own youth so quickly, and we find it only too easy to say, "I let my child develop itself after its own instincts." Think over this, Professor. Remember how the worm has gnawed into your own heart. When the fruit is once attacked, there is no longer any hope for it. It must decay. And the moral beauty of the modern human being is in the same way attacked and decays.'

"She paused, as if absorbed in the ideas which crowded in upon her. As for me, I was so startled and impressed by her words that I could not speak. But she did not expect me to answer, and continued:

"'My own life, too, has been devoured by the worm, only with time the ravages have gone so deep that they seem lost to sight. But I knew well the hardship of struggling against the forces of evil all alone, with no one to give counsel. What I have longed for all my life, and what I have never been able to get, this I want for my child — the true purity of the soul, the serenity of mind that comes from knowledge — in a word, peace. It was at a time of dreadful loneliness, when I had nearly lost all hope in life, that destiny presented me with this child; and more by instinct than by reason I recognised that this was my work in life; that for this purpose I had to come into the world. I educate my child with every impulse of my heart and soul. I agree that to strangers my methods may seem like tyranny. But that I do not mind so long as I am fortunate enough to be able to say that such an idea has never occurred to my child.'

"We sat down on a bench, where both of us remained silent, until at last I felt that I must say something.

"'Your Majesty, it *is* worth the trouble you are taking. I really know the feelings that Princess has for you.'

"At these words she smiled a little mockingly.

"'Have you not found out that I know this also?' she asked; 'that she has told me of what you talked together? You yourself are something of a worm, you know, Professor! However, you see, I am afraid of nothing. You can talk to her about anything you like, but just imagine the chaos in this young brain if a number of Professor Krauses were to talk to her, each with a different set of ideas, and she had to puzzle it all out by herself. How could she recover her peace of mind if every day brought new impressions and new views? The end of it all would be a ruined existence, in spite of all her talents and good qualities.'

"She was silent again, and I could find no words. I would have liked to listen for hours and hours to this wonderful woman. She seemed to have become quite a different being in my eyes. This elegant creature, who had at first struck me as so fantastic and exuberant, this distinguished and fascinating great lady, was, after all, but a tortured and unhappy woman. I felt myself overwhelmed with a respectful compassion for her august grief. What I had mistaken for an affectation, a pose, was perfectly genuine. Her melancholy was not only the result of her son's death; it was of the very essence of her soul. The scales fell from my eyes. I held the secret of the long martyrdom of a life whose sadness had always seemed to me impossible to explain. I knew now the injustice of all those who affect to pity her without believing in her real unhappiness, and who make fine phrases to depict her as a type of Our Lady of Sorrows.

"She is so great, so above all other women. Every one of her ideas is noble, to the extent that ordinary common humanity cannot understand them. She must suffer in the same way as an artist of genius who is denied recognition in his life, and has to wait for death to become known. With the highest ideals in her soul, she ascended to a throne; and there 'the worm' of which she speaks attacked her. There was no one to protect her against it, no one even to warn her. Had she but escaped she would have realised her ideal of what a woman, a mother, and a sovereign should be. Unappreciated as few persons in history have been, she gave up the fight. But she, of whom it has been lightly said that she is misanthropic, has spoiled her life by too great a love for humanity. She does not hate the people; she loves them too much. But, just as a rejected lover shuns the faithless and ungrateful object of his love, so she has shunned them, and like him again she pretends to feel scorn.

" And now she has but one object; she wishes to save her child from her own fate. I hope with all my heart that she may succeed. It seems as if Fate would reward her for her admirable perseverance. . . .

" Such were the ideas flying through my head, when the Empress got up, without speaking another word. Silently we walked towards the house, both of us deep in thought.

"*August* 27*th.* The Empress has gone away again. It was a hard separation for both mother and daughter. I cannot understand why the Empress does not put an end to this torture. I even made a remark to that effect the morning before she left, but she answered: ' No, no; that would be weakness, and quite against my views. She is not yet far advanced enough in her education for that.' Then, turning toward Princess, she said: ' She has both courage and good sense. Is not that so, Weiberl?'

" Princess, who is usually so brave, only nodded her head. She could hardly keep back her tears, which she wished to hide for her mother's sake — and also, no doubt, because such a weakness is forbidden to her."

This ends the extract which I am making from the

Professor's diary. There are other pages detailing his conversations with Frau von Friese and the views which she imparted to him concerning the rigid discipline to which I was subjected. But further extracts would really add nothing to what I have already given here.

CHAPTER XIII

CONFIDENCES

THE days of this sojourn at Ischl, of which the reader has just heard what Professor Kraus had to say, were among the most delightful in my whole life. After my mother's arrival I could spend my time almost uninterruptedly with her. Our pleasure was not marred by those thoughts of a speedy parting that always bring with them the dread of leaving something unsaid which it is most essential to say. This feeling, so often with us, was absent now.

But the shadows which overhung our lives, if less in evidence than usual, were not altogether away. Mother was not in good health at the time. She had many sleepless nights. Through this, however, she spent them all the oftener with me. I would lie with her in her bed or sit by her until late in the night. To me this was a source at once of joy and of surprise; for she did not seem able to endure anyone else with her for long at a time.

It must be admitted that she sometimes sorely tried the patience of those about her. But I cannot remember that she ever had an impatient word for me. What made me prouder still was that she, who was so sparing of her words with others, seemed never tired of talking with me. Even those most closely connected with her did not dare, or, perhaps I should say, did not attempt to hold long conversations with her, on account of her great weariness. Yet I could talk with her for hours without appearing to weary her. On the contrary, she would grow animated and refreshed.

Once I asked her about this; and she told me that, in the first place, she liked the conversation of young girls, who seemed to her more unspoilt than anything else by the influence of the world — as though they still exhaled the perfume which Nature gives her sweetest flowers. And then, as I was moulded after her own ideas, in talking with me she was, as it were, talking with her younger self.

Further, our continual separations had a peculiar influence upon her. With other people she was always conscious that she could see as much of them as she wished, with the result that she grew impatient and tired. With me it was like being in some favourite spot, where she was supremely happy, but from which she knew she must soon depart. Everything grew doubly dear from the fact that it must be left behind. My words were treasured up by her like the wild flowers from the woods, treasured in joy mingled with sorrow that soon they would be with her no more.

Is it wonderful that I should feel happy at the remembrance of her words? And have I not the right to think that, in all those years that we were together, there was no living being for whom she cared as she did for me?

I cannot pretend to recall all the occasions of our conversations or the exact words used. I was no Professor Kraus, to transfer to my diary the talk of each day. My memory goes back to some days, however, with the utmost vividness, and even the very words seem to me still to live. There was an occasion, not long before the time of which I have been writing I should imagine, when, as we sat alone together, I said to her suddenly, " Mother, do you love my brother and sisters as much as you love me?" It was one of those thoughtless, impulsive questions to which I fear that I was rather prone. I could feel, by my mother's trembling hands, how much I had hurt her. She merely answered, however, that the others did not need her now. "And Rudy is no longer alive," she added in a whisper.

My heart ached at the tone of her voice. I could not say a word, but lost control over myself, hid my face in her lap, and broke into sobs. Since the day when the servant had come into my nursery and said, "The Crown Prince is dead!" no mention of him had ever been made in my presence. I had never properly realised that my mother's only son, my brother, could be the same Crown Prince who had died so many years ago. My thoughts were all in confusion. When I raised my face, I saw that, though mother had been weeping, she had mastered herself again. She told me not to grieve over what I had said. For a long time she had been desiring the moment when the last barrier between us might be broken down, and we might speak freely on these subjects too. It would do her good that I should ask whatever I wished.

I was emboldened by her words and said, "Had Rudolf then been your favourite?" "He was my only son," she replied, "a boy with a heart of gold. The world into which he was born was not worthy of him, and his nobility and his faith in his friends cost him his life." "How did he die?" I asked. But she shook her head. "Weiberl," she said, "I cannot speak of this to you to-day. You must first learn something about politics and the creeping baseness of it all."

I went on to ask about my sisters, and pressed her to tell which of us she preferred. Gisela, she said, had been educated by her grandmother, and was married very young. Valerie, although nominally under mother's control, was not brought up according to her wishes. Only with me had she the opportunity of carrying out her ideas. I was all hers, and therefore the nearest to her heart. As I heard her, I felt as if the highest of all decorations had been conferred upon me!

I shall now take the opportunity of speaking of my sisters, though it must be understood that what I say here was not all told me by my mother at one time; nor indeed all told me by her alone, as I shall have to refer to some events which happened after her death. Much of what I have to tell, however, was derived directly from my mother's own words to me.

Of Gisela she never spoke much. The fact of her being brought up by the Archduchess Sophia made a great gulf between them. Then Gisela on her marriage in 1873 to Prince Leopold, second son of the late Prince Regent and brother of the new King of Bavaria, became a Bavarian by residence. Though visiting Ischl every summer, she had and still has her home in Munich. Her husband is a man of no great significance, and a strong contrast to his brother, King Ludwig III, who has both character and charm. Both husband and wife are good-natured, simple, and insignificant — and therefore happy. They have four children. The elder daughter, Elisabeth, created a sensation in 1893 by marrying Baron Otto von Seefried, a mere lieutenant in the Bavarian army. The Emperor Francis-Joseph gave a reluctant consent, but Gisela so strongly resented the match that she has not made up her quarrel with her daughter since. At the time of the marriage my mother was in Majorca, whence she telegraphed to the Emperor, advising that their grandchild should be ordered to Vienna — not to separate her from her husband, but to protect them both from scandal and hostility.

Gisela's younger daughter Augusta married the Archduke Joseph, the elder of the two grandsons of Joseph, Prince Palatine of Hungary, brother of the Emperor Francis II; wife and husband thus being distant cousins.

Of the two sons of Gisela and Leopold, the elder, George, married only two years ago Isabella, daughter of the Archduke Frederick and the Archduchess Isabella. The marriage was a very unhappy one, the bride running away after but two weeks. Having a genuine affection for her mother-in-law, she consented to return. But her husband's faults were too grave to be tolerated, and last year she succeeded in having the marriage declared void by the Supreme Court of Bavaria and annulled by the Pope. The Emperor Francis-Joseph was very upset over the affair, and was almost made ill again. The other brother, Conrad, who is just over thirty and still unmarried, as yet has made no mark in history.

Of Valerie mother always spoke much more freely than of Gisela. She felt bitterly the farce that had been played when it was pretended she should have the control of this her second living daughter. Even when Valerie was quite small this was really not the case. The ordinary relationship between parent and child was not allowed to exist. They did not even have their meals together. Valerie had from her earliest days her own servants and her own cook, who travelled with her wherever she went. So far was the separation carried that when mother went for a summer holiday to Feldafing, in Bavaria, for instance, she would stop at Strauch's Hotel (now the Hotel Kaiserin Elisabeth), while Valerie must not be lodged there but in the house of the clergyman of the place. What intimacy could there be in a state of affairs like this?

Valerie was very timid as a child, so much so that mother found it difficult to extract from her what she really knew. Her education was not at all according to mother's wishes. It was one-sided. She was taught a great deal, while her character was given little chance to develop. She had many teachers and governesses, all of whom idolised her; not one of them ever treated her with the strictness necessary at times for a child's good. No doubt the fact of her being the youngest so long had much to do with the spoiling she received. But it was the educational system which was mainly at fault. Through an original gentleness of disposition she did not grow so capricious as to make the lives of those about her a misery to them. But she certainly became in the end obstinate, self-willed and proud of her attainments. It was claimed that she was very clever. As a matter of fact, she was neither clever nor yet stupid. One of her teachers was the celebrated Joseph Levinsky, the Viennese actor and professor at the Conservatorium. He first taught her elocution, as she had a very weak voice. For long he could make nothing of her, and he was asked to undertake her instruction in deportment as a princess — how to walk, how to carry her fan, etc.

Such things as these she undoubtedly learned. And in the meanwhile her moral nature was starved. She was never shown how to go down deep into the human heart nor to understand the serious questions of life, which was my mother's idea of education. How, indeed, could she grasp the reality of sorrow, when charity was taught her by sending her out in a carriage at Ischl to throw sweetmeats to the peasant children? Although her intimate friends — among whom the principal is the Countess Kinsky, born Aglae Auersperg, once not a little talked of in connection with the Crown Prince Rudolf — use the familiar *Du* (thou) to her, there is no free tone of equality in her friendship.

Valerie was very simple in her tastes, with none of mother's *raffinement*. Although she writes poetry, she is very common-sense, and indeed *bourgeoise*. When she was taken to Corfu once by mother, she said, as she entered the Achilleion, " I hope that you will not leave this to me, for I shouldn't know what to do here with my children! "

Her marriage took Valerie still farther away from intimacy with my mother. Her husband, the Archduke Francis-Salvator of Tuscany, was also her cousin, though only a remote cousin, both being descended in the male line from the Emperor Leopold, elder son of Francis I. The common accusations of unfaithfulness and hereditary illness cannot justly be made against Francis-Salvator. At any rate, they have a large family of children, and her cares as a mother have occupied much of the Archduchess's time. It is perfectly untrue that she is epileptic.

Valerie developed political ambitions early, and in influence over the Emperor, her father, soon displaced both mother and Gisela. Later, before the tragedy of 1914 took off the Duchess of Hohenberg, the morganatic wife of Franz-Ferdinand, Valerie was an effective counter-influence to the Duchess. Of the Duchess I shall have more to say in another chapter. Here I may mention that, while she and Valerie both displayed bigotry in their religion, Valerie is sincerer, franker, and less political in hers. She does not use her faith as a weapon in the prosecution of her schemes.

The home of Francis-Salvator and Valerie is at Lichtenegg. Valerie inherited my mother's château at Lainz. When she stays in Vienna officially, however, she resides in the Hofburg or at Schönbrunn.

CHAPTER XIV

LUDWIG OF BAVARIA

On a certain evening in the August of this same summer holiday, after one of those interminable dull and rainy days which are so frequent in the Salzkammergut region at this time of year, my mother decided to go to bed earlier than usual. She was still in poor health, and felt the need of rest. I came and sat at the foot of her bed. The scene comes back to me vividly. Our conversation had flagged, and for a few minutes there was no sound to be heard in the room except the splashing of the rain in the black night outside. My eyes wandered restlessly, and fell at last upon the portrait of King Ludwig II, which mother had always on the table of her bedside, wherever she might be.

My glance lingered upon the picture, and many thoughts passed through my brain. I had long known what a deep affection mother cherished for him, and had often wondered within myself what was the reason for its depth. But I knew no details of his story — or, rather, I knew scarcely anything about him at all, except that people called him mad, and that mother always indignantly denied the truth of this; and also that he had a special passion for building palaces, to the ruin of himself and the great impoverishment of his country, it was said, though it was admitted that Bavaria had since reaped great benefit from these same palaces, which so many visitors come especially to see. As to how he had died, however, I had heard nothing beyond that it was by drowning. I was very curious about it, particularly since my mother showed such profound respect for his memory, and, as I have told, impressed upon me that I should show the same whenever I might come to Munich.

As these ideas went through my head again now, I broke out thoughtlessly, "Why were you so fond of Ludwig of Bavaria, mother?"

She started violently at my words, and I felt that I should have liked to bite off my foolish tongue. I seized her hands eagerly and kissed them, and then attempted to speak of something else. But she recovered her self-possession quickly, and in gentle tones told me not to feel unhappy. My question had indeed been unexpected; but she would like to talk to me about him. She knew that I must feel bewildered, and it was time that I should be enlightened a little.

Her voice was so soft and low as to be almost unearthly. There was in it the holy resignation of the martyr. A faint smile was on her face, by which she tried to reassure me — the smile of an angel. It passed swiftly, and I knew instinctively that the veil was about to be lifted this night from one of the saddest of tragedies.

And now she spoke slowly and thoughtfully, as if she were recalling incident by incident the story of injustice and cruelty. Again I must state that I make no pretence of quoting the exact words, though it seems to me often that I hear them actually as they came from her lips.

"He was not mad," she began. "They might as well call Louis XIV mad, or any other man with great ideas. The person who was most to blame in the matter was Bismarck. But, of course, one must not say so. Instead, it is common to throw the chief responsibility upon the Jesuits

— who, for once in a way, cannot be justly saddled with it here."

When it was proposed to proclaim the King of Prussia German Emperor, she continued, Ludwig opposed the idea strenuously. There was, indeed, for a moment a question of assigning the Imperial office alternately to the Kings of Prussia and of Bavaria. But Ludwig was young and inexperienced, and at last he was prevailed upon by his advisers, and particularly by his uncle Luitpold, afterwards Prince Regent, to yield to the pretensions of Prussia. As time went by he regretted more and more deeply his acquiescence, and at last was capable of doing anything to reconquer the rights which he had abandoned. By then the Emperor William I was very old — nearly ninety — and illusions could no longer be cherished as to a long continuance of his reign. At his death Prussia had good reason to expect trouble.

Bismarck had staked body and soul to win the Imperial crown for his own country, thereby himself becoming the actual ruler in chief of the German Empire. He could not have endured to see this power passing into other hands than his own, and knew that Prussia was not yet strong enough to keep it against vigorous opposition. The Iron Chancellor realised that if there was a man capable of resisting him, it was Ludwig of Bavaria.

It is generally asserted that Ludwig was destitute of will-power. But this is false. On the contrary, he possessed perhaps only too much of it. It is true, however, that he was not the man to make his way over the corpses of his enemies, calculating and relentless, like another Bismarck. His generous heart forbade that he should act thus. It has also been asserted that he was of a suspicious nature. Alas! if only this had been the fact, then his foes

King Ludwig II of Bavaria

would not have found it so easy to triumph over him. But he was trusting. Indeed, he was no ordinary mortal. His soul was as pure as his body was beautiful. Perhaps that is why he was not allowed to live a long life.

Bismarck, on the other hand, acted in a mean and cowardly fashion toward Ludwig. He could not challenge the King to a frank and open combat, with a fair field and no favour. He found it simpler and more convenient to weave round the King base and unparalleled intrigues.

It was not his fault that more blood was not shed than was actually the case. His prime agent was the King's Chief Equerry, Count Holnstein, who acted as intermediary between him and Prince Luitpold. Holnstein owed everything in the world to his king. He elected to play the part of Brutus. His is the eternal infamy of having conceived the idea of declaring Ludwig mad, after bribing for years everyone about him who was venal, and treasuring up every little scrap of paper, until finally he should be able to bring together a sufficient mass of evidence, so-called, to prove his charge against his master.

Ludwig had many debts, said my mother. Anyone else in his position would have felt miserably ill, for what can be more humiliating than monetary difficulties? Ludwig had been brought up under a very bad system. Until the time of his eighteenth birthday they never gave him a penny of pocket-money. During the year which preceded that in which he was unexpectedly called to the throne, he was allowed a ridiculously small allowance of a few marks a week. And then suddenly he came into possession of supreme power and a considerable fortune; thereby the last chance was taken from him of ever understanding the value of money. On his accession, moreover, not merely was his conduct approved by those around him, but the very smallest acts were extolled as great deeds.

No wonder, then, that he long continued to believe that his power and wealth were illimitable! Still, even if it be allowed that he did very wrong to squander all his fortune, where is the proof of madness? A great part of the world would be an asylum if everyone who spent his money and ran into debt were to be treated as a lunatic. It is unnecessary to argue whether he did any good in his expenditure of money. What harm he did he came to recognise himself only too well. An act of abdication might have been obtained from him, as from his grandfather Ludwig I. It would only have been necessary to appeal to his feelings of honour and self-respect for him to consent in the end.

But proceedings of this kind would have looked unjust in the world's eyes. The second Ludwig's errors had not been gross enough to make a forced abdication the only remedy. The assistance of a loan might be forthcoming to put everything right for him. This was exactly what his enemies feared. Gradually all but a few of his attendants were corrupted, and all his ministers were in time won over to act against his interests, so that the offers of help finally made to him by the Orleans family and the Rothschilds were intercepted and never reached him. It is well known that in the last year of his reign Ludwig refused to give audience to his ministers, conduct which counted very much against him in Bavaria. But there was nothing really remarkable about it. The ministers were in the conspiracy and would come to him, he knew, not merely without advice, still less to offer help, but actually primed with injurious insinuations.

And now we come to the fatal year 1886. I wish I

LUDWIG OF BAVARIA

could give the story, from this point at least, in my mother's own words as she told it that night at Ischl, so vivid and impressive, so full of emotion, so instinct with the tragedy of the affair. I listened as if hypnotised, and never spoke except to urge her to go on.

The King had not returned to Munich in the spring of this year, as he usually did. He remained at his castle of Neuschwanstein. For more than a month past all sorts of rumours had been flying about Bavaria. In the neighbourhood of Hohenschwangau there stood the old palace of the Knights of the Swan, rebuilt by Ludwig's father, and high above it Ludwig's own fine palace of Neuschwanstein. The inhabitants were full of alarm and suspicion concerning a plot against their king.

The general disquiet increased from day to day, until, very early on the morning of June 9th, it became known that during the preceding night a string of carriages had arrived at Hohenschwangau, from which a party of men had alighted at the old castle. It was a " commission " of ministers and doctors, who had come with the intention of forcing the King to sign an act nominating Prince Luitpold to be temporarily Regent of Bavaria while his own illhealth compelled him to take a rest. As soon as Ludwig should have signed, the command of the Regent would have gone forth that he should be taken to Linderhof, on the strength of a report which the doctors had already drawn up (without seeing him for the purpose), to the effect that he was insane.

The loyalty of a few faithful servants wrecked this vile plot. The King's own private coachman, Osterholzer, had made his escape from Hohenschwangau up to Neuschwanstein and brought his master warning while there was still time to provide against the conspirators' arrival. When the commission — whose members were the already mentioned Count Holnstein; Baron von Crailsheim, Secretary of State for Foreign Affairs; Count Törring, a Councillor of State; Lieutenant-Colonel Baron Washington,[1] and the two doctors, von Gudden and Müller — reached the castle of Neuschwanstein, accompanied by four keepers for the "patient," they found to their great annoyance the gates in the custody of the Royal Guards, who forbade admission to anyone whomsoever. After long parleying the King sent out word that he would see Count Holnstein alone. The arch-traitor made but a short stay in the castle. After one glance from Ludwig at the declaration presented for his signature, the ambassador was flung down the stairs. Ludwig had no doubt made up his mind to this drastic but well-deserved punishment when he granted the interview. Almost immediately afterwards the whole party was arrested on a charge of high treason by the old sheriff of the district, Sonntag,[2] who had arrived while they were at the gates.

The conspirators seemed beaten. But Ludwig, over-trustful as ever, commanded that they should be taken under escort to Munich and kept there, instead of detaining them, as he should have, at Neuschwanstein. At the same time he sent an order to Baron Frankenstein in Munich to form a new ministry to replace the existing one which had betrayed him, and announced that he intended to come to Munich himself to appear personally to his people of Bavaria, on whose loyalty he relied. He could not start at

[1] It is worthy of note that both Holnstein and Washington (a descendant on his mother's side of the Grand Dukes of Oldenburg) had been playmates of the King as a boy. When Ludwig was sent a captive to Berg, it was to Washington that the charge of the household was given, though Dr. von Gudden was responsible for the "patient."

[2] Sonntag afterwards died of a broken heart because he had let his prisoners go.

once, however, as he had but few about him, and was very naturally doubtful about the fidelity of some of his servants. He therefore telegraphed to his aide-de-camp and faithful friend, Count Alfred von Dürckheim-Montmartin, to come to him immediately, and to summon to Hohenschwangau without delay a battalion of the 11th regiment of Chasseurs, then at Kempten, whose attachment to him was known. The telegram to Dürckheim, for safety's sake, was sent via Austria, whose frontier was only an hour's distance from Hohenschwangau.

A second telegram was sent — to my mother. She was not in Vienna, nor, indeed, in Austria, but had been for some weeks in Bavaria, at Feldafing. This was a regular resort of hers. In fact, she spent part of eighteen consecutive summers there, staying at Strauch's Hotel, which I mentioned in the last chapter. Feldafing is only about twenty minutes' walk from Possenhofen, where she was born. Since the breaking off of the engagement between Ludwig and her sister Sophie Charlotte, mother had not been on the best of terms with her parents, which was the reason why she preferred to stop at a hotel rather than at Possenhofen itself. Ludwig spent his summers at the castle of Berg, on the opposite side of the Lake of Starnberg, and was expected there this year — though not as he actually came there, alas! a miserable prisoner. The rumours which were flying about Bavaria had found their echo in Vienna, but it had been impossible for mother to get any definite news, especially as Ludwig in his letters to her always avoided all mention of his personal troubles. In her anxiety she left Vienna for Feldafing earlier than usual, hoping there to hear something certain. Before she left she obtained from the Emperor Francis-Joseph a solemn promise that if Ludwig should be compelled to take flight from Bavaria and seek refuge in Austrian territory he should be safe from capture.

For many years Ludwig's courier, a man named Zanders, had been the medium of the correspondence between his master and my mother. He had succeeded in gaining the confidence of Count Holnstein by pretending to act as a spy upon the King. Supposed by Ludwig's other enemies to be one of themselves, he was thus able to learn much and reveal it all to him. It was Zanders who prompted the faithful Osterholzer on June 9th to hasten to Neuschwanstein and give warning of the commissioners' arrival at Hohenschwangau. He was one of those entrusted with the task of bringing Ludwig a captive to Linderhof as soon as he should have signed the proclamation. He had managed to upset this plan without betraying himself, and had reached Neuschwanstein with the rest of the party. With them he had been arrested and sent off on the road to Munich. When they arrived there all had been set free. Zanders then received orders from the conspirators to go at once to Berg and prepare the castle for the King's arrival. It had now been decided that Ludwig should be taken there instead of to Linderhof.

Zanders went to Berg, but took the opportunity, very soon after his arrival, of hurrying to my mother at Feldafing. He was broken with emotion as he told her what had happened at Hohenschwangau and of the King's intention of going to Munich when Count Dürckheim should have joined him. "They will not allow him to do anything," he almost wailed. "They will countermand all his orders, will put the Count in prison, and will rather kill His Majesty than let him speak to his people." What was to be done? Mother was almost beside herself with despair, and unable to think of a plan which promised success. It seemed too late now to convey the King from Neuschwanstein to the frontier. Possibly he was already on his way to Munich and into the hands of his enemies.

As mother and Zanders were in agitated consultation, her Groom of the Bedchamber interrupted them to say that a special messenger was waiting to see her. It was Osterholzer. Ludwig, fearing that his telegram might not reach mother, had sent the coachman to Feldafing with a letter, in which he told her how things stood. He said that he had sent a telegram to Bismarck, hoping to gather from his answer what his real intentions were toward him; and another to the German Emperor, so that he might not later be accused of neglecting to appeal to his natural protector.

After receiving this letter, mother calculated that the King could not be proceeding to Munich that day, and that Osterholzer therefore would be in time to take him a message from her. She wrote to him to let events take their course, to allow himself to be made a prisoner and sent to Berg. From Berg it would be easier for her to arrange his flight than from Hohenschwangau.

Osterholzer dashed off on horseback with this message. Meanwhile, what Zanders had expected had come to pass. Count Dürckheim, reaching Hohenschwangau about four o'clock in the afternoon, had received telegraphic orders from the Minister of War to return to Munich at once. While he hesitated, a second summons came to him, and as an officer in the Bavarian army he felt bound to obey, however reluctantly. On arrival at Munich he was at once arrested and sent to prison. As for the battalion of Chasseurs from Kempten, on its way to Hohenschwangau it was ordered to Munich, and the colonel, thinking that there had been some mistake at first, obeyed. In place of the loyal Chasseurs a detachment of gendarmes was dispatched to Hohenschwangau, with orders to surround the palace of Neuschwanstein and prevent the King's escape.

Osterholzer succeeded in conveying mother's message to Ludwig. Poor man! It was almost the last service he was able to render his master. But Ludwig was not convinced by what mother wrote to him. When he saw the gendarmes in the distance he took them to be his faithful troops. He was soon disillusioned; and then he was compelled to recognise that the advice given to him showed the best and indeed the only way out of his troubles. Those about him, not knowing all, could not understand his sudden great calm. He did not even protest when Dr. von Gudden made his appearance a few hours later, and said to him, in a very brusque and disrespectful tone: " In the name of the Prince Regent, your Majesty is my prisoner! "

At the same moment the four keepers who accompanied him made as though to lay hands on the King. But with a simple gesture the latter put them aside. " Not necessary," was all he said.

Ludwig was not even allowed to travel in his own carriage. A special landau had been prepared for him, with iron bars at the windows, and straps on the seats to fasten him down by if it should be desired. He was scarcely permitted to take leave of his servants. When at the last moment he spoke to his weeping valets, Weber and Mayer, at the carriage-door, Dr. von Gudden addressed him as if talking to a criminal rather than a patient: " Be quick, please! We have no more time to waste! "

It was now four o'clock in the morning, and Berg was

LUDWIG OF BAVARIA 151

reached at noon on Saturday, June 12th. The news of Ludwig's arrival was at once taken to my mother at Feldafing. And now there was very great necessity for caution if suspicion was not to fall upon Zanders. It was Osterholzer who brought the news from Berg. He related that the unhappy King was lodged in two rooms which had hastily been fitted up like cells in a lunatic asylum. The windows had been barred, and holes had been made in the doors, through which the prisoner could be watched constantly. The dining-room had been converted into a bedroom for the doctor.

Mother understood that she must act as quickly as possible if the King was to be saved from utter despair. She had on this same day received a communication from the faithful Chasseurs that they were prepared to shed their last drop of blood for their King, and that a detachment of them was encamped at the moment near Feldafing, and was ready to help whenever called upon. On the following morning, Whitsunday, mother met Zanders by appointment in the woods by the lake side. He told her that Dr. von Gudden was to go to Munich that afternoon to make his report, and would not return until next day. He himself had won over one of the keepers, promising him the protection of the Empress of Austria if the plot should fail, though that was very unlikely.

The King was in a desperate state of mind already from his imprisonment, Zanders said; so that it was decided by mother to take advantage of von Gudden's absence and bring about the rescue the very same evening. A boat was got ready and hidden in the rushes off the shore of the park at Berg. Ludwig was to ask permission to take a short walk in the park after sunset. The keeper who had been won over would accompany him. On reaching the boat the King would row over to a spot on the opposite shore between Possenhofen and Feldafing, where a carriage and four would be waiting in the cover of the woods. Then, escorted by the Chasseurs, the King would drive off at once into Austrian territory. It was to pass under mother's windows at Feldafing, so that she would know that Ludwig had been saved.

At this point in her story, I well remember, mother stopped in great emotion, with her hand to her heart, and when she went on it was in a voice that was barely audible. "I was waiting in my bedroom when the clock in the neighbouring church-tower struck nine. I had retired early, and my suite had all left me at my request. Ten o'clock struck, and still I was waiting. Nothing was to be seen or heard, and the suspense was almost driving me mad. Something ghostly seemed to fill the air. Was it the moon, shining out mistily after a day of rain, that caused those white shapes to glide over the waters of the lake? A deathlike silence reigned everywhere around the hotel, and I seemed to be the only thing alive. Sitting at the open window of my room, I felt as cold as ice from head to foot, and shivered repeatedly. The clock struck midnight. Not another sound still. What could have happened?"

Suddenly there came footsteps under the window. Springing up, mother leant out.

"Where is the King?" asked a low voice.

She understood that it was one of the keepers who was standing there. She told him to come inside, having already arranged that one of her suite should open the door.

"Where is the King?" she asked in her turn when the man had been admitted, and stood trembling before her.

"I hoped to find him here," he stammered.

LUDWIG OF BAVARIA 153

"What has happened? Why has he not come?"

The poor fellow looked at her aghast. At last he managed to tell how he had accompanied King Ludwig to within a hundred paces from where the boat was hidden. There he was ordered to turn back, while the King went on alone to the water's edge. He obeyed, but made his way slowly homewards, after turning his head. Suddenly he saw a man, whom he recognised as Dr. von Gudden, jump from out of some bushes and run towards the King. The latter sprang into the boat, but, though he had time to unfasten the rope which secured it to the shore, the doctor was upon him at once. A violent struggle ensued, the boat swayed more and more, and finally it capsized, and threw them both into the water. The keeper said that he thought that they both succeeded in swimming clear, but that the darkness prevented him from seeing more.

"The King is dead!" shrieked my mother, and fainted away.

Even as she told me now, ten years later, she broke down completely; and pressing me convulsively to her heart, she cried: "Terrible, terrible! In him I lost more than anyone can ever know — and in him, Weiberl, you lost your best friend!"

This account of the facts connected with King Ludwig's death, which my mother told me with her own lips, differs at almost every point from the official statements and widely also from the generally accepted version of the story; if, indeed, one can speak of a generally accepted version, when such a variety of accounts is offered by the biographers of the King. But to me my mother's story is convincingly true.

It seems that the projected flight of the King was betrayed to Dr. von Gudden at the last moment, so that he had no time to send word to Munich. He did not wish, on the other hand, to reveal his knowledge to the other guardians of the prisoner at Berg the existence of a plot making him uncertain who was on his side, who on the King's. Moreover, there were already disagreements and suspicions between the doctors. He therefore attempted to stop the escape single-handed. (Whether he had started to go to Munich and returned, or never set out at all, I do not know.) One thing may be said of him for certain, that he sacrificed his life to his duty, miserable as the duty of the doctor-gaoler may have been. It is unjust to his memory to accuse him — as he has been accused — of wishing to murder the King. Had he so desired, he could easily have found some criminal instrument without risking his own life.

After the keeper gained over by Zanders saw the boat overturn he had run down to the shore and wandered irresolutely along it for a time. The boat drifted out of sight, and nothing else was in view. He waited long, hoping for a sign of either the King or the doctor. He might easily have gone for another boat near at hand and rowed himself over to the Hotel Strauch. But as it was still fairly early he feared to be seen from the castle of Berg. What he did, therefore, was to wander along until he came to the village of Starnberg, at the head of the lake. Here he ventured to take a boat and rowed over to Possenhofen, where he landed and hurried on to the neighbouring Feldafing. He reached the Hotel Strauch after midnight, and, as has been heard, came to my mother. Her protection had been promised to him by Zanders; and besides he may really have thought that the King had escaped.

My mother's piercing shriek, "The King is dead!"

awakened the whole hotel. Some explanation had to be invented to avoid comment and suspicion, and accordingly the story was given out, and has been repeated ever since, that on the same night that King Ludwig lost his life, the Empress Elisabeth had a nightmare vision of her cousin dead by drowning, and woke out of it with her terrible cry, " The King is dead! "

CHAPTER XV

MY "MILITARY YEAR"; AND FIRST LOVE

I NOW resume the story of my own life, interrupted for a time to tell of things more interesting and important. Towards the end of August, 1896, my mother had to leave Ischl for Vienna to be present at a grand reception given to the Tsar and Tsarina of Russia. Our parting on this occasion was harder than ever it had been. She was still far from well, and was unusually depressed. I felt that the strain of separation was almost too much for her strength. Now she would again have no one to give her affection like me in the long sleepless nights when she was alone with her grief and pain. It was really remarkable how much better she was when she had my company. Her restlessness diminished, and she was able to sit or lie still for spells at least.

On the last day of her holiday she said to me: "It is only for a short time, darling. We must have patience. Our separations will soon be over. As we have endured them so long, we will not throw up the game now!"

I whispered through my tears that it was only on her account that I was grieving. For myself, to whom no hardships came, I could bear it better. But she herself had told me how terrible was the solitude in which she seemed plunged, in spite of the devotion of those about her.

For a moment a cloud seemed to pass over her pale forehead — only for a moment, for it quickly vanished.

MY "MILITARY YEAR" 157

But she told me I must never make a remark like that, which might give numbers of poor souls mortification who put themselves to great trouble for her. In my presence, she continued, she never tried to hide her real feelings nor to disguise her sadness when she was sad. But what might be natural enough with me would only humiliate her with others.

When she spoke so gently and lovingly to me, I really would have liked to kneel before her. In spite of all her sufferings, she was still beautiful and youthful-looking, especially when her magnificent hair was loose. As she looked then, so must the Madonna have seemed at the time of her Son's crucifixion. Certainly it would have been a truer picture than those in the churches, where the Virgin is represented as young as on the day when the Redeemer was born.

White still suited my mother wonderfully, especially her white dressing-robe. I remember one morning begging her to undo her hair that I might let it glide through my fingers. This was also a great sacrifice for her, but with a smile she granted my request.

On the day of her departure we remained for a long, long time together, I sitting at her feet with my two arms about her waist. For the last half-hour neither of us uttered a word. When we rose, the eyes of both were filled with tears. We looked at each other, and our gaze said more than any words that we could have spoken. We were both in unusually low spirits. Was it because the clouds so soon to envelop us were even now casting their shadow over our lives? Who can say?

As it was many years since she had last made a public appearance in Vienna, her visit at this time aroused the curiosity and interest of the people to a remarkable degree. The Court, also, was at least as anxious to see her as to see the Tsarina. Upon her return, she brought me some mementoes of the festivities — flowers, sweets, ribbons, bonbonnières, etc.

She told me her impression of the Empress Alexandra. " Poor young woman," she said, " some day perhaps she will be even more unhappy than I have ever been. There is a fatal melancholy about her expression, which touched me to the depths of my heart. She, too, has a mother-in-law who will not make life too easy for her — another of these ambitious creatures!" She also said that the Tsarina, when she greeted her, cried with sheer nervousness.

In October I returned to Vienna. The coming educational year was intended to have an important bearing on my future and was the strictest of all so far. " This is to be your ' military year,' " said Frau von Friese to me. " Contact with young ladies such as you met at your boarding-school is all very well for the first drill, but now you must go under a severer discipline. Now you must learn to be democratic and mix with the poor creatures who do not go to school to amuse themselves, but because they will one day require to earn their daily bread."

She had discussed everything with mother. Her object was to let me know as early as possible what went on in the great outside world of those who were not born to prosperity. " To learn to depend on oneself "— that was her great principle.

This time, she told me, I was not to have anyone at the school to look after me specially. I was to see the world after the fashion of Peter the Great. My incognita must be observed even more strictly than before. I must simply take care of myself and try to imagine as nearly

MY "MILITARY YEAR" 159

as possible that I was just as humble as those with whom I mixed.

So it came about that every day henceforth I had to spend several hours in a public sewing-school, the Frauenerwerbverein, amongst girls all of the lower, some even of the poorest, class. I must confess that it was not very pleasant to me; indeed, every day brought some new torture. In spite of the greatest self-denial on my part, it was recognised from the very first that I was not of the same class as the others, and that I had no real business at the school — for which reason I had a very hard time with the teachers.

We were seventy girls in a room, sometimes even more. The hours were from eight to twelve in the morning and from two to four in the afternoon. We were taught to sew, cut out, and design in a practical way. During all that time we were not allowed to eat anything but dry bread, in order not to soil our work. But Frau von Friese had acted rightly in sending me there. I had a sudden insight into a corner of the world into which I had never looked before. My eyes were all at once opened to the depth of human misery. How thankful I felt that this so-called "military year" was in reality only a case of "playing at soldiers," compared with the life of the other weary, hungry-looking beings, who were but at the beginning of their discipline of sorrow. For the first time I began to appreciate the luxury which surrounded my life. In the evening, when I lay down in my bed, I would not immediately turn out the light. With an indescribable sense of comfort I looked round upon my room. How beautiful it really was, with its plants and flowers, its lace curtains in the windows, its heavy Smyrna rug on the floor, and its dainty white bed and soft white woollen covers! Then I would think to myself how unjust all this was. Here I lay, surrounded by all this luxury, without having done anything all my life! I was utterly ashamed of myself.

I used to recall fragments of the conversation of my poor classmates. "My God, my feet are frozen," one would say. "But I've got to stick it this month in these worn-out old shoes. It's my turn next month. Our young Ferdy wanted some so badly, he couldn't do without them no longer." "What are you grumbling about?" another would retort. "Anyhow, you've got a warm coat. Mine hasn't even a lining!"

And I, for all my "military year," was protected against all kinds of weather. If it was very bad, I drove in my carriage to a neighbouring street — although I must add that after I first heard such a conversation as the above I absolutely refused to drive to school. Nevertheless, on my reaching home, the first thing my maid did was to bring me a pair of warm slippers.

My ideas became very democratic, as those of young people just entering the world of ideas usually are. I desired even to reduce my household! I was quite disgusted with the ceremonious attitude of my old butler when he was serving at table. Every silver dish offended my eye. As much as possible, I denied myself all luxuries.

Mother always endeavoured to be in Vienna on St. Charles's Day, so as to spend it with me. She arrived this time at the end of October, and came to see me on the 31st. Usually she brought me a lot of presents, jewelry and trinkets — besides the six-carat diamond which was given me on my name-day [1] each year. But this year, at my own

[1] The name-day, that of one's patron saint, is far more important in Austria than the birthday. I do not even know the date of my birthday.

request, she gave me very little, and consented instead to my carrying out an idea of helping my classmates, which I had confided to her. In fact, with her habitual charity she improved on my original idea. She told me to find out all the poor girls who could not afford to buy warm clothes, and to get their addresses; then we would send them, anonymously, everything they needed. This we did, mother adding a hundred florins for each girl. They never discovered who the donor was. This name-day was the most joyful in my life, for I was happy in the thought that so many of my classmates were happy too. I should have been very glad to bestow upon them all real fortunes, but naturally I had to curb my desires.

On December 4th of this year mother suffered a great loss in the death of the Mistress of her Household, Countess Goëss, perhaps her dearest friend. I question very much if their great intimacy was known even to those in close contact with my mother, as otherwise the Countess would most likely have been removed. Through the hands of the latter, many secret correspondences and commissions were conducted.

Mother had left Vienna at the end of November, after a stay of a month, and it was in Paris that the news of her friend's death reached her. A few days afterwards it was announced that the Empress of Austria was very ill with neuralgia, and that physicians had been sent from Vienna to Paris to attend her. During her illness I suffered the most poignant anxiety. Few people could have guessed that this sudden nervous attack of my mother's was really the result of shock at the removal of her old friend.

After she had to some extent recovered, she went to Biarritz, where she remained in the utmost seclusion until the middle of January. From Biarritz she went to Mentone as usual. She was accompanied by the Countess Szaray, General von Berceviczy, and her new secretary, Merkati.

This winter yet another new world opened to me of which I had no idea till then. I fell in love — rather prematurely, I fear, for I was only a girl of fifteen. It was a naïve little episode, but the ending was unfortunate.

Laura Kaiser had a few girl-friends, for of course she had not been kept in as strictly as I. Up to this time, after leaving Fräulein von Gunesch's school, I had visited nobody except Elsa von Thyr, with whom I still remained great friends. One of Laura's friends, however, I had known slightly almost ever since I could remember. We had played together several times as small children in the Volkgarten. Her name was Clarisse Mayer. Her parents were very wealthy and kept house in great style. Her mother was a handsome woman, very fashionable and fond of society. Clarisse herself had not been a pretty child, and for this reason her mother treated her rather badly, with the result that she was more than a little shy. I do not believe that I had ever exchanged more than a dozen words with her while we were playing at ball or bowling our hoops together. As Laura did not care much for her I had few opportunities of seeing her. But now that we were nearly grown up, the season of parties arrived for us, since it is customary to give these in Viennese high circles to teach girls how to behave in society. The Mayers' house, in spite of the mother having no wish to play the chaperone too early, promised, in this respect, to be one of the most amusing, and this was sufficient reason for Laura to cultivate Clarisse more closely now. Of course these people believed that I was Laura's sister.

MY "MILITARY YEAR"

I usually spent Sundays at the home of my guardian. One Sunday, however, Mrs. Kaiser said to me, "You are invited to a girls' party at Clarisse's house this afternoon."

As Frau von Friese was spending the day with friends, I could not go to ask her permission.

"Do you think that Frau von Friese will have anything to say against my going?" I asked.

"Oh, what a fuss you always make!" Mrs. Kaiser replied. "I have accepted for you already. I would not have done so; but, if you are not too good to mix with such a mob as you have in your school now, you surely can go to Clarisse Mayer's. Anyhow, I will take the responsibility upon myself."

I was not altogether convinced. In my heart I felt that there was a great difference between a school and a strange house. On the other hand, my scruples appeared ridiculous; for what danger could be there? And, besides, I had been to so few entertainments that I had an inclination to go on that account.

In addition to Laura there were some cousins of Clarisse's and a few other girls, all of the same style — that is to say, all very prim and proper under the eye of Clarisse's governess, of course. We played games until tea-time, and then we all sat around a big table in the dining-room, where tea was served. In the middle of our meal Clarisse's mother entered the dining-room, accompanied by an exceedingly good-looking woman, and behind them a young man of about twenty-five years of age. This was the first time in my life that a young man had ever been introduced to me! He was very tall and handsome, but not what is called a beau. There was a gaiety and brightness about him, especially in his brown eyes, in which there was always a glimpse of laughter.

His features were regular, and his hair brown and wavy. But the most pleasant thing about him was that he himself was obviously quite indifferent as to what impression he was making. In short, he was one of those few people who win their way at first sight by the frankness and simplicity of their demeanour.

There were about twelve girls in the room. He seemed rather amused at being the only man in this society of half-grown girls. I have never been one of those who believe that a girl must fall in love with the first man she meets; and I should not be telling the truth if I pretended that he made any serious impression on me that day. After tea I talked awhile to him. The girls played the piano and danced, and I had a few turns with him. I learnt that his name was Ferdinand Fellner, and that he was the son of a famous architect.

Upon my return home I told Frau von Friese everything that had happened. She was not very pleased at my going to the Mayers'. But, being a very tactful woman, she did not outwardly express her disapproval; and, as I did not say very much about the young man, she did not worry.

A few days after this I went to my guardians', accompanied by somebody — I do not remember whom. I had just walked through the hall to the staircase, when suddenly I heard someone a few steps higher up than myself saying: "How do you do, Fräulein? I have taken the liberty of calling on your parents. I was very sorry not to have met you."

I can only say that I behaved very awkwardly. I stammered something in my confusion, but it was so unintelligible that the young man did not know what to answer and merely bade me good-bye.

MY "MILITARY YEAR" 165

Upon my return home I spoke to Frau von Friese of this incident also. I discussed it so freely that she was not much impressed; or perhaps she acted upon the principle of not paying too much attention to it so as to avoid arousing my interest.

Several weeks after this there was a dance given by Elsa's mother. At first I was refused permission to go. I felt hurt, but did not dare to complain. Elsa, however, begged and begged, and I joined her so far as to ask Mrs. Kaiser to intercede for me with Frau von Friese. I had been so submissive at the sewing-school, and had behaved so irreproachably, that Frau von Friese thought fit to reward me by allowing me to go. Without my knowledge she had already written to my mother, asking her permission. Mother left the decision entirely to Frau von Friese. And so I was told that I might go.

In the evening, when I arrived at Mrs. Kaiser's to go on with her to the dance, she laughingly remarked that she had had an invitation sent to Mr. Fellner to please me. I turned pale and then blushed, but at that time I was totally unconscious that I was in love.

This was my first real dance, although I had studied dancing since I was six and was quite good at it. On my entrance into the ball-room I stood stiffly in front of the row of chaperones, who all sat against the wall. Of course, I was dressed in white — white silk, trimmed with white chiffon. On my shoulder was pinned a large pink rose. My long fair hair was plaited and done in a coronet round my head, just like mother's. I could not help feeling rather pleased with my appearance. The first person introduced to me was the brother of one of Elsa's friends. He looked at my programme and seemed surprised to find it quite empty. He asked me for the Polonaise. Gradually my card filled up, but I was unceasingly watching the entrance to the ballroom. The Polonaise began, and my partner came to fetch me. When he again took up my programme to write his name I had only a few dances vacant.

"The supper quadrille is no longer free," I suddenly exclaimed, in a tone full of anguish.

No sooner were the words uttered than I regretted them, and I blushed with shame. But my daring was rewarded at once, for immediately after I saw before me two sparkling brown eyes in a laughing face. Something seemed to be choking me. Then I heard someone say: "Good evening, Fräulein; I am so sorry I am late. Have you reserved a dance for me?"

"The supper quadrille," I replied precipitately.

"But that is really very charming of you — to show such consideration for me!"

My naïveté probably amused him very much, but I did not notice it, poor little innocent that I was, setting out upon the sea of love with all sails spread. I was happy, gloriously happy, as I had never been before in my life. Does one really know anything about happiness until one falls in love?

I would have preferred not to dance any more, all the others were so tiresome to me; but of course that could not be. To my first partner, who had also put himself down for the fourth quadrille, I was very rude, for when he came to fetch me I am sorry to say I made a grimace.

One little incident which occurred this evening is worthy of record. An old general (whose name, unfortunately, I never knew, since at the time I was not sufficiently interested to ask it) came up to me and said: "Do you know, my dear young lady, I have sat here for ever so long studying you. I really cannot overcome my amazement."

I was so happy at the moment that I could have laughed in the old gentleman's face. Still I asked him at what he was so amazed.

"Did no one ever tell you that you resemble Her Majesty the Empress?" he replied. "Such a striking resemblance!"

In spite of my gaiety I was embarrassed, and remained silent. He noticed my embarrassment and went on: "Well, does not what I say please you? You know, she has been one of the most famous beauties. It is not so much your features — and you are fairer. But there is something about the mouth, the shape of your head, your forehead. And it is not altogether that, either. It is the poise of your head, the back of your neck, your movements, which remind me of her."

But now I had quite recovered my self-possession, and I asked, "Did you know her well?"

"Oh, in earlier years, when the Empress was young, I had many opportunities of seeing her. And I had also the great honour of being presented to her. You remind me so much of her in her youth."

I did not know how to answer this, so I only smiled. Thereby I inadvertently discovered the right way to amaze the old general still more.

"Good heavens!" he exclaimed. "The smile, too! I think I must be going mad." And without waiting to say anything more, he went away, shaking his head like one who has seen some marvellous apparition.

CHAPTER XVI

PLANS FOR MY FUTURE

Now followed days of great happiness for me. I thought of nothing any more except Ferdinand Fellner. At school, during my lessons at home, on my walks, in fact every hour of the day, he was in my thoughts. I would have liked to have told everybody — and yet not for the world would I have mentioned it to anyone! I was rather ashamed of my love. Much as I thought of him, however, I saw him very little. There was nowhere that I could go to see him. I did not visit anywhere. Once or twice I met him on Mrs. Kaiser's reception-days, just enough to keep the passion smouldering. But really I did not confess all this to myself at the time, especially as he did not seem to pay any more attention to me than to any other of the girls. I was too proud to admit the truth. As the weeks passed by I thought myself cured, and told myself that it had all been imagination, that this was not a case of real love.

All this time, mother was on the Riviera, so I had no opportunity to speak to her about it. Almost at the end of March I went with Frau von Friese to Territet, in Switzerland. Mother had written to Frau von Friese the following letter: —

"I simply cannot endure it any longer. It will soon be four months since I last saw her. It is more than I can bear. I cannot spend this spring in Vienna, as my health makes it necessary for me to go to some watering-place. So I should have to wait an eternity to see her. But, since she is now such a big girl, the interruption in her studies will not harm her a great deal. To get away from that dreadful school for a while will be a great relief to her."

So once again I passed a whole month with mother. We lived in the same hotel, and every morning from seven to half-past eight we walked out together. The first thing she did, of course, was to put me in the confessional. For my part, I told her at once all my experiences, but so as not to alarm her I added that my whole love-story had only been an affair of the imagination; because, had it been a case of true love, I should not have recovered from it so quickly.

"Weiberl," said my mother, "I trust that you are too reasonable to deceive yourself as well as me, and that it was really only a passing fancy."

Her words were accompanied by an anxious, sorrowful look. It was far from my desire, however, to give a serious turn to this affair, and so I merely laughed to put her at her ease.

Mother's illness now seemed to weary her more than ever. She was tortured with sciatica. For hours and hours she would lie awake at night. But she was always patient as an angel and never complained. That silently borne pain made such an impression upon me that I can never forget it, and even to this day I seem able to bear any pain myself by remembering what my mother had to undergo and her quiet fortitude through it all.

My many diversions drove my love-affair into the background for the time being. We made constant excursions into that beautiful country, and the scenery alone was enough to make one happy. And mother was still really the only person for whom I lived. When I examine my feelings to-day, I can truthfully assert that in the affair with Ferdinand Fellner I did not deceive her or myself. To be all alone with her, day after day, made me happy beyond a wish. At that time I would have given him up without even a sigh, my only idea day and night being mother. She, on her side, spoiled me now as never before. Upon every possible occasion she showered presents on me in a way which she had not hitherto. Up to this time I had not been very much spoilt in this respect. Mother did not want to make me too vain. I always received beautiful Christmas and name-day presents; but until this year, 1897, she never had given me anything on other occasions. Now she bought me all sorts of beautiful things, by which she thought to give me special pleasure.

Nor had I ever yet had any money of my own, even though sometimes, as mother held in her hand her purse — that oblong leather purse that she always carried — I might look longingly at it. On such occasions, when my desire became too evident she would say to me: "What are you looking so intently at my purse for, you greedy little girl? You should be quite happy that you have nothing to do with money."

To which I might perhaps reply: "Oh, mamma, it must be lovely to buy something by your own self!"

Once, when my longing for a purse of my own was more than usually keen, she asked me, I remember: "What do you want to buy? If you wish for anything you have only to speak to Frau von Friese, and if it is anything reasonable you will get it."

I was not able to buy even a bunch of violets, I complained, if I should fancy it. By speaking of flowers, I suppose, I thought I should soften her.

"Babe, don't be childish," she answered. "You have plenty of flowers. If you want more, you have only to speak to Frau von Friese, and the florist will send you all that your heart can desire."

Yes, but sometimes in the street, I said, there might be a flower-girl, or some poor boy selling spring flowers, and I was unable even to buy a bunch from them.

Was I not always with someone who had money, someone who might give me enough credit to lend me a small sum of money? "However," she continued, "if your heart is really set upon this, I will give you so much." With these words she opened her purse, and carefully, with two fingers, fished out a ten-kreuzer piece (about twopence-halfpenny, or five cents), which she handed to me with an amused smile.

I do not think she was ever so liberal to anyone else! I have mentioned already this strange little trait in her character, that with all her generosity of heart and charity she hated to part with small sums. This time at Territet was the first occasion on which she ever gave me a considerable sum. She had promised to go with me on April 10th to a little farm, famous for its beautiful hand-made embroidery, the work of the peasant-women. At the last moment she was prevented, by the unexpected arrival of Archduke Franz-Ferdinand, who, on his way to Montreux, wished to pay her a call. She came early to tell me that she could not go to the farm. I was both disappointed and angry at the change in our plans, and was at no pains to conceal my feelings. I do not think that mother was much better pleased.

I should go with her there another time, she promised;

but to make up for the disappointment now I might, if I wished, go and spend the day with Frau von Friese at Lausanne. And for once in my life, I might buy something that I liked, and pay for it myself. As she spoke, she produced her familiar oblong purse, and took therefrom — to my surprise and delight — a twenty-franc gold piece! With this, the first money I ever spent on myself in my life, I bought a manicure-set.

Every day of this visit to Territet we were together at least in the mornings, when our walks were directed principally through the sombre stretches of gigantic oaks which surround the place. In the early morning the forest exhaled a delightful fragrance, and the stillness and quiet of the glades seemed the natural consequence of the fairy revels which must have been held in them the night before.

"How beautiful is this forest!" exclaimed mother one morning. "These giant trees, which may have stood here for centuries, are a connecting link between the present and the past. If they could talk, what strange stories they might tell us of the Valkyries, and the warriors and heroes of bygone days, who may have trod where we are now treading."

The remark seemed not so much addressed to me as the unconscious utterance of her private thoughts. Or was she talking with her dead friend, the only real friend she ever had, the only one to whom she would lay bare her soul without any reserve?

I had begun to realise what Ludwig of Bavaria had meant to her. And I understood better still when she began talking to me about him again on one of these mornings at Territet.

"Weiberl," she said, "you cannot imagine what a

noble being he was — far too noble for this world. He understood how to enjoy life as few people do. He revelled in it with the prodigality of a genius."

I asked her if it was true, as people sometimes said, that he had helped Richard Wagner in his operas.

No, never, she answered. Besides, Wagner had written most of his works before Ludwig came to his assistance. But still, perhaps, without him Wagner the musician might never have become Wagner the great. Not only was the merit of discovering Wagner's greatness Ludwig's, but Wagner himself admitted that near the King he became a different person. Far more important than the mere material aid given to him were the spiritual inspirations which Ludwig brought to him through his own noble individuality, and the atmosphere with which he surrounded him. The sublime masterpieces of Wagner were all his own; but, if his music helped to rouse Ludwig's poetical nature, Ludwig in his turn could accompany Wagner to wonderful regions whither others could not follow him. He admired him intensely, and it is this admiration which genius requires to make it expand. Ludwig arranged splendid feasts for him, with the sole intention of giving inspiration to his muse. And he was the most charming host imaginable — when he loved his guests.

"Mother dear," I asked, "were you often his guest?"

Of course, particularly when she was at Feldafing, she replied. During the last years of his life, when he was so overburdened with debts, he used to shut himself up to avoid his ministers, who harassed him terribly. But she and he always continued firm friends, and it made her very happy that at the moment she came near him he seemed to forget all his troubles. Their little luncheon-parties, tête à tête, would always remain among the pleasantest memories of her life. They generally took place on Rose Island in the middle of the Lake of Starnberg. Every dish and every flower on the table were of his selection. Nothing was too good for those for whom he cared. He would have given his life for them. How cruel it was that he should have to die!

"He at least suffers no more," she concluded, "but we two remain . . . to mourn for him."

Many a time on our walks, after having spoken of him, she would repeat, "He is no longer with us . . . but we must mourn for him."

We left Territet on April 27th for Geneva; or, rather, mother left on that day, and I followed her on the 28th, as she had arranged to spend a day at the château of Pregny, a few miles from Geneva. The Baroness Adolphe Rothschild had given her an invitation to come over to Pregny and see her hot-houses, which she now took the opportunity of doing.

On the night of the 28th we stayed together at the Hotel Beaurivage, Geneva. Here, as usual, I crept from my bedroom to hers to spend the evening with her. But she was so restless and nervous that it ended in my remaining with her all night, and sleeping with her in her bed. It was on this night that she first spoke to me of the measures which she had taken to provide for my future.

"Thank God!" she exclaimed, in accents of great weariness, "these continual separations are soon coming to an end. I am beginning to grow quite impatient, and I long for the day when I can have you openly at my side."

My only answer was a sigh, and, seeing how sad I looked, she went on to assure me that there was not very

PLANS FOR MY FUTURE

long to wait now — only through the next winter. In the meantime we must both of us be reasonable. My education must receive the finishing touches, to fit me to resist the temptations which awaited me. I had no idea yet of the extent of the intrigues of Court life. I must acquire more self-control and stability to live among these people without falling a victim to their snares. Vienna was the most difficult of all Courts. Men valued their friends only for the profit to be derived from them, and sacrificed them without a scruple when it seemed advantageous to their own interests. It was a great mistake to suppose that there were fewer crimes committed at Court nowadays than in former times. The only difference was that to-day the methods employed were more complicated, but none the less scandalous for that. In the face of all this she trembled for me. She wanted to protect me. But she never had any talent for intrigues. She was powerless even to meet those directed against herself. She had always been too confiding, and it was still impossible for her to believe anyone capable of treachery without indisputable proof. That was the real reason for her reserve towards everyone. She had always to be on her guard against falling into a trap. Happily they bothered little about her in their intrigues now. She was no longer interesting enough! But she suffered sufficiently in hearing how they sold and betrayed others.

"How happy I shall be," I exclaimed, "when at last I can be always at your side."

"Don't you think I also shall be glad, Weiberl?" she answered. "I shall find more rest then, and shall be better able to remain in one place. We will pass our winters in Corfu together. I love Corfu, though it always makes me melancholy. It is too vast and magnificent for me. But with you there it will be quite different. How unspeakably happy I should be with you there! And how you will love the spring, when everything there is in flower!"

Then she gave a great sigh and fell suddenly into melancholy again.

"Dearest, dearest mother," I hastily asked, "are you not feeling well?"

"Perfectly well, Weiberl," was her reply, "only these things seem to me such castles in the air. I cannot think that such happiness is for me. I cannot think that such a thing as peace still awaits me on this planet. So many years life has been a burden to me that now, when it has regained its value, I cannot believe that all will come right."

I was trembling all over, and vainly striving to hide my anguish. I understood only too well what she meant but avoided saying; she feared that, at the moment when life again meant something for her, death the inexorable would carry her away. She looked pityingly on my distress, and said: —

"Weiberl, don't be alarmed; I was foolish to speak like that, but the thought that something like that might happen has weighed upon my heart for a long time past. Do not allow my foolish fancies to worry you. After all, everything has been foreseen and provided for. *In case of my sudden death before I am able to take you out of your retirement, I have all the documents at Lainz, explaining everything concerning you. Amongst these papers are directions written by my own hand concerning your future. These also state openly why I did not wish to rear you in the poisonous atmosphere of the Court — you, my last-born child!*"

PLANS FOR MY FUTURE

At these words I burst into tears, and hid my sobbing face on her breast.

"Weiberl, be reasonable," she said. "Why do you cry? I am not dead yet, dear. But is it not wiser to take precautions?"

She ceased, and a deadly quiet seemed to pervade the room, which oppressed me by its silence. Her words sounded like a farewell. And so, in a measure, they were; for sixteen months later in this same hotel, probably in this very same bed, she passed away for ever.

CHAPTER XVII

THE COURSE OF LOVE

On the day following that of the melancholy conversation which I have just reported I left for Vienna. My mother accompanied me to the railway station, but returned purposely (for these precautions were still necessary) to spend the day in an excursion with the Countess Senyey. Then she came on to Vienna by special train at an early hour in the morning.

She only remained in Vienna on this occasion for ten days, during which period I saw much less of her than usual. My sister Gisela had come over on a visit from Munich, and mother's health was very poor. Her doctor, indeed, advised that, instead of passing the spring as she regularly did at Lainz, she should go to Kissingen for a cure.

Short as was her stay in Vienna, during it she received a very severe shock. My youngest aunt, Sophie-Charlotte, Duchess of Alençon, was burnt to death in the terrible fire of the Bazar de la Charité in the Rue Jean Gougeon, Paris. On May 5th mother came to me in the morning to say that she had had very bad news, a telegram announcing that Aunt Sophie was missing after the fire, and that it was feared she had perished.

Of the girls in the Bavarian ducal family Sophie had naturally been the pet. My mother's junior by ten years, she was still a small child at the time of the Imperial wedding, and mother continued always to look upon her as a child — as elder sisters will. A certain estrangement had been produced between them, I have already said, by the rupture of Aunt Sophie's engagement in 1867. Various legends are current about this rather strange affair. When it was announced at the beginning of the year that King Ludwig was engaged to his young cousin, the Bavarians as a people were well pleased. But at Court the case was different. There was a great deal of jealousy and intriguing against the Duke's daughter, especially on the part of some of the King's immediate relatives. When the postponement of the wedding — which was only a diplomatic way of stating that it was not to come off at all — was announced in September, the country was upset, while the Court rejoiced.

Aunt Sophie had not done anything very awful to provoke the King to break off the engagement. She was, however, rather too lighthearted and irresponsible for the idealistic Ludwig. He interpreted her little mistakes as evidence of a grave lack of tact, if nothing worse. And the intriguers, of course, did their utmost to poison his mind against her. He made no excuse to the Duke for rejecting his daughter, and communicated his decision very abruptly, simply stating that he would now never marry. The Duke Maximilian was terribly offended. He was a very ambitious man with regard to his daughters' marriages, taking their happiness, apparently, very little into account. My aunt Marie-Sophie, Queen of Naples, never even saw her husband before her union with him, and was married by proxy at the age of fifteen — to be sadly disillusioned when she reached Naples, and found what manner of man was King Francis. The Duchess Ludovica was still more ambitious about her daughters than the Duke. The whole family was very much upset at Sophie-Charlotte's misfortune, and very angry with King Ludwig. But my mother's affection for Ludwig was unaltered, and this was the cause of coldness between her and the rest of the family, especially Aunt Sophie herself. Yet she continued to feel towards her a semi-maternal love, and her death aroused very painful associations.

The effect of the new shock was serious to mother's health, although it is most cruel to pretend, as some do, that at this time she was in the least degree out of her mind. The truth is merely that she was overwhelmed with grief, and could think of nothing else. She was so utterly miserable and restless that she simply fled to Kissingen, where she hoped to find a little peace.

Now Frau von Friese, too, had been ailing all the winter; and although she also was one of those rare persons who never complain, I knew that she was not as usual. Mother, who could so well read the people for whom she cared, had several times during our stay in Territet remarked how ill Frau von Friese looked. Again and again she pressed her to declare the nature of her illness, only to be met by the assertion that it was nothing serious. My governess grew more miserable daily, but after our return from Territet, seeing what trouble mother had of her own, she continued to conceal her condition from her as before. She also concealed it from me for fear I should tell my mother. Soon after mother had left Vienna, however, she suddenly broke down from the strain she had undergone. To me this was perfectly unexpected; and even now I had to guess at the state of affairs, for all details were kept secret from me. I was told merely that Frau von Friese was ill, not how serious her illness was. She still went about every day, for lying down seemed to make her worse; so that I was buoyed up with a false hope about her. My despair can be imagined, therefore, when one morning, about a week after mother's departure, she said to me: "My dear, I am going home to Denmark; I hope it will do me good."

I threw myself on my knees beside the couch where she sat, and clasped my arms around her neck, crying, "Frau von Friese, Frau von Friese, you are more ill than you care to let me know." And I began to sob. I implored her to tell me the worst. I would tell mother. But no, I said again, I would not, for her sake; she had already all the grief she could bear. Only let me know what was the matter.

In spite of her pain, Frau von Friese could not forbear a smile at my nervous anxiety. "Darling, don't take it so tragically," she said. "I hope to be much better after my trip home. Promise me to be reasonable." She had intended, she continued, to speak to my mother before she went away. However, when she saw how trying the last few weeks had been for her, she decided not to do so, but to arrange everything herself. She would not be away longer than a month. For this short time I would be under the care of Mrs. Kaiser. She had written the previous day to my mother, telling her not to be alarmed and asking her permission to take a short holiday. She had begged forgiveness for not having informed her of her condition before, since she had only concealed her illness to avoid giving her any fresh trouble. She knew mother would have worried about finding a suitable place for me while she was away, only to come in the end to the same decision as herself — that is, to leave me in the care of the

Kaisers. Even if Mrs. Kaiser was not very reliable, there was no one to whose care she would more willingly entrust me than Mr. Kaiser.

Mother sent her answer by return of post. What could she do but agree? It was certainly very hard for her. In her kindness of heart always unwilling to hurt anyone, she did not complain; but in the few lines enclosed for me, in her letter to Frau von Friese, I could detect how miserably unhappy she was. She wrote: —

MY ONLY DARLING,

Frau von Friese must leave you for a short time. There is nothing to be done but to leave you at the Kaisers'. Dearest, be careful of yourself, and beware of all dangers which may surround you.

YOUR MOTHER.

My grief was profound, not merely because I was separated from both mother and Frau von Friese, but still more from the knowledge that the two persons whom I loved most in the world were both at the same time ill and unhappy, while I was unable to be of the slightest assistance to either.

Although Mrs. Kaiser and Laura were both most kind to me, and tried their best to cheer me up, the first few days were almost unendurable. Still, it was May, and in May Vienna put on all her beauty as no other capital in the world could. Then its parks, with their splendid drives, bordered by long avenues of stately chestnuts with velvety turf and exquisite flower-beds about them, stood forth in glory. Then the Prater became the rendezvous of Viennese high society. Then the Freudenau, at the time of the races, was a blaze of fashionable magnificence.

On every day there was a great stream of carriages along the Hauptallee (the principal avenue of the Prater), in which could be seen the equipages of all the old aristocratic families, those proud names which made the Viennese Court world-famous for its pride and exclusiveness — the Liechtensteins, the Montenuovos, the Schwartzenbergs, the Metternichs, the Fürstenbergs, the Kinskys, the Harrachs, and a hundred other illustrious houses, whose fame is inseparably interwoven with history.

At the beginning of the Hauptallee were the coffee gardens and restaurants where the citizens resorted to spend their leisure in social gossip, to the accompaniment of the famous Viennese waltzes and the Austrian folk-songs played by military bands. Here, under the stately trees whose leaves whispered strange tales of past glories or mournful defeats, the middle-class frequenters gathered to enjoy their beer and cheese, or drink their coffee and eat little Viennese rolls, in full view of the great avenue along which the carriages of their more privileged fellow-citizens passed. Often must some young girl, walking by her mother's side, have sighed with envy as she saw her more fortunate sisters driving by in splendour.

Far down the avenue, quite away from the other cafés and standing aside from the Hauptallee, was the Krieau, a sort of idyllic little farm planted in a great park. Here, in spite of its simple appearance, you could get anything just as at any other place. This was the exclusive resort, patronised only by the most distinguished people in art, literature, finance, politics, and society. It was here that all the noble dames and cavaliers came to sip their coffee, their tea, or their chocolate, in aristocratic seclusion, and to rest from their drives. For a couple of hours in the afternoon empty carriages with impassive footmen and beautiful horses surrounded it. You would imagine yourself at the entrance of a theatre rather than outside a restaurant. As the habitués were all more or less known to one another, the assembly was like a daily tea-party given by the same hostess — a very different kind of place from such a rendezvous as the Pré Catalan in Paris, for instance, huge, full of strangers, and unfriendly, unless you bring your own friends with you. Very few foreigners knew of the Krieau; but it was none the less one of the most interesting and curious resorts in Vienna in spring. Here you might see the city's *haute volée* in intimate intercourse. Here wit and beauty reigned supreme. Here, quite at their ease, and without the stiffness inseparable from formal gatherings, they gaily chatted of social events, political affairs, or the latest theatres. The fashionable costumes combined with the gay badinage to produce an atmosphere of frivolity; and the stranger surveying the scene would readily have believed that the passage of time in Vienna brought to all nothing but prosperity and pleasure.

And now it was spring, and of course the Krieau was the one desirable resort for Laura and her mother. So several times a week we drove down the Prater and had tea there. This was done, perhaps, as much for my pleasure as for theirs; and certainly, in spite of my worry, I rather enjoyed the new world thus introduced to me.

On one of our very first visits to the Krieau, as we were sitting with a few lady friends of Mrs. Kaiser's, I suddenly heard a voice behind me saying, " Good afternoon, ladies."

At the sound of the voice I was as though struck by lightning. I felt myself grow cold and pale, and then hot, as the furious blushes covered my face. A strange

THE COURSE OF LOVE

kind of excitement came upon me. I knew, as will easily have been guessed, that Ferdinand Fellner was there . . . and it was spring.

After this we met nearly every day, although always with Mrs. Kaiser and friends of hers. We never saw one another alone nor for more than half an hour on any occasion. Yet even this was sufficient to cause me to fall completely in love with him. It was very wrong of Mrs. Kaiser to countenance these meetings, but her foolish good-nature made it impossible for her to foresee the consequences. And perhaps, too, she hoped to distract my attention from my sorrows. From the day of our first meeting I did, indeed, begin to grow more cheerful. To my youthful imagination it seemed that it was the hand of fate that had brought me once more under the care of Mrs. Kaiser that we might meet again. Suddenly the sombre hues of life were changed.

There were other reasons, too, for the dispersal of my gloom. Toward the end of May I received a letter from mother. She wrote that her stay at Kissingen had benefited her very much, and that she was about to leave for Schwalbach, where she proposed remaining during the month of June. Frau von Friese also wrote that, though her health was not yet satisfactory, the mere fact of being once more in her native land, among her own people, made her feel better, and she was very hopeful for the future. Why then should I not be happy? And, despite my great affection for Frau von Friese, I knew that were she to return I should no longer be able to meet Ferdinand Fellner. The flight of years had developed my independence of character, and at a moment like this my heart cried out for freedom. With Frau von Friese at hand such a thing would have been impossible. Under her strict discipline, what a sad figure I should have cut, had I even dared to hint that I was in love! She would probably have resorted to extreme measures — and doubtless she would have been right. But nevertheless my love was rather that of the child than of the woman. It was not even platonic. If I must analyse my feelings, I should say that I was in love with the physical beauty of Ferdinand Fellner, for his mental qualities (it seems to me nowadays) were rather mediocre. Yet there was never in my mind the slightest thought of approaching nearer to him. A kiss was unthinkable. To place my hand in his would, in my innocence, have brought no feelings of self-consciousness or shame. There was nothing for which I can really blame myself.

A great part of June passed, and found me still awaiting Frau von Friese's return to join my mother at Ischl. But toward the end of the month I received a letter from mother, in which she told me that Frau von Friese was about to undergo an operation, and consequently would be unable to return for about six weeks. How desperate should I have been at another time, and how calmly did I now receive the news! Yet I could not help feeling regret when I read the following in mother's letter to me:

"All this is so unexpected, my poor child, that, being at this distance, I am unable to make any different arrangements for you. I know that Mr. and Mrs. Kaiser intended to travel this summer, and I do not like to cause them to change their plans for my sake, much as I should have preferred to know that at any moment I wished for news of you I should find you always in the same place, instead of at some hotel without either me or Frau von Friese at your side. For a moment I thought of sending you to Ischl under Fräulein Hain's and Pirker's care; but this is impossible without Frau von Friese. Moreover, it would cause deep offence to Mr. Kaiser, and as I cannot afford to make any enemies, I suppose I must submit. I ought to be accustomed to it by this time, but — *c'est plus fort que moi!* I know that it is silly, and that nothing will happen. It is probably the state of my nerves which causes everything to appear to me in so tragic a light. As for you, my dear Baby, be reasonable, and do not be too much grieved at all this. Such is fate, and we must bow to the inevitable. Let us hope that Frau von Friese will soon recover and that you will be able to join me shortly. Towards the 15th of July I am going to Ischl. After a short stay there I shall go to Karrersee in the Tyrol. About a month later, after August 18th if nothing occurs before then, I hope to be able to let you come. Oh, darling, I dare not think that I shall be unable to see you for such an eternity."

This last sentence was like a cry of grief to me. I felt so miserable; but what was I to do? She had written " such is fate," and as for my fate, did I not think I knew what that was to be?

For the time being I had to part from Ferdinand Fellner, who promised to meet us again toward the end of July, or early in August, at the little summer resort of Veldes, in the Carnic Alps. I am afraid my greatest anxiety was lest Frau von Friese might recover too quickly, and so spoil my well-laid plans. How selfish and frivolous I had become!

I enjoyed the journey greatly. For the first time in my life I travelled like an ordinary tourist, halting at various places on the way, and stopping at charming hotels, where I was not obliged to remain in my own room, but had my meals like the others in the public dining-rooms. Now at last could I thoroughly understand my mother's passion for travelling, that passion which made ignorant people call her mad.

We spent several weeks journeying through the province of Salzburg, and a great part of the Tyrol. Fortunately for my plans, Frau von Friese recovered slowly, and wrote that she would be unable to travel before August, so that I could look forward with pleased expectancy to our little sojourn at Veldes.

We arrived there in the last days of July. Veldes is a pretty little place on the shores of an emerald-green lake, and is surrounded by majestic peaks, covered by the everlasting snow. There are — or were then — only a few villas; but there was the cosiest little hotel imaginable. On the day of our arrival we made the acquaintance of all the other guests in the place, so that it can readily be understood that their number must have been limited. There were just enough to make it interesting; about forty or fifty in all. But if the company was small, it was all the more select. There was not a single uncongenial person in the little circle, not one whose presence was undesirable. It was the height of the season, and so there were every day picnics and excursions, as well as dancing, bathing, and tennis — at that time fully established in fashionable society.

A few days after our arrival Ferdinand Fellner joined us. His stay was limited to three days, for he had to join his regiment at Agram to serve his requisite four weeks. Short as was the time, we had more opportunity here than in Vienna for untrammelled conversation. Yet the charm of the situation lay rather in the growth of our mutual feelings than in anything that was said between us. I really wonder sometimes to-day why I found this young man so fascinating. From my childhood I had been serious and meditative, while he did not seem anxious to utter two reasonable words consecutively. It must have been the contrast between us which attracted me. His exuberant cheerfulness and his gay lightheartedness, so typically Viennese, were a revelation to me. He touched a new chord in my life, one which my education had never touched, but had left undiscovered. I had never noticed before that my life had been so terribly strict, not to say austere. Indeed, I did not realise it even then. I only felt extremely happy. During these three days we were constantly together, always in the company of others, yet always alone. Three days together in the country brings people nearer than three years in the city. Onlookers might have thought that we spoke of nothing but love, whereas, as a matter of fact, not one word of love passed our lips. But I was so innocently stupid that I never for a moment imagined things could have been different. I knew that I was in love — and that was all I knew about love.

On the last evening of his stay at Veldes there was a little dance. The heat of the evening caused many of the guests to seek the fresh air outside. Feeling rather tired, I looked for rest and seclusion farther down the terrace, where it jutted out into the lake. I was all alone there. Behind me was the glittering hotel, from which came snatches of laughter and strains of music softened by the distance; before me lay the darkness of the lake. Above, the myriads of stars looked down in soft radiance on the world, and all around the gentle breeze played, enveloping me in its cool freshness. The deep hush of the outer night was broken only by the croak of the frogs in the adjacent meadows or the quick splash of a leaping fish as it fell back upon the surface of the lake. Suddenly a shooting star flashed along the blackness of the sky. I bethought myself of the superstition that a wish made before it faded out of sight would be fulfilled; but before I could settle what the wish should be the glittering meteor had disappeared into the darkness. Was I then so "wunschlos glücklich," as we say in Germany, so "wishlessly happy"? Perhaps.

Into the dreamy peace of my introspection there broke the sound of a quick, light step, drawing nearer, and then I heard Ferdinand Fellner's voice saying: —

"I have been looking everywhere for you, and now at last I find you in this solitary corner! What are you doing here? Has mamma been scolding you so that you have come here to get over it; or are you admiring the moon and the stars?"

"Nothing of the kind," I answered laughingly, "only sometimes I have the feeling that I cannot breathe among all those people, that they are keeping all the air from me, and then I run away."

Out on the lake some one was playing on the horn "When the moon shines bright." Oh, the memories of my childhood, the happy times long gone by! It was as though mother were sending me a signal through this song, which she had so often sung to me when I was a little child.

All of a sudden I started. A slight breath touched my hand, which was resting on the arm of the basket chair in which I was sitting. Quickly I withdrew my hand. I felt myself changing colour, but I could not speak. I had a sensation of choking, and my eyes were filled with tears. I touched the back of my hand as if it had been wounded.

In the darkness all this was invisible to Ferdinand Fellner. At my silence he burst into laughter. Then he clasped me to him and pressed ardent kisses on my lips. Violently I tore myself from him and fled.

For half the night I could not sleep. I was too excited. I did not know whether to laugh or to cry over what had happened; but after a time I felt very happy. Now I was sure that he loved me. At this idea every fibre of my being quivered with joy, and my cheeks were burning.

However, my happiness was troubled. I felt as though his kiss were visible, like a scar upon my lips. The next morning I did not dare at first look Laura or her mother in the face.

Unfortunately, Fellner was leaving the same morning, and I had no further occasion to speak with him alone. He breakfasted with us, was as gay as usual, and behaved as if nothing extraordinary had happened. Then he left, and I was alone with my reflections. One minute I would say to myself that there was nothing in such a kiss, that it was only my ignorance which made me think it seriously meant. The next I remembered that he had pressed my hand at parting, and had said, "Take care of yourself, and be good." He had said the same thing in Vienna when we separated, but that was before the kiss. For more than a week I wearied myself out with my thoughts, and things remained unchanged, save that the passing days served to increase my infatuation as well as my longing to see him and ask him what he had meant.

While I was thus troubled, Mr. Kaiser announced one day at lunch that he had had news from Frau von Friese, who was returning from Denmark. I was to meet her at Villach on August 14th, and to go on with her to Karrersee, where we were to join my mother. He informed me also that they were returning to the neighbourhood of Vienna, to stay near the Semmering.

This news was not unexpected to me, but in spite of that, on hearing it, I blushed, choked, and was speechless for a moment. I recovered myself as quickly as possible, pretending that it was my joy which had momentarily robbed me of my voice. After the first shock my pleasure was indeed unfeigned, and as soon as I had had time to realise the situation I was even glad of the opportunity to tell mother everything. But it was not only joy that I felt. I reproached myself for not having thought of her at first, and suddenly felt how I had neglected her in not before asking her advice. And yet at this my heart sank. Could I not guess what would be her advice? How blind I had been! Who was this young man, and who was I? My only answer to these questions was a despairing sob.

On August 15th I arrived at Karrersee, where mother had already been a few days. She had left Ischl a week earlier than usual on account of the disastrous floods produced by the unceasing rain, which had rendered further stay there inadvisable for her health. Had it not been for this, according to her usual custom, she would have remained at Ischl over the 18th, so as to be with the Emperor on that day, which is his birthday.

My poor mother had by this time so learned to read my face that she immediately noticed something unusual about me. In the very first minute of our meeting she fastened a long look upon me, a look which caused me to turn my eyes downwards in shame.

I had arrived in the afternoon, so that mother had just time to slip into my apartments for a few minutes, to greet Frau von Friese and to hold me in her arms. She had no opportunity to talk much. It was therefore arranged that I should come to her room at ten o'clock, so as to make sure that she should have retired and that no one would disturb us.

Having travelled for nearly two whole days, of which the hours between Meran and Karrersee were spent in an old country carriage, which had shaken me considerably, I was very tired. I therefore lay down immediately after dinner, requesting Mina to wake me at half-past nine in case I should have fallen asleep. But, tired though I was, I could not sleep. I had noticed mother's searching glance, and knew that my confession could not be postponed to another day — knew, indeed, that she would ask for it at the very first. So I lay on my bed, shivering with cold one minute, and in a burning fever the next. What would she say? Would she be angry? Poor darling mother! I knew she would not be that; but she would be grieved, and that was worse. I looked at my little watch. Time was going so slowly. Or was it flying swiftly, oh, so swiftly? There was still half an hour more to be spent — an age before I *could* unburden my heart — a breath before I *must!*

The door of my room opened slowly and cautiously. I struck a light, thinking it was Mina. I almost fell back upon the pillows. It was mother, her face deeply serious — or, it would be more true to say, exceedingly mournful.

I sprang from the bed and went toward her, taking hold of her hand and pressing it to my lips. She did not speak. She took my hand in hers and went slowly towards an armchair, where she sat down. I followed mechanically and seated myself at her feet.

My heart was beating so loud that she must have heard

it. So much did I tremble that she was obliged to put her arms around my shoulders to support me, and then, in her sweet angelic voice, she asked me what had happened.

I scarcely knew what I was saying. I tried to stammer out a few words, to the effect that I could not help it, but that I was very ashamed of myself; and then I hid my face in her lap. But she lifted my head firmly, and compelled me to look her in the eyes. Resistance was useless, I knew, and I made no struggle. She commanded me to speak freely, to keep no secret from her. In a softer tone again she told me not to suppose she was cross, but only to remember how in the past I had told her everything and trusted entirely in her.

The confessional, however, was hard now as it had never been before. She had to put questions to me before I could proceed. Slowly and painfully she drew from me at length the whole story. When I had finished she looked at me in an agony of apprehension. Was I sure that I loved the man? she asked. "I suppose so," I brokenly replied; whereat, for the first time, she could not repress a smile. Why did I only suppose? she asked. Because sometimes I wished I had never met him, I explained, and yet when I did meet him my heart seemed to stand still. . . .

The sadness came back into her face when she reminded me that I had told her nothing at all about the matter when we were at Territet together. I was in torture when she said this, and tried desperately to prove to her that I did not then acknowledge the truth to myself, and so deceived not only her but myself also. I begged her to believe that, now I saw all, I recognized the folly of my dreams, and knew that I had been thinking of impossibilities. I was much too young to choose for myself. It was for her to choose, not me.

This was my last effort, and after it I lost all control over myself and burst into bitter sobs. I knew that it would have been a terrible blow to mother if I had told her that I still wished to marry this young man. Ferdinand Fellner was not for me. I had said good-bye to my first dream of love. How difficult it would really be to forget I did not then understand; but it seemed bad enough even at the time. I realised that I had practically taken a vow to put him out of my heart — for her sake.

Mother lavished affection and consolation upon me. She knew how hard the task was, she said, but I must be strong and trust her, as I had always done before. Then she got up from her chair, and, looking into my eyes, she continued gravely: —

"Once, when you were quite young, do you remember, dear, you asked me to lead you? The way is full of thorns and renunciations. But now you are on this path, and there is no turning back. You asked me, too, to give you the spurs if sometimes you refused to continue along the hard road." Suddenly her voice choked with emotion, and she breathed, rather than spoke, her last words: "And to-night I had to give them."

I hid my face on her shoulder, and wept silently.

"Go to bed now," she whispered. "Try to sleep and not to think, and only remember you are with mother."

And with that she said good-night, and left me.

CHAPTER XVIII

A TYROLESE HOLIDAY

IN spite of my mother's command and my own good intentions, I remained awake many hours, sobbing as if my heart would break. Only when the morning twilight first began to steal through the windows did I find a troubled sleep. But not in vain had I for years been disciplined in self-control. For her dear sake alone I did not wish to betray my grief, and so I soon managed to appear bright and cheerful. If mother suspected possibly that in the depth of my heart it was otherwise, she was too wise to open the old wounds by talking much about them. She hoped that my youth would soon enable me to banish even the memories of this experience.

I remained at Karrersee with my mother nearly a month. As the place was so small, consisting in fact of little save the hotel, we were compelled to rise early to enjoy our daily morning walks without attracting attention. And this was necessary to avoid not merely the guests, but also the Countess Sztaray and General von Berceviczy, who accompanied her to Karrersee. They were very glad to be able to enjoy the comfort of their beds in the early morning hours. But the intimacy of the place made it less easy for us to be together than mother had expected. It is true that her suite knew of my presence indirectly. It was more of a farce than ever. If I met any of her people we each pretended not to know who the other was.

A TYROLESE HOLIDAY

They usually tried to hide from me — to my great amusement. Etiquette being considerably relaxed, however, all the suite, and especially the Countess Sztaray, could practically enter and leave mother's apartments unannounced. This unusual informality led to my being compelled to secrete myself behind mother's bed one rainy afternoon to avoid a chance encounter with the Countess, who entered unexpectedly with an important message, or at least one that she chose to consider important. It was, as a matter of fact, only a letter from the Countess Harrach, her newly appointed Mistress of the Household, who had written in the name of the Emperor to ask if Her Majesty had decided to be present on September 28th at the reception of the King and Queen of Roumania in Budapest. Of course, in Vienna it would have been imperative that this should be communicated at once to the Empress; but here, at Karrersee, the case was quite different.

I do not know which at that moment was the more to be pitied — mother, who almost lost her presence of mind, and did lose her temper, or the Countess, who realised at once that she had made a mistake. Mother scarcely gave the Countess time to deliver her message before exclaiming: "No, certainly not! Tell them not to annoy me with their tiresome festivities, and to leave me in peace during my holidays." With this she made an impatient little movement of her hand, as though to brush away a fly — and the Countess Sztaray was already outside the door.

At this time mother was so anæmic that the doctors ordered her to take raw meat, especially the juice. Now she loathed meat, and the sight of blood was abhorrent to her. The juice, therefore, she usually poured away into the flower-pots as she had no other means of disposing of it without those about her seeing what she was doing. She dared not absolutely refuse to take it, lest the doctors should force something worse upon her. As for the raw meat, she would keep it hidden in paper until she could carry it away and get rid of it. Sometimes, at my special request, she ate some of it — loving me too well to refuse me even this. She had little faith in physicians, and trusted to Nature rather for help. She adhered to her system of bodily training (prompted to a certain extent by personal vanity, as I have said before), and this must have increased her nervous malady and physical weakness.

This summer, as already related, my mother broke through her regular custom of spending the Emperor's birthday, August 18th, with him at Ischl. The guests in the hotel at Karrersee, as everywhere else in Austria, celebrated the day with a banquet, followed by a dance in the evening. Mother and I both absented ourselves from them and spent the greater part of the day together. On the previous day, in honour of the occasion, the English guests had presented an address to mother, through the Rev. Mr. Bennett, who was staying at Karrersee.

As the summer of 1897 was rather rainy, our early morning walks often constituted the only time of the day spent out of doors. I had my own suite of rooms with Frau von Friese and my maid. I took all my meals in my room, so saw very little of the other guests, and they saw equally little of me. After my barely averted encounter with Countess Sztaray, mother preferred to come to my rooms rather than that I should visit hers. Accordingly she spent hours with me there, often taking her meals with me. Everything was brought into the little ante-room, and from there set before us by Mina. I have often won-

A TYROLESE HOLIDAY

dered what the hotel servants thought of the life I led while I was there. As Frau von Friese had not yet fully recovered, and remained mostly on the balcony leading out of her room, perhaps they thought it was on her account that I lived such a secluded life.

Mother was very kind to Frau von Friese now, as ever, and when we were together she was usually with us. Indeed, they were on such terms of intimacy that all formality was entirely dispensed with. There was absolutely no constraint in their intercourse, and Frau von Friese always came or went as she felt disposed.

I had my own table service, as mother never liked the ordinary hotel ware. She did not object to drinking from a poor peasant's cup at a little mountain farm, but she always said there was nothing more unappetising than hotel plates and dishes. And, in fact, in spite of all her travelling, she used them as little as possible.

At table Mina's waiting was reduced to the minimum. She served us once each, then placed the dishes in the centre of the table and retired. After that we helped ourselves. This was very different from our custom in Vienna, where a certain state was kept up through the presence of Pirker and Leopold, who would have been horrified at any breach of etiquette.

Mother thoroughly enjoyed these little meals of ours at Karrersee, and one day exclaimed: —

"Here at last I can enjoy a meal in comfort — nobody to watch me all the time, and eat as I like! Really, Frau von Friese, we made a great mistake in not ordering the same arrangements for your home in Vienna. But I suppose Pirker never would have given his permission!"

At these words Frau von Friese and I burst into laughter, for really poor Pirker was a terror to the entire household without exception. Mother used to say such things in a very humorous way, quite unlike anyone else. And she always made her most amusing remarks with a perfectly serious face.

CHAPTER XIX

A THUNDERBOLT

ABOUT the beginning of October I returned to Vienna, after having spent over two weeks with the Kaisers at Reichenau. Now that I was again away from mother, life seemed wearier than ever. Moreover, my relations with Frau von Friese were, for a time at least, somewhat strained. I felt that she strongly disapproved of my love affair, and was offended that I had not confessed all to her before. She seemed disappointed in me, and made me feel it. Besides, she had not recovered her usual good health, and so had good reason for being low-spirited. She who had formerly been so cheerful and talkative was greatly changed.

She now ruled me with an iron strictness, and was very stern with me at all times. She talked in a very abrupt manner; and as for me, I scarcely dared to speak a word to her unless asked to do so. My life became extremely mechanical, every day the same — lessons, walks, meals, and sleep. Not a moment's recreation was there; not a single opportunity to do as I wished. For years past the evening had been my time of recreation, when I read or played the piano or did needlework. During the last year I had been at least once a week to the opera, to a concert, to some other place of amusement, or to Elsa's home. This brought some slight variety into the monotony of my life. But this autumn Frau von Friese gave me special lessons every evening from half-past seven to half-past ten; three consecutive hours of work after the lessons of the day. "This will make us both tired and sleepy," she said. "We need it, so as not to lie awake in bed."

I understood what she meant. But how harsh I found this measure of hers!

In the mornings I went to a class to learn dressmaking, this time with Laura, while in the afternoons I took lessons in commercial subjects, such as book-keeping, shorthand, etc. My going again to the sewing-class was a species of penance decided upon by Frau von Friese after my return from Karrersee. Mother was asked to agree to this by letter. As she had always approved Frau von Friese's dispositions concerning me, she did not deem it wise to interfere now, so she wrote expressing her consent. Thus my time was fully occupied from morning to night.

The sewing-school was a private one, belonging to a Fräulein Fritzi Weigl. The pupils were of a better class than those of the previous year in the Frauenerwerbverein. Although a few expected to have to make their living by the knowledge acquired there, the great majority only came to learn dressmaking, so that they might save the expense of a dressmaker in after years. Nevertheless, there was not a single girl there of Laura's social standing, and once again I felt out of place.

The month of October passed slowly and monotonously. On November 1st my mother returned from Gödöllö, as was her custom every year, for All Souls' Day, and my Saint's Day, the 4th of the month. Now at least I was happier again.

About this time, also, we had a little change in our sewing-class, which made it pleasanter for Laura and for me. This was caused by the entrance into the class of

A THUNDERBOLT

three young girls who were more our equals, the Baroness Marianne Devez, Hanna Taschermann, and Bertha Habrda. Fräulein Weigl's pupils sat at tables with room for about six at each.

Until this time Laura and I had sat alone, but now these three new girls were placed at our table. Neither of us was personally acquainted with them before this, though Laura knew them all by name and sight. The day after their arrival — it was, as a matter of fact, St. Charles's Day — in great delight I told mother about our new school companions. No sooner had I pronounced the name of Bertha Habrda, however, than I was stunned by mother's outcry. "Habrda?" she all but shrieked.

Then catching hold of my two arms and bending her terrified face towards mine, she cried again, in a voice absolutely hoarse with emotion: "Habrda? Did you say Habrda? Are you sure?"

I was so frightened that I could not answer. My mother did not seem to expect it, for she continued: "Do you know what her father is? What is his position?"

"I only know he is Hofrath [Privy Councillor] Habrda," I stammered.

I had never seen mother so much excited in my life. She kept on clenching and unclenching her fists, in impotent anger, exclaiming again and again: "Oh! the scoundrels, the scoundrels!"

I caressed and kissed her hands in an endeavour to soothe her. But it was of little avail, for she went on in the same harsh, strained tones: "Tell Frau von Friese to come at once to your room."

I got up immediately and fetched my governess. When we came back mother had to some extent regained her usual composure.

"Frau von Friese," she said, "I wish Lintchi to leave that sewing-school at once."

"As it pleases your Majesty," Frau von Friese replied. "But may I ask why?"

I was afraid mother would lose her temper again; but she only turned first very red, and then very pale as she said: "Do you know the name of Habrda, Frau von Friese?"

"No, your Majesty, I never heard the name before Lily mentioned it," was the quiet answer.

"Perhaps it will suffice if I tell you that the last police superintendent in charge of the personal safety of the Crown Prince was Johann Habrda — and his daughter is at the same school as mine!" (Here Frau von Friese gave a little cry of astonishment.) "Now you know why I do not wish my girl to remain any longer at this school."

Frau von Friese stood in silent thought for a moment and then asked: "Does your Majesty really believe then that there is some hidden motive for placing these young girls near Lily?"

"You are too optimistic, Frau von Friese. I am sure of it," answered my mother, with deep feeling.

"I ask your Majesty's permission," calmly continued Frau von Friese, "to do a little reasoning. In the first place, is it probable that Hofrath Habrda would use his own sixteen-year-old daughter as a spy? This is absolutely unlikely. That being so, what can he expect to get through her being there?"

"He will use his daughter, without her knowing it, simply as a detective, so as by this to find out facts about my child."

"No, your Majesty," was the reply. "Had he desired

he would have found an easier way to discover what he wished."

During this conversation I stood staring at them both, turned almost to stone with surprise and apprehension.

" What is it, mother? " I asked at last, doing my best to master my excitement. " Who knows of our secret? Why should the police interfere? It is none of their business, for we are not criminals."

" My dear, dear Weiberl," said mother in a low voice, " you have no idea of the many things with which the police meddle." She continued in tones full of anguish: " Must I inch by inch destroy your youth entirely? Must I tell you of all the crimes which are committed every year? Do you know how many people have disappeared in this city, and are still disappearing every day, without anybody knowing what becomes of them? "

" Oh, mamma, then do you believe that something might happen to me? " I exclaimed. The idea seemed to me rather interesting than terrifying now. In my heart of hearts, I thought it more the product of mother's nervousness than anything else. I imagine that Frau von Friese was of much the same opinion, for she said: " I must ask your Majesty's pardon for what I venture to say, but I really think she is carrying her anxiety a little too far. Her Majesty is very imprudent about her safety, and now she sees things far blacker than they really are."

" So then, to speak plainly, my dear Friese, you do not agree with me? You think it simply a coincidence? "

" Yes, your Majesty, and I do not believe that there is the slightest danger for Lily in remaining at the school. And let us even suppose that there are grounds for suspicion. What a good training this will be for her to meet the world! "

At these words poor mother hid her face in her hands to conceal her despair, for she knew that she would again be obliged to submit to my implacable governess.

Frau von Friese continued in the same calm, even voice, ignoring my mother's emotion: " I have to be hard, your Majesty. I am the one who has taken in hand the task of preparing this child for life. I must not blind myself. What can she learn if she is always to be sheltered? How can she learn to protect herself? No, as I said, here is a splendid opportunity for her. If this is really some trick, is it not by our good fortune that they were so simple as to make their action easily discoverable? Unfortunately, your Majesty, I imagine them to be more skilful. We have to beware of the traps we are unable to see, not those like this."

And so I continued to go to the school. Mother, however, thought it time now to enlighten me about the tragedy of my brother's death, of which hitherto she had always refused to speak. What she told me I will in my turn relate.

CHAPTER XX

MAYERLING

"RUDY never committed suicide! Rudy was murdered!"

These were my mother's words. What indescribable despair did they convey — the despair that dries up the source of tears and turns sleep into an evil dream! The state of her soul since the death of the Crown Prince was not one of ordinary sorrow over a bereavement, but something far worse. Blended with the terrible anguish caused to her by the loss of her only boy was a feeling of intense, concentrated hatred for those who had been the authors of his death. Her heart cried out for vengeance; and this mother's wrath was all the more desperate because her own exalted position prevented her from tracking down the guilty ones, who were themselves of high standing, or sheltered behind higher personages still to save themselves from attack.

Yes, Rudolf was murdered. This is the true solution of the riddle of Mayerling, and I am grateful to Fate that for me has been reserved the duty of revealing the true story to the world.

In order to make things clearer to me my mother gave me a detailed description of the manners and customs of the Court of Vienna. I have already, earlier in this book, said something upon this subject, but even at the risk of wearying the reader with repetition it is necessary to return to it again here. At the Viennese Court far more than at any other Court in the world, not only the members of the Imperial Family, but all, be they men or women, who are admitted within the sacred precincts, lead a life very remote from that of the outside world. Here a long roll of ancestors is still the only passport, and whosoever cannot produce one, if indeed he can gain admission at all, is eyed with severe disapproval. The inhabitants of this select place think themselves much too good for the rest of mankind, who are mere *canaille* in comparison, and they actually believe that it is by the grace of God that they have a right to the privileges and comforts of life. They dwell in splendid luxury, while others who are not "high-born" spend their last penny and work their fingers to the bone in their service. These aristocrats play indeed at charity because it is good form, *comme il faut*, and also because it is a very pleasant stimulant to look upon the misery of others from the midst of one's own happiness.

The Spanish etiquette still reigns at the Court of Vienna, which was there in the reign of the Emperor Charles V. Whatever the occasion may be, a birth, a wedding, a funeral, a glad or a mournful ceremony, the feeling of an outside spectator must be the same; he is carried back three hundred years into the past. The same state of affairs prevails with regard to the government of the Imperial Family, over which the power of the Emperor is absolute. The same again is true of the household, everything must be in the same rank, in the same order, down to the smallest detail of State livery. All is Spanish, all is narrow and arrogant. And, of course, all who claim to belong to the Court fashion their lives on the same model.

In contrast to this pomp and almost Oriental luxury, in contrast to this conceit of exalted birth, stand the self-de-

Baroness Marie Vetsera

Crown Prince Rudolf
(*From a water-color miniature*)

Mayerling

nial and renunciation, the gentleness and tolerance inculcated by the Church, the all-powerful Roman Catholic Church. The inevitable results of these contradictory influences are deceit, immorality, and intrigue. Hypocrites, slanderers, and treacherous dealers abound. Everyone has his own father-confessor, from whom he receives absolution; for the Church has no wish to lose the favour of these great folk, and is content if appearances are maintained. So clergy and Court are the best of friends, and appearances *are* maintained excellently.

It is necessary to have lived among these people in order to understand the various causes which drive them to become bad; how in one case it is fear, in another ambition, in another weakness of character, in another inborn vice. Anyone amongst them whose mind is of a different cast and who expresses different views is looked upon as an apostate, and his life is that of a prisoner, wearily dragging around with him the chains of his captivity.

What wonder is it, then, that a deep and liberal thinker like the Crown Prince Rudolf should try to set himself free from such surroundings?

Rudolf in his childhood had been brought up in the narrowest of ways, as might be imagined when it is said that the sole control of his early education was in the hands of the Archduchess Sophia, his grandmother. As a matter of course, he was taught to believe implicitly in the "divine right of kings"; and, until the time came when he began to observe and think for himself, he was contemptuous of others' feelings and arrogant in his behaviour. His nature was close, defiant, wilful and passionate, and he preferred his own company. When a little boy he liked to play alone, and got angry if anyone else touched his toys. As he got older he showed a taste for reading, and took much interest in everything connected with animals and plants, about which he never seemed able to learn enough. Had he not been born a Crown Prince he would probably have become a naturalist, for he possessed the requisite ability and strength of will, loved the active open-air life, and was gifted with more than average intelligence. When he grew up, he became less reserved — under the influence of her who was his mother and mine — especially in the society of the people whom he felt to be sympathetic, and he lost the haughtiness which had been implanted in him.

It has been brought as a charge against Rudolf that he was exceedingly frivolous and frittered away his time in the company of frivolous women. This is mere invention. By temperament he was very serious, and the consequence was that cheerfulness with him often showed itself in noisy gaiety; for it is hard for natures like his to preserve their balance in such circumstances. But his amusements were not dissolute ones. An Imperial prince, however, readily incurs suspicions of this kind. Rudolf's chief amusement was to drive out with his favourite coachman, Bratfisch, to the suburbs, and there to pay a visit to some small inn. Here he would stay till late at night over his Heurigen — that is to say, wine of the current year — listening to the singing of popular songs or talking with the ordinary people sitting about him. These night excursions of his were not merely an idle device for killing time. They were prompted by the instinct of the inquirer, the spirit of Haroun-el-Raschid — a spirit, by the way, which also showed itself in Ludwig I of Bavaria. How much more practical was this method of investigating the ways and thoughts of the people than the usual systematic plan which crams the minds of princes with useless rubbish. Rudolf by his conduct soon gained the hearts of all his people and made himself more popular than any other member of the Imperial family. " Our Rudy " was his name everywhere, and it was with feelings of confidence that men looked forward to the days when he should reign over them.

Through the whole course of his childhood he had been treated with such an exaggeration of strictness where religious matters were concerned that, when he had grown to be a thinking human being, he felt an utter repulsion for the Church and he never attended its services unless actually compelled to do so; and he habitually ridiculed the hypocrisy of the clergy. But in time, as he discovered the extent of their trickery, and particularly that of the Jesuits, and realised what a harmful power they wielded in Austria, he ceased to laugh at them and began to meditate how he might one day cut himself free from them. He sought his friends among the men of science, the writers and artists — and became a freemason. Now masonry in Austria is quite a different thing from what it is in any other country in the world. It is forbidden. The Church in Austria has such strength that it has succeeded in having masonry declared illegal. To be a freemason, therefore, is to break the law. The meetings of this necessarily secret society, when discovered, are broken up and the members are prosecuted in the courts. And the Crown Prince of Austria was a freemason!

Of a certainty Rudolf was neither the frivolous creature nor the libertine which his enemies endeavoured to represent him as being. But their point of view — or, rather, their plan of campaign — is intelligible enough. They had to be prepared for troublous times when he should mount the throne. The Prince took as his ideal and model the Emperor Joseph II. This monarch, who reigned from 1780 to 1790 and was the brother of the unhappy Marie-Antoinette, made matters very uncomfortable for the clergy and the nobility of his empire. He specially decreed that all religious orders whose members would not "keep school, or preach, or help the sick and dying, or distinguish themselves by study," should have their property confiscated. With the money thus acquired he founded schools, hospitals, lunatic asylums, orphanages, and other charitable institutions. He soon went on to interfere with the internal affairs of the Church in his dominions and to regulate the order of the services and the details connected with processions, pilgrimages, indulgences, etc.; in fact, to subject the Church entirely to the authority of the State.

In order to put a stop to these measures, the Pope of the day, Pius VI, condescended even to go to Vienna and beg the Emperor not to proceed with his reforms. But he strove in vain. The reformation went on. The Jesuits were banished from the Empire. The Protestants, on the other hand, who had suffered terribly in Austria for the past hundred and fifty years, obtained all manner of alleviations. The Jews were granted freedom of movement. Hitherto they had been forced to live in their ghettos and to wear the yellow patch on their clothes as a distinguishing mark.

The nobles did not come off much better than the Church. Innumerable privileges which previously had been theirs were done away with. What affected them most painfully was the abolition of serfdom, by which a great portion of their possessions was taken from them and made over to the freed peasantry.

The last-named measures were allowed to continue in force after the death of the Emperor Joseph. But under his successors the Church of Rome secured a complete restitution of her lost rights. In particular the religious orders and the monasteries were restored. And the Jesuits, above all, regained their position, their power now spreading farther than ever.

Rudolf never concealed his aversion to the Church, and to the Jesuits in chief; and, as I have already said, they could anticipate no good for themselves from his accession to the throne. It did not take long, therefore, for a party hostile to him to form at the Court. It would be difficult to name all the members of importance in this party. But it can be stated definitely that at its head stood the Archduke Karl-Ludwig (Charles-Louis), brother of the Emperor and father of the then heir-presumptive, the Archduke Franz-Ferdinand. Karl-Ludwig had never forgiven his elder brother for being born before him and thus obtaining the Imperial crown. Yet he had a great influence over Francis-Joseph, and probably it was for this reason that he was chosen to head the party against the Crown Prince. He was well fitted for the post, since no one could match him in creeping hypocrisy.

My mother heard nothing about the vile intrigue until after the death of Rudolf. The latter was unequal to coping with the machinations of his enemies. His very uprightness was in itself an obstacle to him. It prevented him from being able to judge clearly the baseness of other people. Besides, the effect of his early education had been to foster in him a goodly portion of self-conceit, which never left him. He could not imagine that anyone could set himself up as a rival to him.

Perhaps Rudolf's greatest misfortune, however, was his indifference toward the military profession. Not that he felt any personal dislike against soldiers; but he did not take the slightest interest in them and their pursuits.

Consequently this party, which is so powerful in Austria and is the only one that has any influence besides the Church and the nobility, was estranged from him. The Emperor, on the other hand, was a thorough soldier and could not forgive his son for his indifference to military matters. Their relations with one another constantly grew more and more strained; which, of course, was grist to the mill of Rudolf's enemies.

As soon as the Crown Prince was allotted his own Court, which took place on his sixteenth birthday, when he legally came of age, he began to surround himself with people who did not belong to the Imperial Court circle — for the most part scholars and literary men. At the age of twenty he had established a small society about himself, which was very select but was certainly not fashionable. Among them, to the horror of the Court, there were even journalists; and, worse still, they were mostly of the Jewish persuasion! This was intolerable, and must be put an end to.

Attempts were made to entice Rudolf into feminine society. But, if one may say so, he was somewhat undeveloped on the sensual side and took no particular pleasure in it. Occasionally he noticed himself his lack of enjoyment in the alluring things of this life, and then, as if he were ashamed of his deficiency, he would plunge into some wild dissipation, toward which he felt all the greater repugnance when he had come to his senses again. The instigator of these orgies was Count Charles Bombelles. This man, a son of the Emperor Francis-Joseph's tutor in boyhood, was first tutor and then controller of the household to the Crown Prince Rudolf.[1] Bombelles might have suc-

[1] It was his uncle Charles René, Grand Master of the Court to Ferdinand I, who was the third husband of the Archduchess Marie-Louise.

ceeded in drawing the Prince into this life of vice had not the Empress interfered in time and exhorted the Emperor incessantly to prevent the ruin of their son.

To Francis-Joseph, looking on Rudolf in more ways than one as an unnatural son, there only appeared one remedy — marriage. If my mother's advice had been taken and Rudolf had been sent away on a voyage round the world, his own wish would have been fulfilled and everything would have turned out differently. But the Emperor's advisers, his chief ministers, and his confessor, Father Laurenz Mayer, whose influence far exceeded the Empress's, were against the plan. Was not the Crown Prince already democratic enough? they asked. Were not his ideas already sufficiently perverse that he should be sent to bring home still madder ones?

And so, instead of taking a voyage round the world, he went to look for a wife.

Here again came an opportunity for fresh intrigues. Among the few eligible princesses of the day the two best-looking and most attractive, the Infanta Maria-Anna of Braganza, later Grand-Duchess of Luxemburg, and her sister Marie-Antonia, later Duchess of Parma, were not considered.[1] If only those in authority had consented to wait a few years — and Rudolf was barely twenty — he would have had a wider and better field for choice, and he himself would have been maturer and more capable of appreciating the gravity of the step which he was taking. As it was, he allowed himself to be misled by frivolous advice, especially from Count Bombelles. His advisers said

[1] They were daughters of Miguel I, King of Portugal. Their brother, Miguel II, the Legitimist claimant to the former kingdom of Portugal, married the Princess Elizabeth of Thurn and Taxis (since dead), daughter of my aunt Hélène. Marie-Antonia is the mother of the Archduchess Zita, the new heir-presumptive's wife.

to him that it would be useless to wait for some princess from fairyland. The heir to a throne must have sober, common-sense ideas concerning marriage. As he would probably never fall in love with the woman he would be permitted to marry, it was a matter of indifference upon whom his choice fell. So the poor, inexperienced Crown Prince, still himself at an awkward age and not yet very attractive in looks, an idealist at heart but profoundly unconscious of his own idealism, submitted and married Stephanie, daughter of Leopold, King of the Belgians.

The selection of Princess Stephanie was not fortunate, as she shared none of Rudolf's interests. She cared for nothing but dress and entertainments, and in her manner was tactless and impatient.

Following mother's advice, Rudolf at first took pains and did his best to bring into harmony his wife's interests and his own. The effort was not a success. The youthfulness of both parties was the chief obstacle to their happiness, mother said. She herself, who from the beginning had strongly opposed the match, tried to the utmost of her power to bring the two together. But Rudolf was far from being easy to guide, and in the first year of the marriage things went very wrong indeed.

It was hoped that affairs would improve upon the birth of an heir. Unfortunately, this proved a delusion, not merely because it was a little girl that was born, but also because the doctors now announced that the Crown Princess would never be able to bear another child. This was not merely a disappointment; it was the total ruin of the hopes of Rudolf and of the whole Court alike.

There was now complete coldness between the two young people. They might simply have gone their own way — Rudolf not being a jealous husband — had not his enemies thought the time opportune for them to intervene. The Crown Prince being perfectly indifferent, they must try to arouse Stephanie's jealousy. She would never have become jealous of her own accord. But they gradually instilled into her mind that her husband was occupied with the scheme of having his marriage annulled, in order to be able to marry someone with whom he was in love, the Princess Aglae Auersperg. There would be nothing to prevent this marriage, were Rudolf free, for the Princess belonged to one of the mediatised princely families, and therefore, according to the Austrian idea, was eligible to marry even a Crown Prince. The whole story was an invention, but Stephanie was thrown into a perfect panic, and became an easy tool in the hands of the enemy. Agents of the secret police were placed at her disposal, who made up and brought to her the most harrowing stories of her husband's manner of life. The unhappy woman, instead of enduring in silence or with quiet dignity asking him to explain himself, overwhelmed Rudolf at once with reproaches and insults, refusing absolutely to believe his categoric denials.

Terrible scenes now took place, which would have been unworthy of a washerwoman and a stableman. The scandal reached the ears of the public. The Crown Princess herself helped not a little to spread it about by speaking of her wretchedness to everyone who had the patience to listen to her.

In reality Rudolf, not having a very strong constitution, was obliged to avoid a life of dissipation and to dwell in comparative retirement. Political matters occupied his attention more and more, especially those concerning the spread of liberal ideas. Many a night which Stephanie was induced to believe spent in wild orgies, was spent in secret meetings with men of like views to his own. It is probable that had he found peace and quiet in his married life, he would not have been so ready to pass his time thus. As it was, he used politics not only to gratify his personal leanings, but also to escape from his home and the troublesome thoughts aroused there.

In order to be able to lead a life free from disturbance, he resolved to buy an estate in the neighbourhood of Vienna. Up to now he had resided, when not at the Hofburg itself, at the castle of Laxenburg, which was not far away. It was necessary that his new place also should be near the capital, and he decided on the hunting-box of Mayerling. So cunningly had his enemies woven their intrigues that he remained totally unsuspicious that his choice had been influenced by them. Mayerling was all but next door to the Cistercian monastery of the Holy Cross (Heiligenkreuz). The estate being really too small for purposes of hunting, the amiable monks offered a lease of their grounds in case his Imperial Highness should make up his mind to purchase Mayerling. As this had been the only objection to the estate, that it was not extensive enough, the unsuspecting Prince accepted their offer and bought Mayerling. The result was that he, who thought himself at length alone and undisturbed, was under closer observation than before.

The man who acted as intermediary between the Crown Prince and the monks was the police commissioner, Johann Habrda, the guardian of the personal safety of the former. Habrda owed what advancement had been his so far, to the abbot of the monastery Father Grünbeck, to whom he naturally felt under an obligation.

Rudolf's political activities were of too mild a nature to furnish his enemies with material for a scandal; and, more-

MAYERLING

over, as his sympathies were all in favour of liberty, an attack on him for this would only have increased his popularity. On the other hand, they had so far completely failed to demonstrate to the public satisfaction that he was a dissipated character. And, to make matters worse, there were serious scandals connected with the sons of the Archduke Karl-Ludwig, Franz-Ferdinand and still more Otto. The misdeeds of the latter have so often been enumerated in the Press and in books that I am glad to say I can abstain from mentioning any of them here. They are so repulsive that those who have never heard of them may congratulate themselves. I have only alluded to them in this vague way to point out that if people in Court circles behave scandalously there is no necessity for a campaign to spread the unsavoury stories. They make their way abroad, and do not remain, as in my brother Rudolf's case, mere idle gossip of the Court. Of the things done by the Archduke Karl-Ludwig's sons there were many eye-witnesses among the people, both middle and lower classes. Can anyone say the same about Rudolf?

The efforts to compromise the Crown Prince over his disagreements with his wife failed entirely, and the blame seemed always to fall upon the unhappy Stephanie. Years passed, and no opportunity offered itself to damage him.

But Rudolf had never yet loved passionately, and it was the awakening of passion which put his ruin within his enemies' hands. He fell in love at last — and fell very deeply.

The utter baseness and unscrupulousness of the plotters, my mother said, was in no way more revealed than that they employed the innocence of a young girl, who knew nothing of the scheme, to bring about their ends. It was enough for them that they found a convenient, unsuspecting tool. What mattered it if she too were ruined?

The Baroness Marie Vetsera's unusual beauty is a matter of common knowledge. Her mother was by birth a Baltazzi, daughter of a wealthy financier from the Near East. She had married an Austrian baron, by whom she was left a widow with four children. Her reputation in Vienna was certainly not very good, but in consequence of the great state which she kept she was at least tolerated in Court society. Her frivolous character was a very useful circumstance to the conspirators, for in consequence of it she lent herself willingly to suggestions of a noble love affair for her daughter.

I never heard from my mother how the Crown Prince became acquainted with Marie Vetsera, and doubtless she did not herself know. Recently, however, the missing link in the chain seems to have been supplied. The Countess Larisch,[1] in her book published in London last year, furnishes an explanation. It is true that she says that Marie Vetsera first wrote to my brother, and that he consented to her offer of friendship. Now it is impossible that a letter addressed by her directly to him could have reached his hands unseen. And what intermediary could she have employed between herself and the Crown Prince — except one? Either as a practical joke or as a piece of good-nature, the undertaking of such a commission will probably seem to most people as going a little too far. And with regard to good-nature, the Countess makes little attempt in her book to conceal that she hated both my mother (who had made a great favourite of her in childhood) and the Crown Princess Stephanie. Good-nature, therefore,

[1] Daughter by a morganatic marriage of Ludwig, eldest son of Maximilian, Duke in Bavaria. (See p. 29, footnote.)

seems an inadequate theory to explain the assistance which she gave, on her own showing, to bring about numerous interviews between Rudolf and Marie Vetsera. More than this I need not perhaps say. After all, the question is not one of great importance. Fate surely decides such matters, whatever the nature of the instruments it uses.

Rudolf was a lonely, unloved man, who in the course of time felt the necessity of finding some object of his affections. The strange thing was that what happened came about so much later than had been expected.

His enemies lay carefully in wait. Not until the passion had broken into a blaze did they begin to fan the flames. His jealousy must now be stirred. The Archduke Otto and the Duke of Braganza vied with one another in paying attentions to Marie Vetsera, who was regularly besieged by admirers. Rudolf, as a matter of course, did not wish to be the last.

Every detail was faithfully reported to the Crown Princess Stephanie by those who were so glad to have found at last some material for their purposes. Stephanie on her part was not content with reproaching and abusing her husband, but in his presence expressed herself in an abominably provocative fashion regarding the woman he loved, designating her in terms which would never, even, have been expected in the mouths of women much lower in the social scale than herself. Nor did she attempt to control herself in the least when others were present.

The indifference which Rudolf had felt for his wife up to now turned to hate and loathing. His situation was all the more intolerable because for the first time he felt really to blame and did not quite know how to defend himself.

The result would have been the same in any case. A

complete breach was now made. Rudolf refused to live any longer with Stephanie, and forbade her to set foot in Mayerling. His meetings with Marie Vetsera were all the more frequent.

My mother only heard little by little what was going on. She was really powerless. On the one hand, she could not possibly approve of her son's behaviour; on the other, she felt the deepest sympathy with him. She would have dearly loved him to give her his full confidence, but this, of course, was impossible — it was against the ideas of the day, and she was an Empress, and above all the Empress of Austria. The curse of the Spanish etiquette again came into play. Down to his twelfth year Rudolf had been brought up away from her. Till then she was a stranger to him. Not until after the death of his grandmother, the Archduchess Sophia, did she exert any influence over his character. And even then the strict rules of etiquette made a dividing gulf between mother and son which could never be bridged.

Furthermore, mother had suffered too much at the hands of her own mother-in-law to be quite devoid of sympathy with Stephanie. Her own docility and her tactful behaviour toward the Emperor, which was in such striking contrast to Stephanie's conduct toward the Crown Prince, had availed her nothing; but her failure had made her understand only too well the difficulties of the position. Her powerlessness, in spite of her comprehension, made her all the more unhappy.

In the meanwhile the relations between the Emperor and his son had not improved. The former had received hints about the political activities of the latter, and, angered at the new proofs of his son's apostasy, he forbade him to associate with a number of learned men whom he had made his friends. Among them was the famous and universally esteemed naturalist, Brehm. As might be imagined, such a step did not tend to calm Rudolf's excited nerves. He withdrew more and more from the life of the Court. And now Marie Vetsera found that she was about to become a mother.

Poor Rudolf! He was very fond of children, and deeply attached to his little Ersie. According to my mother, Ersie was a good little girl, though neither very talented nor even intelligent. As she grew older she was terribly spoilt. Rudolf always lavished affection upon her. Many of the pranks which he played with her reached the ears of the public. It was always he who, to the last year of his life, disguised himself each December 6th as St. Nicholas to amuse her. It was only when the saint reproved her for having lately acquired the habit of throwing her hat and gloves out of the carriage-window, for fun, that she recognised him. He was very unhappy at the idea that he would never have another child. And now he was suddenly convinced, for some reason, that Marie was going to bear him a son. At the idea he was transported with joy, and totally new thoughts entered his head.

Hungary was under the Salic law, which allows divorce to the sovereign and entitles the children of any wife legally married to him to ascend the throne. The Crown Prince was, if possible, even more popular in Hungary than in Austria. He could attain what he wished there; Marie could become his wife and could wear the Imperial crown.

But this was only to be his last resource. Before he took so extreme a step he intended, for his father's sake, to try to have his marriage annulled by the Church. Being, as I have said, on the worst possible footing with the priesthood, he required some friend who would act as mediator.

And now he committed an error which was destined to complete his ruin. He confided entirely in his brother-in-law, Duke Philip of Coburg —" that idiot," as my mother scornfully called him. Philip of Coburg was married to Stephanie's sister, the much discussed and slandered Princess Louise of Belgium, and was no happier in his marriage than Rudolf. It must have been this circumstance which drew the two luckless husbands together, for otherwise they had no interest in common. Philip was depraved and brutal, and really was singularly lacking in mind. Fully convinced that he was doing Rudolf a favour, the Duke communicated all that he told him to the Archduke Franz-Ferdinand, with whom he was on very friendly terms, and whom he knew to be an ally of the Church.

Now at last the moment had arrived so long wished for by the Crown Prince's enemies. Franz-Ferdinand advised recourse to a priest named Gottfried Marschall, formerly his own tutor. Marschall was complaisant and insinuating in his manners, and was able, by an appearance of *bonhomie,* to gain Rudolf's confidence. He seemed to enter entirely into the latter's plans, and even advised him that, to avoid the possibility of interference, he had better send a letter direct to the Pope himself instead of employing an agent. In this letter he was to ask His Holiness to aid him to the extent of annulling his marriage.

Rudolf must assuredly have been blinded by his passion, for how else could he have believed so readily in the broadmindedness of the priest?

"Those abominable traitors!" cried my mother, when she had reached this point in the story, "they had calculated everything. He must die, because his life was a source of constant danger to them."

Her mingled agony and righteous wrath made it hard for her to continue, but at last she proceeded.

Pope Leo XIII did not condescend to answer the letter. There is no need to point out what an insult lay in this alone; but that was not all. He sent the letter to the Emperor through the Nuncio then accredited to the Court of Vienna, Monsignor Galimberti.

On January 28, 1889, about three o'clock in the afternoon, the Emperor sent a message to my mother requesting her to come to his apartments. They were residing, as usual in the winter, at the Hofburg. To her astonishment, on entering the Emperor's study she found the Nuncio in his company — a very unusual occurrence. In a few words everything was explained to her. She protested indignantly, it is true, that even if her son had done wrong, he was being treated in an unheard-of fashion. But the Emperor stopped her with a gesture, and said that this was for him alone to judge. She had been asked to come merely that she might be present at an interview with the Crown Prince, who had been summoned and was expected every minute.

It was about half-past four when Rudolf was announced. Poor mother! She had not even a chance of giving him the slightest warning. As she told this, in sentences cut short by dry, suffocating sobs, the scene seemed to rise vividly up before my eyes.

"And to think that it was thus I was to see him for the last time!" she cried. Words of comfort would have been a profanation to such grief, so I waited for her to go on.

To judge by his troubled expression as he entered the

room, Rudolf must have known already that something was wrong. The Emperor, however, left him little time to think about it. Without any introductory words he almost threw in his face the letter to the Pope, and demanded from him, in ill-controlled anger, whether he had taken leave of his senses to expose himself so and bring shame upon his whole family.

For an instant the Crown Prince stood speechless. Then suddenly, looking the Nuncio contemptuously from head to foot, he said with the utmost bitterness: " I ought to have known what kind of help was to be expected from you! Baseness and meanness can always be looked for there!"

Turning to his father, he reproached him for placing him in so ridiculous a position, for treating him like a mere schoolboy. But as he had been challenged, he added, he would state unreservedly what he would otherwise have tried to explain with more circumspection.

Truly he did not mince matters. It was the fault of his father and his father's advisers that he had been made unhappy. They had all desired his ruin, or else they would not have given him such a wife as her to whom he was now to be chained all his life.

Fearing that his excitement would carry him too far, mother went up to him and gently caught hold of his hands. But Rudolf only became the more passionate, and, after pressing his burning lips to her hands, he begged her not to take the side of the others, when she did not at all think with them.

The Emperor grew anxious at the effect of this upon her, and impatiently broke in. " Do not speak like that," he commanded, " nor try to make us believe you want your marriage annulled merely because you are unhappy with your wife. It is a disgrace for a young man like you not to maintain appearances better."

Rudolf must certainly have lost his head altogether to dare to answer as he did his father and his Emperor. He told him that he had no right to speak to him in that fashion. Stephanie was both stupid and ugly, and he had been forced to take her, while his father had married, of his own free choice, an intelligent and beautiful woman, with the result — but I need not here repeat what Rudolf in his fury said.

Things were not taking the course desired by the Nuncio. It might be expected that the next minute the Crown Prince would be ordered out of the room, before he himself had had the chance of saying a word. He therefore had recourse to his dignity as a prince of the Church to come forward as a peacemaker, and to take the liberty of speaking uninvited. Suavely he called the Crown Prince's attention to the fact that it was not worth while to quarrel with his family for the sake of some woman.

At these coolly uttered words Rudolf turned deadly pale. With an unnatural calmness he strode up to the priest, halted in front of him so close that their faces almost touched, and, emphasising each separate word, he gasped out: "Whom — do — you — mean?"

"Your Imperial Highness knows very well of whom we are speaking."

"Then," shouted Rudolf, "will you dare repeat that again?"

"Why not? I repeat only what the birds on the housetops are already chirping to one another, that the Crown Prince, for the sake of some worthless person —"

The Nuncio got no further, for two resounding boxes on the ear from the Crown Prince put an end to his speech, accompanied by the words, "Wait, you —— priest! Once for all, I'll make you pay for this!"

The Emperor up to now had kept calm only by the exertion of all his will. He now saw that there was nothing to be done for the moment, and ordered Rudolf to retire, asking him to give his word that he would not see Marie Vetsera again before he had had a quiet discussion with him.

My mother would have detained him, so that father and son might not part in such anger. But the Emperor silenced her, and Rudolf left the room unreconciled. He went off at once to Mayerling, where he shut himself up in his private apartments, although Duke Philip of Coburg and the Duke of Braganza were on a visit there. Loschegg, his valet, heard him walking up and down restlessly nearly all the night, as he, Loschegg, afterwards told my mother.

It was from Loschegg and from Bratfisch the coachman that mother heard, after the catastrophe, most of the details of what had taken place. Loschegg was a friend of Bratfisch, and therefore confided to him early next morning that their master must have met with some serious trouble, since he had apparently not closed his eyes all night. Now Bratfisch filled a very exceptional position in the Crown Prince's service, somewhat like that of a court jester in times of old. Rudolf talked over everything with him, and put great trust in him. When, therefore, the coachman asked to be admitted he was at once brought into his presence.

Rudolf told Bratfisch about the events of the previous day and then gave him a letter, which he was to deliver personally to the Baroness Marie Vetsera in Vienna. In this letter he begged her not to be anxious if she did not see him for a few days, and promised he would keep her informed by letter.

When Bratfisch reached the Vetseras' house in the Salesianergasse he was surprised to find that apparently the Baroness Marie was expecting him. He gave her the letter and asked for an answer. She informed him, however, that she was going back with him at once to Mayerling, and asked him to drive off to the Ringstrasse, so that she might not be seen from her home going away with him. Bratfisch did not fail to notice the girl's tear-stained eyes, and conjectured that, having already had news of the events at the Hofburg, and fearing the Crown Prince's eventual submission to his father's will, she wanted to be at his side at once. Being an unceremonious, queer fellow, he did not hesitate to beg her not to try to force matters, but to listen to His Imperial Highness's instructions, assuring her the latter was more than ever determined to stand by her. But she shook her head, and, with her tears welling up again, declared that she must go back with him at once, for if she hesitated only twenty-four hours she would be forced to marry another man. And she went on to tell him — she too looking on him as a friend rather than a servant — that the previous evening the Nuncio's secretary had come to her mother, with the Emperor's confessor, Father Laurenz Mayer, to tell her that the Emperor knew of the Crown Prince's affection and plans for her daughter, and had ordered that she was to be married to someone else — a certain nobleman — within twenty-four hours.

It was probably the Emperor's intention thus to put an end, once for all, to this love affair. But, said my mother, the schemes of the conspirators against Rudolf here were quite different from the Emperor's. It was not to their interest to bring matters to such a conclusion. Otherwise Marie Vetsera would never have succeeded in getting away unchecked as she did.

When she reached Mayerling, Rudolf could not believe his eyes, and his anger was unbounded when he heard what a trick was to have been played upon him.

Commissioner Habrda had arranged to report at the Holy Cross monastery all events that took place at the hunting-lodge. It was Loschegg and Bratfisch who told my mother, later on, how they had discovered that Habrda, having the Crown Prince under observation constantly during the past year, had reported regularly at Mayerling to the Abbot Grünbeck, or in Vienna to Gottfried Marschall. Scarcely therefore had Marie Vetsera reached the hunting-lodge when the news was taken to the monastery, and from there transmitted at once to Vienna.

In the course of the morning one of the most esteemed journalists in Vienna, Edgard von Spiegel, had been received by the Crown Prince, and this too, of course, was reported.

The Nuncio in Vienna is not only the accredited representative of the Pope at the Court, but also the highest spiritual authority for the Imperial family. In the latter capacity Galimberti thought it his duty to inform the Emperor of what was going on at Mayerling. But he represented the Crown Prince's conduct as if he had intentionally disobeyed his father's command and sent Bratfisch to fetch Marie Vetsera to Mayerling. Then, choosing his time well, he told the Emperor that the secret police had discovered that for a long time past the Crown Prince had been conspiring with Hungary against both

Crown Prince Rudolf

Crown Prince Rudolf and his Fiancée Princess Stephanie of Belgium

Emperor Francis-Joseph

Church and State, and had the intention of flying to that country with Marie Vetsera, whom he would doubtless marry there.

These last details, as well as what follows next, my mother heard from Prince Rudolf Liechtenstein, Grand Master of the Horse to the Emperor, and one of her most devoted friends.

After what the Nuncio told him, the Emperor sent Prince Liechtenstein to summon Baron Bolfrass, head of the military department of the government. To Bolfrass he gave orders to take a detachment of soldiers and go to Mayerling, where, in the name of His Imperial Majesty, as well as on behalf of the relatives of the Baroness Marie Vetsera, he was to demand her surrender by the Crown Prince. In case of resistance, the latter was to be arrested with all due form and consideration for his exalted rank. The hunting-lodge was to be surrounded by a military cordon and then to be searched. All this should, if possible, take place at night, so as to attract less attention.

Prince Liechtenstein hastened at once to my mother to inform her of her son's danger. Instantly she in her turn hurried to the Emperor. She found him in a state of speechless fury. It was in his nature to be able to control himself for a long time, but when his anger did break out it took him long to subdue it again.

Mother insisted that the aim of all these machinations against her son was his destruction; it was this his enemies desired. But the Emperor would not hear of it, and refused to yield. The evidence produced by her he considered ridiculous and incredible. He asked her whether she had already forgotten Rudolf's behaviour on the previous day, and whether, after that, she wished to persuade him that there was a plot against the Crown Prince. On the contrary, it was he who was plotting — plotting high treason and the dishonour of his house.

"And it is you," cried mother in despair, "who will bear the blame of his death."

"Better death than dishonour!" replied the Emperor grimly, little thinking what terrible words he was uttering.

Mother was about to hasten away, horror-stricken, but the Emperor, either repenting of his violence or unwilling to give her a chance of informing Rudolf, took her by the hand and attempted to calm her. The case was not so tragic as she tried to make out, he said. This would merely be a good lesson, such as Rudolf required, and one that he would remember.

So an hour passed by, and with it all possibility of mother doing anything for Rudolf.

At Mayerling, Marie Vetsera had spent the whole evening alone in the Crown Prince's study, which he had placed at her disposal, while he, to avoid comment, passed the time until midnight with his friends in the dining-room. The visitors all declared afterwards that they had known nothing of the Baroness Vetsera's presence in the house; and the equerries on duty with the Crown Prince, Counts Hoyos and Bombelles, said the same. At all events, they all thought it wise to pretend to have known nothing.

They went to bed comparatively early, as they were to be up betimes the next day for hunting. Rudolf did not intend to accompany them; he dared not leave Marie for a moment without the protection of his presence. But, of course, he did not say a word about this to the others. Whether he really had the plan in his head of an escape to Hungary is unknown. It is not improbable, however, for he had had this solution of his difficulties in view for long.

MAYERLING

According to Loschegg's account, about one o'clock everything was silent in the place. His own room was in the private suite of the Crown Prince, quite close to the latter's bedroom. He had scarcely got off to sleep when he was awakened by a knock at the entrance door to the private apartments. He sprang out of bed to call his master. But the Prince, having been in a state of feverish excitement all day, had been lying awake and was already up. Swiftly telling Marie to conceal herself and taking his revolver, he went to the door of the ante-room, but he did not open it. Who was there, he asked. A messenger from His Imperial Majesty, was the answer, Baron Bolfrass. Rudolf declined to receive him at that hour, and asked him to return in the morning.

Baron Bolfrass persisted in his demand for admission. The Prince again declared that it was impossible. Bolfrass grew more and more urgent, and said that he would be obliged to force an entrance. Understanding the danger to which he was exposing himself if he still refused, Rudolf hastily assured himself that Marie was in safe hiding, and then let Bolfrass in.

So far Loschegg had been at his master's side. Now he was compelled to withdraw, but he remained listening at the door and overheard almost everything.

Bolfrass demanded Marie Vetsera's surrender. Rudolf obstinately refused it. For a time they parleyed. Then Loschegg heard the Baron raise his voice, up to now quite low, and say: "In that case, I am compelled to have the house searched and to arrest your Imperial Highness in the name of His Majesty!"

There was silence for a few minutes, then steps were audible outside, and Loschegg heard his master cry: "The first man who dares enter I shall shoot down!"

Upon this, without waiting a moment, Loschegg rushed into the room. But already a shot rang out from the Crown Prince's revolver, and a man fell — a gamekeeper. There was no time for reflection now; the room was full of people, who could scarcely be distinguished in the dim light. Other shots were fired. The Crown Prince fell, was beaten, trampled upon, and disfigured beyond recognition. Marie Vetsera, who, regardless of her own safety, had probably rushed in at the beginning, also fell, with a shot in her back.

Who was the guilty party? Who fired the fatal shots? It would be impossible to say. Certainly there was not one, but several criminals. And were they not, after all, mere tools in the hands of an infamous gang?

Bratfisch noticed, looking out of a window casually a short time afterwards, that the lodge was surrounded by soldiers. He said also that the Duke of Coburg called together all the servants and employees at Mayerling, and made them all swear upon their word of honour to keep silence.

Almost immediately Habrda turned Loschegg and Bratfisch out of the private apartments. He was playing the master, who only twenty-four hours previously had assured them of his friendship.

The dreadful task of taking the news to the Hofburg fell to Count Hoyos. He himself was limping from the effect of the blows which he had received while trying to help the Crown Prince.

Prince Liechtenstein was the first to whom the horrible story was told. He had promised mother to bring her word as soon as he received information from Mayerling.

These two gentlemen were at their wits' end as to what was to be done. At last they decided to go first of all to the Empress, and as gently as possible to break the news to her, before communicating with the Emperor. But no sooner did they stand in her presence, before they could utter a word, she whispered faintly, looking as though turned to stone: —

"*They have murdered him!*"

CHAPTER XXI

AFTER MAYERLING [1]

IN the preceding chapter I have recorded as faithfully as I could what I learnt from my mother's own lips concerning the life and death of my brother Rudolf. I wish now to add a few remarks of my own about the affair of Mayerling, and then to say something about the situation produced thereafter.

It is easy to see that such a story as has just been told could not be made public. It was not merely a question of defiling the honour of the house of Habsburg and the reputation of several more or less high personages, but the prestige of the religious hierarchy, that rotten pillar of the Empire which could only be kept standing by the greatest exertions, must also be preserved. The safety of the Crown, of the very State itself, was at stake. Thirteen years later the whole world shuddered at the tale of how the Servians had butchered the wretched King Alexander and his Draga, claiming to save their country from destruction. But my brother, the Crown Prince Rudolf, was no perverse creature like Alexander of Servia. What must one be prepared for if the truth about Rudolf's death became known? The throne would have been forfeited for ever by those who coveted it so. The clericals would have lost their power, the secretly fermenting troubles all over the Empire would have come to a head, especially in

[1] Before reading this chapter the reader must be warned that the bulk of it was written before the terrible affair of Sarajevo. See p. 262 for the additions since made to the chapter.

AFTER MAYERLING

Hungary. The peace of all Europe would have been imperilled.

There is a German proverb which says:—

> " Aber nichts ist so fein gesponnen
> Es kommt doch an die Sonnen."

(Nothing is so finely spun that the sun does not shine through.) Let us hope that the day is not far distant when the régime which brought about the death of the heir-apparent will be destroyed for ever.

That the reactionary party is still all-powerful can be proved from the careers, before and after Mayerling, of two of the most active members of the conspiracy. Gottfried Marschall, who till then, in spite of his having been the Archduke Franz-Ferdinand's tutor, has risen no higher than the rectorship of the Votive Church in Vienna, from this time onward advanced rapidly. He soon became Bishop-Coadjutor of Vienna; and there is no doubt that if he had not died before the old Prince Bishop, Dr. Gruscha, he would on the latter's death have stepped into his place.[1]

But the case of the Rev. Gottfried Marschall is quite unimportant compared with that of Commissioner Johann Habrda. In modern times Austria can show no other example of such a career. To appreciate fully its astonishing character, one has to know what a Golgotha is the ordinary career of Austrian officials. They cannot live on their pay for a number of years, during which they are practically beggars, and even at the age of thirty they have but a mere pittance. If a man has influence, money,

[1] Marschall did not die on good terms with his former pupil, Franz-Ferdinand, for the reason that he was opposed to the Countess Chotek and would not use his influence at the Vatican in her favour.

and intelligence, he can advance a step on the ladder of promotion every three years. But that is the shortest time in which it can be done. Habrda was only in the seventh class — that is to say, the lowest but three of the ten which had to be gone through — when he was appointed commissioner in the service of the Crown Prince, and had taken fifteen to eighteen years (I cannot be certain of the exact figure) to rise even so high. It is clear, therefore, that before Mayerling he was not one of the lucky ones. After the Crown Prince's death, however, he passed through the remaining seven classes in the space of eight years — an average of little less than one class a year as against the previous one class in five or six years. In 1897 he became President of the Viennese Police, the most important police official in the Empire. In addition he was created a baron and received all the highest decorations a man can get except the Golden Fleece. This was a man whose father was a poor carpenter, scarcely able to provide for his son's early education. Is it necessary to argue from what quarter came the protection that was extended to him? How was it that the commissioner to whom the care of the Crown Prince was confided was not dismissed at once after the catastrophe? How was it that, so far from being dismissed, he was, on the contrary, overwhelmed with honours and dignities? Is not this man's career a living proof of the truth of my mother's story?

By one of the little tricks Fate plays, the evidence is preserved which makes for truth and justice. The people of Austria-Hungary have, in the career just described, the grain of sand which can bring to an end the working of the machinery that caused Mayerling. If they desire, they have the power to obtain satisfaction for that crime. But will they desire?

AFTER MAYERLING

With the death of the Crown Prince Rudolf the succession left the male descendants of the Emperor Francis-Joseph and went to those of his brother Karl-Ludwig, after the death of the latter in 1896. In that year the Archduke Franz-Ferdinand became heir-presumptive, the reversion of the throne being to the elder son of his dead brother Otto.

The Archduke Franz-Ferdinand has been mentioned several times in this book, but not discussed at any length. My mother did not often speak to me about him; most at the time when he spoilt our little excursion at Territet. To her he appeared dull, utterly lacking in idealism, and devoid of personality. As a boy he was mild compared with his brother Otto, who early showed signs of becoming the ruffian that he later on was universally acknowledged to be. He was very affectionate to his sister Margaret-Sophia, who afterwards married the Duke Albert of Würtemberg and died in 1902. He was always on good terms with his stepmother, Maria-Theresa of Braganza, his own mother, Anunciada of Bourbon-Sicily, having died when he was quite young. His clinging to his wife, in the face of strong opposition, and his care for his little family proved that he was by no means deficient in domestic affection, which must be counted to him for virtue.

After Rudolf's death very little was seen of the Archduke Franz-Ferdinand in public. In fact, he seemed to be very much hidden away. This was, no doubt, partly due to the state of his health, for his lungs were affected, and consumption was recognised as present. He was obliged to spend time in the pursuit of health, some of it on a long sea-voyage. His condition improved, but he did not become robust, and during the past two or three years reports of his shattered constitution were renewed.

He began to be more visible to the public after his marriage in July, 1900, to the Countess Sophie Chotek. In fact, he might often be seen thereafter walking down the Prater. He is decidedly *bourgeois* in very many of his ways. He is good at business, for example, and by some might be styled mercenary. He owns a dairy, which is called after his name, and has also entered into competition with the leading monumental mason in Vienna, Eduard Hauser. Such a trait does not endear him to the Viennese.

A legend has been spread of his " strong will " since he was officially recognised as heir-presumptive, but it has no foundation in fact. He had no will before his marriage, and it is his wife who is the strong-willed one. But he has strong prejudices, as for instance, against Italy, hating the house of Savoy as despoilers of the Church. On the question of the rights of Hungary, too, he feels deeply. Indeed, by his attitude over this question he first became prominent in the politics of the Empire, using his influence with Francis-Joseph against the Hungarians. He is a firm advocate of increased armament, working hand in hand in this with General Conrad von Hötzendorf, whose appointment as General of the Staff he warmly advocated.

No one ever speaks about the Archduke Franz-Ferdinand without mentioning the word bigotry. But truly he has some reason, apart from his own leanings toward this form of religious fervour, to be a bigot. His father was bigoted, his stepmother is bigoted, and, more important still in his case, his wife is bigoted.

There is no necessity to say much about his marriage with the Countess Chotek, since the facts are so well known. She was a Bohemian lady-in-waiting to the Archduchess Isabella.¹ Franz-Ferdinand fell in love with her, the Archduchess discovered the secret, and dismissed her. Franz-Ferdinand, playing upon his uncle's fears of a new addition to the ever-growing list of scandals in the Imperial family, forced him to consent to a marriage, which, however, could only be morganatic owing to the Countess not being of royal blood, nor even of one of the families eligible for marriage with royalty.

The Countess Chotek after her marriage entered the Imperial Court as the next in rank to the last lady of the old princely families. This did not suit her at all; but she had the Emperor to win over to her side before she could improve her position. She was clever enough to do this, but only by degrees. He created her Fürstin von Hohenberg upon her marriage — Fürstin, though translated Princess, being lower in rank than Duchess. About five years ago she insisted that she ought to come immediately after the Archduchesses. Her pretensions were supported by the conduct of the German Emperor, who paid her marked attention upon the occasion of a visit by her to Berlin, and Francis-Joseph gave way. He made the heir-presumptive's wife Duchess (Herzogin) of Hohenberg, whereby she now ranked as she wished, immediately after the Archduchesses.

Nor did the Duchess of Hohenberg's ambitions stop there. She aimed at dominating the old Emperor. Indeed, until about four years ago, she felt herself so strong that she thought she could supplant the Archduchess Marie-Valerie. My sister, however, was not so easily beaten. A curious scene took place at Pola, where a warship was to be christened, and the god-parents were Franz-

¹ The Princess Isabella, of Cröy-Dulmen, married to the Archduke Frederick of Austria, a descendant of the famous Archduke Charles. The Archduke Frederick is the wealthiest of the Archdukes.

Ferdinand and Marie-Valerie. But when the Duchess of Hohenberg and Marie-Valerie met they quarrelled so badly that their two husbands had to take them away, not unnoticed by their suites.

The Duchess is clever, it has been said. At one time she used to mask her cleverness, but now it is generally recognised, and concealment is impossible. One of her most useful possessions is a very flexible backbone, and it is through this that she has been able to conquer the Emperor. She has a good business head, like her husband, and is a successful speculator. She is lacking in refinement, especially in her manners. Yet she has tried in her pose to imitate my mother — in vain, as may be imagined. She speaks German with a strong Czech accent, which creates a bad impression when she is heard for the first time.

She has borne her husband three children, the eldest a girl and the others two boys, and the marriage from the domestic point of view has turned out happily enough. The marriages of princes, however, are never considered purely from the domestic point of view.

The fly in the ointment for the Archduke Franz-Ferdinand and his wife is, of course, that their union is only morganatic and that she cannot become Empress, while their sons are not eligible to ascend the throne. Franz-Ferdinand's heir, imperially, is his nephew, the Archduke Karl-Franz-Joseph, elder son of the infamous Otto. That is to say, the nephew will be heir unless the Austrian constitution and the family law of the Habsburgs are both amended. It is fairly certain that Franz-Ferdinand originally intended to get all the rights he could for his wife (and therefore for his children) out of the Emperor. But he now sees that the aged Francis-Joseph is not strong enough to do what he wanted him to do. Consequently the game has to be played differently. Franz-Ferdinand and the Duchess of Hohenberg have most powerful allies, the Jesuits. In return for binding themselves to them, body and soul, husband and wife have all the resources of the order behind them. The advice which they have received is to keep very quiet and do nothing to provoke opposition yet. It is even thought that the rumours of Franz-Ferdinand's shattered health are purposely spread that he may be thought to be now a negligible quantity. His interest in Balkan affairs, his anti-Italian activity at the time of the war in Tripoli, and above all his quarrel with Count Aehrenthal, were no doubt considered to have brought him into unwise prominence, necessitating a temporary retreat.

The curious attitude of the heir-presumptive and his wife toward the Hungarians is probably also part of this subtle scheme. Franz-Ferdinand opposes Hungarian pretensions and pays no more than bare official visits to the country. The Duchess avoids it entirely. Such conduct has been denounced as foolish, but those who advise it know their business. The Hungarians are an enthusiastic people when they conceive an affection for anyone, as my mother learnt early in her life. She was an idol to them from the moment they saw her. Such enthusiasm in Hungary provokes a very different response in Vienna, and is therefore to be avoided by the heir-presumptive. The Duchess of Hohenberg will show herself in Hungary after her husband's accession to the throne. She will then wipe out the memories of past indifference. So at least it is hoped, though it is doubtful whether the Hungarians will forgive her anxiety to clericalise their country and her use of her influence in favour of making the Hungarian divorce laws more stringent four years ago.

What makes it specially needful for Franz-Ferdinand to go carefully is the existence of a strong party in opposition to him. If the Crown Prince Rudolf, the Emperor's own son, had a cabal against him, how could the Emperor's nephew, saddled with a wife whose existence threatens State and family laws, escape? The heads of the opposition now are the Archduchess Marie-Valerie, the Archduchess Maria-Josepha, widow of the Archduke Otto and mother of the next heir; and the Archduchess Isabella. My sister's hostility needs no further explanation. Maria-Josepha, a handsome, simple, and upright woman, who now leads a very retired existence, was, as long as her husband lived, the first Archduchess of the whole Court, as prospective Empress. Her enmity toward the Duchess of Hohenberg can also easily be understood. As for the Archduchess Isabella, it is no secret that she was seriously annoyed with Franz-Ferdinand because he did not take to wife her daughter rather than her lady-in-waiting.

The photograph here reproduced is a curious one inasmuch as it shows the three feminine heads of the opposition in a group together. Their male companion is the Archduke Ferdinand-Karl, younger brother of the Archdukes Franz-Ferdinand and Otto. Like Franz-Ferdinand, he has made a morganatic marriage, his wife being Bertha Tschuber, a Viennese professor's daughter and a very charming woman. He is known as Ferdinand Burg, and lives exiled from Court, while she has been created a Baroness.

The strength of the party opposed to the present heir apparently lies in the number of members of the Imperial family which it includes. Austria-Hungary swarms with Archdukes and Archduchesses, owing to the custom by which the title extends to all legitimate members of the

Archduchess Isabella (standing), Archduchess Marie-Josepha, Archduchess Marie-Valerie (right), and Archduke Ferdinand-Karl

family. The sympathy of such is naturally in favour of legitimism, which excludes morganatic unions. The Emperor Francis-Joseph found this the case when he extended his protection to the Duchess of Hohenberg, and was angry at the difficulties put in his way. On one occasion at Court he positively commanded his granddaughter Elisabeth, Rudolf's daughter, to take her seat next the Duchess. But Elisabeth herself had married out of her rank, being the wife of Prince Otto of Windischgrätz.

Since the above was written, the Archduke Franz-Ferdinand and his wife were brutally cut off by the hand of an assassin at Sarajevo, Bosnia, on Sunday, June 28th. I have thought it better, however, not to alter what I wrote, but rather to add a few pages to this chapter, first concerning the crime and its effects, and secondly concerning the new heir-presumptive and his wife.

There can, of course, be no two views as to the assassination, which has been denounced all over the civilised world. The Serb nationality of the murderer recalls the fact that the late Archduke was in favour of crushing the Servians, whom he did not like. [Among the races composing the population of the Empire he favoured only the Czechs, his wife's people.] In return the Servians hated him, so that there was a special motive for the crime. It is difficult, however, to resist the suspicion that there was more behind it than has come out, or perhaps will ever come out, and that Servia alone should not bear all the blame. Be that as it may, it cannot be doubted that the removal of Franz-Ferdinand and his wife came as a relief to many. The Court as a whole watched with apprehension the way in which the old Emperor was harassed by the two parties, the adherents and the enemies of the late heir-apparent;

and from its point of view the future looks much more peaceful now. The Duchess of Hohenberg was the main cause of fear, not her husband. There were those who regarded her as a potential Catherine de' Medici, whose ambitions might work incalculable harm. Now that she is dead they breathe again.

About the new heir-presumptive these people feel that it is permissible to entertain hopes. The Archduke Karl-Franz-Joseph is not an important man; the training of an archduke does not tend to produce such. He is not only young in years — being born in August, 1887 — but also young for his years. He might even be called childish. He is credited by gossip with having been to see " The Waltz Dream " fifty times; and he has a strong liking for cinema shows. About six years ago he was put for a week under "house arrest" for firing at targets in the neighbourhood of a powder magazine, which was certainly a foolish escapade. But he is not known to be worse than unduly young. On the other hand, the Emperor Francis-Joseph, who was already an old man when his grand-nephew was a baby, has always watched his development with interest and had much to say with regard to his education, about which his father Otto naturally troubled little. From the beginning of his life almost, or, to be precise, from the age of two, Karl (as he is called in the family) was regarded as a possible heir-presumptive. After the Crown Prince Rudolf's death there stood between him and the throne only his grandfather, the Archduke Karl-Ludwig, who was fifty-six years old; his uncle, Franz-Ferdinand, whose health was very precarious; and his father, whose accession was out of the question. Therefore his eventual rise to his present position had always to be kept in view by the Emperor and the rest of

Archduke Franz-Ferdinand and Family

Archduke Karl-Franz-Joseph and the Archduchess Zita

the family. Doubtless this is partly accountable for the fact that he and Franz-Ferdinand were not on good terms, the nephew never paying a visit to the uncle's country home at Konopischt, in Bohemia, although he lived quite near.

Karl-Franz-Joseph came over to England for the coronation of King George V, being the representative of the Emperor on that occasion.

In his looks, the young Archduke is by no means so striking as was his father, being in fact rather slight, though his figure is good. Of his attainments the principal one is that he speaks languages well. He is very clerical in his views, as was also his mother.

But the new heir is very much of a closed book, and his tendencies, being kept under, are unknown. A fate which seems to threaten him is that he may become the puppet of parties. At present the chief influences with him, as also with his wife, the Archduchess Zita, are his mother Marie-Josepha, and her aunt Maria-Theresa, who was the Archduke Karl-Ludwig's third and last wife.

The Archduchess Zita herself, the prospective Empress, may have a rather good influence over her husband, if she can manage to keep it — which is very difficult for an Austrian archduchess to do. She was one of the nineteen children of the late Duke Robert of Parma, by his second wife Marie-Antonia of Braganza. The duke was a very wealthy man, who cheerfully saw his duchy swallowed up by the kingdom of Italy when he was allowed to keep his riches. The Duchess came of a pious race, and her daughter Zita is convent-bred and somewhat bigoted. But her convent was in the Isle of Wight, and her experience of foreign lands has prevented her becoming too narrow, though she remains *bourgeoise*. She is now, at the age of twenty-two, decidedly a nice woman, neither given to intrigue nor fond of the limelight. Whether she will make a good Empress is perhaps a question. Self-effacement may well be carried too far.

The little son of the Archduke and Archduchess, Franz-Joseph-Otto, is not yet two years old, while their daughter's age is only reckoned by months.

I have made a very long digression, and must now return to my own story.

CHAPTER XXII

I GO UNDER FIRE

As the result of Frau von Friese's arguments with my mother, I continued to attend Fräulein Weigl's school; and really, as one day followed another, the coincidence of Bertha Habrda's presence there looked more and more innocent. Mother became somewhat reassured — the more so as she intended that I should pass the greater part of the winter at her side.

On November 24th she left Vienna for Biarritz. "I shall let you come to Paris shortly after Christmas," she said to me on the 22nd, when she came to say good-bye to me.

"To Paris!" I exclaimed in ecstasy.

"Yes, dearest. I never thought of it before. The place is so big that we shall be better off there than anywhere else. We shall be together again in the same hotel, and I will remain there the whole winter with you. In the spring we will go again together to Switzerland, so that my Babe will be all the time at my side."

Was I happy? I cannot say how happy. The long winter, usually so horrible, would this year be all delightful. I should rejoice to get away from Vienna, to rid myself of all my forbidden dreams of love and banish their memory in agreeable distractions.

Mother had left, and I spent my time daily from nine o'clock to two in the sewing-school. She had solemnly warned me to be on the *qui vive,* and this was really the only thing which made it worth while for me to go; for to this day I hate any work with the needle, and it was not less distasteful to me then.

The three new girls were very friendly to me, and we spent some very pleasant hours together. Hardly had my mother left Vienna when Laura asked them to come to her mother's reception-day, which they did. I was not allowed to go, and so did not meet them there. But some time after Bertha Habrda asked if we might come to see her. Just at this time her father was nominated President of the Vienna Police, the highest position in the entire police-force of Austria. The family had magnificent apartments, comprising the whole of the first floor of the police building in the Ringstrasse.

I was a little suspicious — but, I must confess, at least as much of the Kaisers as of the Habrdas. It struck me considerably that Laura had invited them immediately after mother had left Vienna. Why had she not done so either before or a little later? Of course mother had forbidden me to mention her suspicions to the Kaisers, and so they were unaware that she was at all alarmed. The matter seemed to me worth more than passing attention.

Well, as I have said, Bertha invited me together with Laura. They believed, or affected to believe, that we were sisters, and some excuse had been made for my absence when they came to visit the Kaisers. Bertha gave us the invitation at the school. I had expected it, and so also had Frau von Friese. The day after Bertha was at Laura's home, my governess had said to me, " Now you will be invited to President Habrda's."

" Yes," said I, " and what shall I do? "

Was I scared? she asked. Not in the least, I replied;

I GO UNDER FIRE

but nevertheless, unconsciously, my heart was beating so rapidly as to make me uncomfortable.

"Now don't tell fibs to me, my dear child," said Frau von Friese, with a smile. "Your mother would be tortured at the mere idea of your being there. But you are not a baby any more, Lily, and it is no longer necessary to make you believe it wrong to keep something secret from your mother, if it is for her peace of mind and for the sake of her health. On the other hand, I wish you to have both courage and self-control, which you cannot without the opportunity to exercise them. In short, I want you to go to the house of the President of Police. There is no danger. If there was I would not dare to send you. But I too have my spies, who are very reliable, and during the hour that you are there they will be near you to guard you, although I know it is a needless precaution."

Noticing my continued excitement, which my very inability to speak betrayed, she told me that it was just because she knew I should be walking as if on needles that it would be so good for me to go to the Habrdas. I must learn to go under fire. And there was something else which she had to tell me, which would astonish me greatly. Although there was, as she said, no immediate danger, she no longer suspected that there was a plot against me, she knew it! I must not think that my double existence, my life as Miss Lily Kaiser and my other secret one, was unknown to the people who had nothing to do except discover such matters. The day after my mother had told her who Bertha Habrda was, she had set her organisation [1] to work, and they had found out that Habrda had orders

[1] I know the name of the police commissioner who was the chief of those whom Frau von Friese called her "spies"; but as he is still living and in the police it would not be right to divulge it. He was a good friend to Frau von Friese. At the same time he was on friendly terms with Commissioner Georg Bayerl.

to become personally acquainted with me. Indeed, he was told that to some extent his nomination to the just about to be vacant Presidency of Police depended upon his success in this matter.

"But why Habrda in particular?" I demanded.

"Because," said Frau von Friese, taking my two hands into hers and looking gravely and earnestly with her great steel-grey eyes into mine, "because he has already shown himself to be a reliable man."

"Oh, very well!" I cried. "He was my brother's police-superintendent, and now you wish me to go to his house. I will go — with a revolver in my hand, to blow his brains out and so make one less in the company of scoundrels!"

At this outburst Frau von Friese laughed aloud, and now taking my face between her hands, she said: —

"No, you little volcano, not to do that, but to look in the scoundrel's eyes. Take a good look at him, and learn in one lesson what you have to expect from such a man. Further, you will meet at his house all the men of whom you have to beware. First of all there will be Chief Commissioner Camillo Windt, who in a short time will be head of the secret police. Then there will be Commissioner Georg Bayerl, in a few weeks' time to be the superintendent in charge of the Emperor's safety; and Chief Commissioner Stuckhart, though he is of less importance; and others, at all of whom you must look as hard as they will look at you. They will talk little, or not at all, to you; but they will stamp your features on their memory. They must see in you a thoughtless young girl, who does not pay any attention to them. Still less must it occur to them that you have any suspicions. Clever plotters as they are, they never would believe that I should let you

I GO UNDER FIRE

go there if I was even slightly aware of what was going on."

At this moment Frau von Friese was really beautiful. Her cheeks flushed with excitement, and her eyes shone, though the tone of her voice was still soft and even. She was once again, after so long a time, my dear old cheerful Frau von Friese. I threw both my arms about her neck and kissed her vehemently. The escapade was much to my liking. I had now lost all fear. And so, about a week later, I went to visit at the President's home.

In spite of my courage, I must admit that I felt a little troubled when I entered the great building, at every corner of which was a policeman. On the landing of the stairs to the first floor, barring the way to the President's apartments, was a high iron gate. There came over me the impression of entering a prison as I passed through it, and I seemed already to feel the chains clanking about my feet. But all such feelings passed away immediately I entered the private hall, where a footman took our cloaks.

There were only a few girls and ladies present; no gentlemen as yet. The Habrdas were descended from very simple middle-class people, as was most evident even at this time when they were at the height of their power. At tea we all sat down round the table quite *à la bourgeoise*. Frau Habrda poured out the tea. It was very cosy and old-fashioned, and I laughed to myself in thinking of what I had expected and what I really found. While we were drinking tea, a short fat little man, with keen small eyes, entered the dining-room. "Here comes papa," said Bertha. She introduced him to Laura and myself, as we were the only persons he did not seem to know. He sat down at the table, very friendly to all and full of fun.

"Which is the elder of the two young ladies?" he asked, looking at me. "You both seem to be of the same age."

"How is it those two sisters do not in the slightest resemble each other?" he said again. While he was making these remarks, the little piercing eyes were roving from one to the other. I realised that he would soon make me feel uncomfortable with his banter. Immediately I felt a secret repugnance for this man; and, perhaps for the first time in my life, I was sorry not to be an openly acknowledged Archduchess of Austria. How pleasing it would have been to me to have been crushingly arrogant to the man. Looking at him I could not help thinking, "You coward, it is you that let them kill my brother!"

After tea we were shown over the apartments, President Habrda accompanying us. Adjoining the living-rooms were his official apartments, which could be thrown open to communicate with the private rooms, if needed for large receptions.

"Do you want to see my workshop, too?" he said jokingly; and with this he opened the padded door which separated his office from the rest. The girls played about a little and seemed rather amused at the handcuffs lying on his desk. In the meantime, he engaged me in conversation, explaining to me that it happened sometimes that he even had to use them himself on obstreperous prisoners. By this time the other girls had passed into another room, while I was forced to remain. I could scarcely any more take in half of what he was saying to me. I kept impressing on myself, "Keep calm. Don't show any embarrassment! It may be only a test to see if you are suspicious." But, to tell the truth, I thought myself lost already, expecting the floor to open under my feet every moment. I did not dare to suggest we should follow the others for fear of precipitating my disappearance!

He talked of matters quite uninteresting to me, and all the while his little eyes seemed to pierce me through. But I resisted these looks successfully. The longer they continued the calmer I grew, until at last he said, " Shall we rejoin the rest? " Thereupon he reopened the door, which had closed automatically. I felt as if I had a new lease of life. Only with difficulty was I able to suppress my sigh of relief at what seemed to me a narrow escape.

It did not appear to me that the President was a good dissimulator, for he treated me with far too much distinction among the school-friends of his daughter. Perhaps he intended thereby to embarrass me. If so, he did not succeed.

When I re-entered the large reception-room, I found that a few other guests had arrived. They were mostly very insignificant people. One only of them had the same piercing eyes as my host. He was introduced to me as Commissioner Camillo Windt.

" Oh, that is you," I thought to myself, " the chief of the secret police. You have a bad face, and I must beware of you."

Commissioner Georg Bayerl was also there. There was nothing remarkable about his face, though he was rather good-looking. He was clearly one of those who obey the orders of others.

As Frau von Friese had said, they did not speak to me; but, every time I happened to glance towards Camillo Windt, I noticed that his eyes were fixed on me.

After another half-hour we left. I was glad to have got it over. Going downstairs, I went first, hurrying on before Laura and Mina, and I smiled as I noticed how my poor maid hastened to my side as if to protect me. I could not speak because of Laura's presence, but I had much ado to prevent myself exclaiming: " Well, I have escaped all right!"

When I returned home I noticed that, in spite of her outward calm, Frau von Friese was very uneasy, and she could not refrain from clasping both her arms about my neck and pressing me to her for a few minutes.

"I was nearly lost, little mother," I said laughing. "That is to say, nobody tried to do me any harm, but had they wished to they had a splendid chance." Then I gave her all the details of my visit. She was so moved that at first she could not speak, and I had to reassure her by telling her again that no one had really tried to harm me.

From this day on, unless I went out with Frau von Friese, the faithful Pirker followed everywhere in my steps. I could no longer move without having one of them at my side. Frau von Friese strongly impressed upon me that I was never to leave the school by myself, and that at school I must keep with all the girls and never be alone for a moment. As for the Kaisers, I soon found out that they were quite ignorant of what was going on. Laura was too young to understand, Mrs. Kaiser too indifferent and careless. As for Mr. Kaiser, whatever suspicions he had, he did not say anything to his wife about them. But, on the very next day after my visit to the Habrdas, he came quite unexpectedly to my home in the Strohgasse. He wished to speak to Frau von Friese quite alone, he said. I could not imagine what was the matter with him. After he had gone, Frau von Friese said to me, " Poor old gentleman, he questioned Laura yesterday on her return; and after what she told him, especially when she said that the President seemed to have taken quite a fancy to you, he became very much worried and came over at once to warn me."

From this day forward, Mr. Kaiser nearly always came himself to fetch me from school. He was really a very worthy man, in spite of an insupportably irritable temper.

The greater part of December passed by, with me expecting every day an order from mother to join her in Paris. On the 18th Frau von Friese received these few lines from Biarritz: —

"Still the same sorrow, still the same troubles. Will write in more detail from Paris. Shall probably ask you to come there for the New Year."

This was disappointing. I had expected to be with mother on her birthday and for Christmas, but I was too much accustomed to these disappointments to fall into despair over them.

On the 26th we had further bad news. Another letter came, in which mother wrote: —

"Since I have come to Paris, my health seems to have grown worse. I tried Metzger's massage-cure, but it did me more harm than good. My physicians tell me that I must lose no time, but go south at once. I feel it myself. I can't stand Paris. I am leaving on the 28th for Marseilles, where the Countess Trani will meet me. I do not know how long she intends to remain with me. All this means turning my plans upside down and makes me worse than ever, so that now no cure can help me. I feel that my place is beside my child, and everything seems to conspire to prevent my having her with me. As she grows up, all kinds of dangers are coming upon her. At night I get even less sleep than before. I always imagine that something has happened to her. My heart ceases to beat when I get your letters, for fear of bad news. I can't help it. I am frightened to death of H——. He is capable of anything. Day and night I dream of my darling being caught in some trap and tortured to death. I must make an end of all this, but I have also to wait for the right opportunity, and sometimes I feel that for the present I am unable to undergo such great excitements. As I say, I do not know when my sister is leaving me again, nor where I shall settle down. Just now the Miramar is awaiting me at Marseilles, so probably weeks will elapse before I can let you know where to join me. Poor darling, what a disappointment for her again. Make her life as pleasant as you can for her, dear Friese, and please, for God's sake, watch over her and protect her."

I was perfectly desperate at this news. My poor mother was so ill, killing herself with useless worry — and I was unable to be at her side. I kept on thinking that she was going to die. I was in such despair that Frau von Friese no longer knew what to do with me. She made inquiries concerning the real state of mother's health, and was told that, although it was very poor, there was no real danger of anything serious. This reassured me a little, but I could not overcome my melancholy still.

The greater part of January passed without further news. Frau von Friese took me about, to the opera and to concerts; but music, far from cheering me, had a saddening effect upon me.

My aunt Mathilde, Countess Trani, mother's youngest living sister, decided in the end to spend the winter with her. They went to San Remo, where they intended to remain a few months. So once again mother had to write postponing our reunion.

"During March," she said, "I shall again be at Territet, and there we will at last meet once more. The physicians want me to try all kinds of cures, but my only real help lies in you, darling."

The delays seemed endless. I became terribly discontented, and a sort of jealousy sprang up in me against my aunt, who was keeping my mother from me. The real fact of the matter was that mother, if not dangerously ill, was at least so bad that it would have been impossible for her to meet me in our usual way, for she could not go out alone without a companion. I am now strongly inclined to think that her state was due, in great part, to her belief that I was in grave peril and surrounded by enemies; or perhaps she had even found out that I was really in some danger of which I myself was unaware. But at the time it seemed to me that mother was putting me aside for my aunt's sake. I thought that she might possibly have arranged for me to join her earlier than March, and a horrible feeling of loneliness came over me.

All this time I continued to attend the sewing-school. One day we were sitting as usual round our table, when Bertha and her girl friends told us, choking with laughter as they did so, that Commissioners Windt and Bayerl were coming that morning to pay us a visit in school. We were not to let Fräulein Weigl know that it was a joke, as they would come as though officially to inspect the school. For a moment I thought myself that it was really a joke, but the next I shrewdly suspected that they were paying a special visit to see me.

Of course, poor Fräulein Weigl trembled when she heard the word "Police," and did not know what to think of the two gentlemen sitting down at our table, talking and chatting for half an hour. It seemed to her so extraordinary a proceeding that she could scarcely believe that they were there officially, or even that they belonged to the Police. To satisfy herself as to this last point she asked them to produce their badges, which they promptly did. If Fräulein Weigl was astonished at this, it at once confirmed my suspicion that they were there for some other purpose than a practical joke. Of course, it was not within the duties of their departments to inspect schools. What had the chief of the secret police to do with this? Still more, what had a commissioner in special charge of the Emperor to do with it? On the other hand, was it credible that they should use their office for the purpose of a joke upon an inoffensive schoolmistress, and risk the loss of their high positions, or at least expose themselves to a severe reprimand?

More than ever I felt the necessity of being on my guard.

CHAPTER XXIII

THE END OF LOVE'S YOUNG DREAM

TOWARD the end of January, Elsa's mother and a few other ladies prominent in Viennese society got up a sort of dancing class, in which their young people might be taught some of the national dances, such as the Czardas and the Polish Great Mazurka. I had learned all these long before, but Frau von Friese thought it might be some distraction for me, and so arranged that I should attend the class under the care of Mrs. Kaiser and the watchful eye of Pirker, who shadowed me everywhere. Frau von Friese scarcely knew Frau von Thyr, as they had only met accidentally at the home of the Kaisers; and as Frau von Thyr was a conceited and arrogant woman, Frau von Friese had not been very cordial to her. I suppose that Frau von Thyr really knew something about me, and also what Frau von Friese's position was. While, being widow of a field-marshal and very well connected at Court, she preferred not to be too closely in touch with my affairs, on the other hand she was flattered to know that her daughter was my only intimate friend. But to her Mrs. Kaiser had to appear as my mother, and I still had to go under the latter's care wherever I might be invited. Moreover, I was too young to come out yet, and these dancing lessons were only a preparation for a later introduction into the social world, for one of the essential things in Austrian high society is that all its members must be perfect dancers. This was one of the few things in which I may boast that I was perfect. I did not particularly wish to go to the class. However, as my mother had said that this was to be my last year spent in retirement, I was indifferent as to whether I continued for a short time more under the guardianship of Mrs. Kaiser, which had already continued so long. I was eagerly looking forward to the time when I could rejoin my mother, and that was all I cared about. I felt that I was better when near her, less passionate and quick-tempered, and more accustomed to do my best to be dignified. As I grew older I felt the uncongeniality of the sphere in which I was moving. However, the society at these dancing-lessons was very exclusive, according to the general opinion, even to the point of being stiff and uninteresting.

The first lesson was a sort of introductory dance, at which others were present in addition to those actually joining the class.

I had not seen Ferdinand Fellner for months, although I spent some of my spare moments in dreaming of him and storing up his memory more and more in my inmost heart. Never, after the interview with my mother, had his name been mentioned by myself, nor by anyone else in my presence. It might easily have been imagined that in the lapse of time I had forgotten him.

I had taken Elsa partly into my confidence with regard to my love-affair, telling her that Mr. Kaiser thought Fellner not serious enough to marry me, and had refused his consent on account both of this and of my extreme youth. Elsa was by nature rather discreet and uncommunicative, and, although she could not but know that my life was one out of the ordinary, she had never asked me about it, while I had not told her anything about it. Frau von Friese had expressly warned Mrs. Kaiser that Fellner must not

THE END OF LOVE'S YOUNG DREAM 263

be present at these lessons, and that, if he were, she must be informed, so that I might absent myself on those occasions. I guessed from what Elsa said that this was Frau von Friese's order. For my governess personally conducted herself in my presence as if she had entirely forgotten the affair.

How it happened I do not know. There was a misunderstanding somehow. Nothing could have been more unexpected by me when, shortly after I had entered the ballroom, I heard a familiar voice behind me saying, " Good evening! What a surprise it is to meet you here! "

I was so troubled that I could not speak, and the hand I gave him trembled. He also seemed troubled, and for a moment looked quite pale and embarrassed. To hide his agitation and tide us both through this awkward situation, he forced himself to assume his usual mood and said gaily, " How wonderfully you have changed! How many hearts are you going to break to-night? "

All my resolutions melted in a moment. I simply could not resist, and so I danced too much with him that evening. During the first hour I tried hard to control myself a little; but after that I abandoned myself to the enjoyment of those few hours. I justified my conduct to myself by saying that I was not harming anyone; that it was my last farewell, and, above all, that I should feel happier with this memory in my heart.

Mrs. Kaiser was sitting with a number of other ladies and paid little attention to me. In fact, she did not notice Ferdinand Fellner until some time after our meeting, and I managed not to let her see me with him. I was engaged for supper with someone else, but I ventured so far as to tell Fellner to sit at my right side and not to engage himself to another partner. Supper was served at little tables in different rooms, and here again I managed to escape Mrs. Kaiser's eyes.

He seemed more serious this evening than usual, while I, on the contrary, was more lively than was my wont. My partner at supper, finding that I paid very little attention to him, conversed altogether with his neighbour on the other side, so that I had leisure to talk to Fellner. The latter was so noticeably quiet that at last, near the end of supper, I asked, "What has happened to you? I do not seem to recognise you any more."

He paused, and then said slowly, "In the first place, I am preoccupied about my final examination; and then . . ." He paused, and looked at me. As I did not say anything, however, he went on: "Can't you imagine? Don't you know what is on my mind?"

I continued silent. I could not collect the thoughts as they rushed through my head. I only felt of a sudden inexpressibly sad.

"You do not care to reply. But I, who have so rarely an opportunity of talking to you, shall not waste it this time. I know your people think me dissipated and untrustworthy. I called three or four times at your home, only to be told each time that you were not in. I understood from this that I was no longer welcome there, and so I remained away. I was not sure whether you would be here; but as I heard that her Excellency Frau von Thyr was to be one of the patronesses, I hoped you might be present, and therefore accepted the Baroness von Buschmann's invitation. Otherwise I should not have come, as my time is quite absorbed by my work. But now I have at last found an opportunity of speaking to you, and I shall make use of it."

I still sat staring at him, unable to find a word to utter;

THE END OF LOVE'S YOUNG DREAM

and he continued. Was I displeased with him, he asked, for speaking like this? Could I not guess that he had been striving for months and months to conquer himself? He grew more impassioned still as I remained speechless. At least I should tell him that I knew of his love for me, and that I would accept it. He had worked so hard at his examinations, to prove himself worthy of me. After his final he would be a qualified architect, and his father would take him into his business. The firm had a world-wide reputation, and he could say without conceit that no girl could have a reason for refusing him.

Then he seemed to lose his head. Did my father prefer some idler from one of the embassies, he demanded — some man of title? He, too, could be a baron. His father had already refused the honour, but could have it still, if that were what I wanted. "Can't you understand how tortured I am?" he concluded. "As soon as I am through my final I shall go straight to your father. I must have you!"

Suddenly the veil fell from before my eyes, and I was as if awakened from a dream. I must stop him, must not leave him in uncertainty any longer. Painfully forcing back the tears, I said, "Ferry, even if I can understand what you say, *perhaps I am not allowed to understand you.*"

I spoke as gently as I could. I wished at one and the same time to comfort him and to destroy for ever all his hopes. But he altogether misinterpreted me, as I saw at once.

"Oh, you are an old-fashioned girl," he answered with a laugh. "It can easily be seen that you have always been kept as if in a convent. You are afraid of papa's strong will. Perhaps he has already disposed of your hand. Let me see what I can do. I will soon make him give his consent."

I was just on the point of saying, "For goodness' sake don't act too hastily," when everyone began to rise from the table. My partner, with a low bow and many apologies for being compelled to disturb me, offered me his arm. Behind me Fellner laughed, saying in a joyful voice, "Arrivederci! Later on!"

But I had no opportunity to speak to him again. Mrs. Kaiser had at last noticed that he was seeking me out, and every time he tried to approach me either Laura or Elsa was immediately at my side, so that at last I was compelled to go home, with my heart full of anguish and almost in despair. One moment I wished to whisper to him that I would try to meet him somewhere, but immediately my conscience disapproved of an action which at that time seemed to me dreadful — apart from its being impossible.

With all this my passion had blazed up stronger than ever. How masterfully he had spoken! He was quite changed since last summer. He had suddenly become a man. But then again the thought forced itself upon me on what a desperate and hopeless struggle I was embarking. My anguish at the idea of his going to speak to my guardian was indescribable. More than ever I longed for my mother's presence. I should have thrown myself at her feet, imploring her to give her consent to this union. It seemed to me that it was destiny which had caused me to be brought up away from the Court, whereby it had been possible to meet him.

But, alas! mother was far away, and I was alone with my torturing thoughts. I had the most intense need of someone in whom to confide. But who was there? And now I committed a great error, for I deceived the one person above all in whom I should have had confidence, Frau von Friese. Instead of going at once to her, I trembled at the very thought of doing so. Her first impulse, I felt, would be one of indignation, and afterwards she would lead me into the right way. But I had no desire for the right way then. Frau von Friese would have induced me to abandon my fantastic ideas at once, while I on the contrary wanted to find someone who would indulge my passion. Still, the great reason for my refusing to speak to her was, as I have said, fear. I knew how implacably severe she could be, and this time she would have been quite pitiless.

Finally I took a step which should have been the very last to be dreamt of. I placed myself in the hands of Mrs. Kaiser, hoping that she, who knew the whole affair from the beginning, would help me. At first she seemed rather alarmed. The next moment she laughed over this "folly" of mine, as she called it. Yet it did not escape me that her manner of speech was rather forced, and I was not at all favourably impressed when she concluded: "Well, I think that was carrying a joke rather too far. You will see that the young man will not reappear. There is only one way to make sure. Let us wait until his examinations are over."

And so I waited patiently. Naïvely I failed to realise that through my confession to Mrs. Kaiser I had given her just the opportunity which enabled her surreptitiously and without great difficulty to bring the whole affair to an end.

When the date of Ferdinand Fellner's examination was past my uneasiness began to grow again. Had Mrs. Kaiser been right? Was all that he had said a jest? If that were so I never could endure such an outrage quietly. I was speculating vainly what was to be done when, quite unexpectedly, I saw in a newspaper that his mother had died suddenly. Of course, I immediately found an excuse for him and waited patiently again. But, though I had heard nothing from him since our last meeting, I could not consider myself free. I should be obliged to attend the dancing class while he was in deep mourning. I could not do that. But what excuse was I to find? This was my plan for the first week. I rubbed the skin off the ankle of my right foot with the heel of the left, and so made what looked like a serious enough wound to prevent me from going out. I thought that before this could have time to heal I should hear from him. But no news came.

My next step was certainly most audacious and imprudent. I must have parted with my reason to ignore completely my mother's strict orders and overlook the grief I should cause her. I wrote to Ferdinand Fellner. In my letter I asked him not to be surprised and hurt if its contents seemed to him rather frivolous. It was intended as an apology if I should again attend the dancing class. As I had heard nothing from him since our last meeting, I was no longer able to stay away without exciting the suspicions of my friends. Besides I did not really know whether I was called upon to do so. I begged him to write back to me.

As the answer must come to my guardians' address, to prevent its being intercepted before reaching me I bribed one of the kitchen-maids to be on the lookout for it. A few days later, after I had suffered tortures, the girl handed me a black-bordered envelope. The letter's brief contents were as follows:—

THE END OF LOVE'S YOUNG DREAM

DEAR MISS LILY,

After the sad event which has just happened, I do not feel at present in the mood to talk about anything like the subject of our last conversation, and therefore beg you to consider it unspoken.

Now I knew. But how dreadful was that knowledge! It was my first stunning blow. With it departed my childhood and the confidence which I had hitherto had in everyone. I lost that innocent pleasure in life which had been mine. I had been heartlessly deceived; or at least I thought so, for of course, at the time, I blamed him for all and never imagined that there had been any outside interference.

In later years, when I learned that Mr. Kaiser had given Ferdinand Fellner to understand the impossibility of his plans concerning me and had advised him to withdraw, I changed my ideas a great deal. But nothing could give me back my lost youth. I never saw him again. He, too, I afterwards heard, was in despair at the unhappy ending of the affair. He abandoned himself to a wild and ruinous life, which made him ill for years, and finally caused his premature death.

Only after I received the unwelcome intelligence contained in Fellner's short letter did it occur to me in what a disgraceful manner I had behaved towards my mother. My sole consolation, and it was a faint one, at this unhappy moment, was that at least I was able to save her from a worse grief I might have caused her. As I recovered from the blow I could readily understand how much greater the misfortune would have been had his answer been favourable to my wishes. Now I could see how utterly impossible it would have been for me to plead with my poor mother for her consent.

I had scarcely had time to think much about this, however, when, like a flash of lightning across the sky, came the following telegram from mother to Frau von Friese: —

"Bring Caroline at once."

Brief as was the message, I could read in it that mother did not send it just now by chance alone, and I was afraid to meet her. Yet, in spite of my fear, I longed for her as the only comfort I had, the only person who could give be peace again. I think I shall never forget this interview if I live to be a hundred years old.

Mother was sitting alone in the drawing-room of our apartments in the hotel where Frau von Friese and myself were staying at San Remo. This time I did not stay in the same hotel as mother.

She was even paler than usual, and her features wore a hard, marble-like expression such as I had never seen before on her dear face. At the sight of her I trembled from head to foot. Usually we hurried into each other's arms; but this time she remained motionless. Suddenly she seemed to lose patience, and then she said in a voice that was almost harsh: "Do you dare to come again before my eyes?"

This beginning was totally unexpected. I felt my tears choke me.

"You have deceived me and lied to me. I suppose you come now to do the same again."

This too was said severely, though her voice had somewhat softened, with less anger and more reproach in it. I remained silent. I had already feared that she might have heard something of what I had done, but I had continued to hope that I was mistaken. Her manner of greeting me, therefore, came like a bolt from the blue.

THE END OF LOVE'S YOUNG DREAM 271

My fault must have been depicted to her as much worse than it really was.

Misinterpreting my silence as obstinacy, and irritated at the absolute quiet which reigned, she grew angrier again; but this time it was a deadly quiet anger, for she spoke now in an almost icy voice. "Madame the Archduchess (Frau Erzherzogin) does not seem to have heard that I have spoken to her," she said.

For the first and only time in my life she addressed me by this title, as though wishing to remind me of what I seemed to have forgotten. I really did not know what I could say, but I felt that I must give some sort of an answer if only to show my willingness to speak. With a superhuman effort I forced out the words, "I have heard, mother."

Then suddenly something seemed to restore to me my strength, and determinedly keeping back my tears, I exclaimed loudly: "I never lied to you, mother, and it is because I do not wish to do so to-day that I have taken so long to make my reply." All my pride had returned to me, and I continued: "When I gave you my promise in the Tyrol last summer, I intended to be faithful to my word. Circumstances turned my head, but, even in the moment of my greatest passion, I never thought to keep a word of all this secret from you. I thought of rebellion, perhaps, but never of deceit."

And now I told her of all I had suffered; how lonely I had felt, especially since she had seemed to prefer Aunt Mathilde's company to mine; and how, really, it had been more my pride than anything else that had induced me to write to the young man. With this I took out the black-bordered envelope and gave it to her.

She did not know of the letter's existence until now, and

this at last convinced her that I had intended to speak to her. It was the final necessary proof that I had meant to be true to her. She was deeply moved and pulled me toward her. Then, holding me motionless in her arms, she looked at me with those sad eyes of hers, in which the tears had come, and whispered: "My poor, lonely girl!"

Her expression as she spoke I can never forget; and even now when I am feeling most miserable, I am restored by thinking of those words: "My poor, lonely girl!"

After we had sat together like this for a short time, she began to speak again: "We have to give up many things in this life, child, which seem to us sacred. You have early to learn to bow to this rule. Perhaps there will some time come a day when people will tell of a princess who had to renounce what was sacred to her for the sake of the people."

"But how could it be I, darling mother?" I whispered in reply. "What have my sufferings to do with the people? It would be a great consolation to me if it were so! But what am I to them?"

But now mother put both her hands over my eyes and said: "Once you promised me blind obedience, and I promised you to make you reach the goal of your ambitions."

Hearing her words I bowed down and fervently kissed her hands. And with this my first dream of love was shattered for ever.

CHAPTER XXIV

OUR LAST DAYS TOGETHER

I REMAINED but twenty-four hours in San Remo and then returned to Vienna for a short while. I well remember in what a state of depression I was and how I cried all night while the sleeping-car bore me away from my mother again.

We were not long separated this time, however, for I passed barely a week in Vienna and then joined her once more at Territet. Here she recovered to some extent from her nervous state, and, if she could not stand the strain of long walks, we were at least able to take short rambles in the neighbouring woods. In the evenings and at night we talked for hours of many things, but chiefly about my future.

How amusing it would be to watch the astonishment of all the people who knew nothing of my story, when they were at last enlightened!

"I myself will go with you to pay a visit to Frau von Thyr and her daughter," said my mother. "And then all those girls who were your companions at school — what will they say? But, Weiberl, you won't be conceited, will you, when all these people suddenly bow down before you and everybody turns round to stare at you in the streets? On the contrary, it must prove to you how light and frivolous the world is."

And should I know my father and sisters? I asked.

"Yes, of course," she answered; but I felt a certain strangeness in the tone of her voice.

Somewhat embarrassed at this I continued: "I wonder how I shall get on with them."

"Very well, I hope, dear. Anyhow, they will not trouble us much."

But I was afraid of Valerie, I said. I did not know why, but I did not think she would like me. Mother, however, told me it was wrong to entertain such ideas. Valerie was good and kind, and would try to take me under her sisterly wing. Probably she might insist upon the fact that she was the elder sister, whom I must therefore respect. But, as I was a reasonable person, who understood the weak points of others, I would give in and get on very well with her.

On one of the last days of our stay, mother said to me: "When I return to Vienna I shall have to settle all the matters connected with bringing you out. This year is the right time."

"How will you manage to do it, mother?" I asked excitedly.

"Very simply," she replied. "The Emperor will have to announce officially to Parliament that the Empress and he have a third daughter living, who has been educated away from the Court, and who will be introduced on the occasion of his Jubilee. It will not make any trouble whatever. All is in order, the papers and everything. That is all that will be necessary."

So the time of separations was almost past, the date of my recognition was almost at hand. The days dragging out their slow length were scarcely bearable to me in my increasing impatience. This time I gladly accepted the parting from mother. Was I not longing for news that my future was decided upon?

We returned to Vienna in the first week of April, and

I schooled myself as best I could to await the outcome of mother's mission. But she did not let me hear anything for a few days; and then Frau von Friese received only a line or two, stating that she was suddenly indisposed and must leave almost immediately for Kissingen. She only came to bid me good-bye. In answer to the questioning look in my eyes, she said, "My poor darling, I feel so miserable all at once. For the moment my nerves will not allow me to undertake what I intended."

I kissed her hand, and made no answer. I guessed that there was some quite other obstacle than the question of her health. But, as I wished to make her believe that I was confident, I kept silence.

She remained with me only a short time, during which I could see how she was tortured by the thoughts which she wished to keep to herself. Only at the last, when she put her arms about me and gave me the farewell kiss, did she lose countenance. There was one heart-breaking sob from her. Neither of us said a single word more. It was useless. We understood without words.

Mother remained away nearly two months, going first to Kissingen, and after that to Bruckenau. The weeks crawled by for me with the most deadly slowness. I was so depressed that nothing now had any interest for me. I tried to be reasonable and succeeded fairly well in the daytime; but at night I could not get any sleep. The remembrance of that long last sob of mother's remained in my heart. What did it mean? I knew that there must have been some trouble about me, but I could not imagine what was its nature. I indulged in all sorts of conjectures as to her meeting with the Emperor. I fancied that he had been abrupt, perhaps had refused point-blank to do what mother asked. But why he should set his face against me I could not make out. Or had mother had to fight against others, with whom she was not strong enough to contend? It was a great enigma, unsolvable by me.

Toward the middle of June mother returned to Vienna. She was slightly better, but what was wrong with her was mental rather than physical trouble. It was given out officially that she needed a complete rest, and that Professor Nothnagel had told her that if she wished to recover speedily she should see as few people as possible, and not even her own family. The truth, of course, was that she was at the moment on such terms with the family that she declined to see any of them.

Frau von Friese's health was not completely restored yet, although she was much better than before. Professor Nothnagel told her that she should go for a cure to Franzensbad, as her blood was in a poor condition. At first she thought of taking me with her, but this idea was discountenanced by mother, who did not wish me to be absent from Vienna while she was there. So Frau von Friese went alone to Franzensbad, while I remained at my own home in the Strohgasse with Fräulein Hain.

During the month of June the Kaisers were again at Vöslau, and I was often with them for the week-ends. Almost every day I met mother in a corner of her park at Lainz. I was brought to a side entrance by my coachman, Franz Schneider, and by Pirker, who accompanied me to our meeting-place. There he left me and waited sometimes for hours until I returned. This dear old servant was the one person besides Frau von Friese in whose care my mother trusted me. He was like my own shadow to me. Nothing could be a sweeter reward to him than to hear mother say one morning: "Pirker, you are my greatest comfort. I don't know what I should do without you. As long as I know you are near my daughter, I feel that she is safe."

I must say here that mother was not very well pleased at Frau von Friese's leaving me so often alone, although she could do nothing to prevent it, for my governess was with me of her own good will, and not by regular appointment. Frau von Friese, for her part, was of the opinion that my mother was needlessly anxious about me, and never would believe that I was really in danger. Moreover, the police commissioner who acted as her confidential agent had assured her that there was nothing planned against me at present, and that everything seemed safe.

In spite of Professor Nothnagel's advice, mother seemed to have trouble about her all the time. I would almost have given my life that she might tell me what was going on; but all I could find out was that, as I have already said, she was on bad terms with all the members of her family.

On July 2nd she left for Ischl. Frau von Friese was to return in a week's time and to accompany me there too. "I hope things will get on better now," were mother's last words. "I think that you will be able to join me again toward the middle of the month."

And now Frau von Friese had returned from Franzensbad, and everything was in readiness for our departure. We only awaited the final order from mother. On the 18th came the letter we were expecting, but, to our astonishment, not from Ischl, but from Munich.

"I am on my way to Nauheim," she wrote. "Left Ischl quite unexpectedly. Will tell you all when we meet. Join me at once at Nauheim."

More trouble, I thought to myself. And I was not mistaken. This time mother concealed nothing from me. She told me that for many months she had been taking steps to effect my recognition, but that new difficulties kept cropping up. As long ago as the previous autumn she had talked matters over with the Emperor. At first he had been quite willing to discuss the subject. But gradually those in his confidence had turned him against it. He suddenly made an objection to my broad-minded system of education, said he was afraid this would have a bad effect at Court, and so on.

Mother did not know what to do, when she was approached by the Jesuits through the medium of Cardinal Steinhuber. The Cardinal in his younger days had been religious instructor in the house of my grandfather, the Duke Max in Bavaria, and had taught the daughters. He was, therefore, personally acquainted with my mother.

The Jesuits' proposal was that if they assisted mother with regard to me she must use her influence in support of certain privileges which they claimed in Hungary; and, secondly, she must send me to a convent for three years. She could not agree to these conditions, and particularly not to the latter. She had a great affection for the Hungarians, and would not work against their prejudices, while as to me it is hardly necessary to say that she never dreamt of yielding. Such a plan would either destroy the fruits of a careful education or else would entail upon me a life of misery, as it was too late now for the convent rule to influence me.

I believe that the Cardinal personally did all he could to help mother. But the Jesuits would not abate their terms in the least. The only result was that they became more hostile to us. In vain mother tried to win over the Emperor single-handed.

There had been violent scenes at Ischl. Mother threatened to appeal to Hungary. She suddenly left Ischl and

OUR LAST DAYS TOGETHER

went abroad, causing, as she wished, the more sensation because she almost invariably stopped at Ischl over the Emperor's birthday.

When she told me of all this she added excitedly: "And Austria shall not see me again until you have been given your rights. They know that I adhere to what I say. I have given them proofs of that. They *shall* come to me!"

And now one morning she hastened, full of joy, to meet me, waving her hand to me from afar in token of triumph. She was happy, as I had not seen her for a long time.

"Weiberl," she called out, when she was still a little distance away, "you see, they *are* coming to me now! I knew it. I had a message to-day from the Emperor. He wants to meet me here, or else in a few weeks' time at Territet, or somewhere in Switzerland, to talk matters over with me again. He wishes to make his announcement on December 2nd, and we will fix the date when I am to present you to him and your sisters."

Hearing her words, I began to tremble. I felt as if a great weight were pressing upon my heart. Why did I hesitate for some time before I could join in my mother's pleasure? What was it that almost made the tears come to my eyes? Why did I feel so sorry for mother at that moment? Why did I throw myself into her arms to avoid the necessity of speaking? I could not have explained my emotion at the time. But to-day I know that it was one of those uncanny presentiments which flash upon the soul and prepare it for what is to come.

I stopped about three weeks with mother at Nauheim. As usual, the time was all delightful while I was near her. But how awful, how ghastly it is to be compelled to add that this was the last time that we were ever together! It is beyond my powers to describe this final stay with her. When I try to recollect that time, so full of sunshine, my eyes are blinded with tears, and I cannot see what I am writing.

How could anyone else realise what sufferings are mine again and again, whenever I think of this unconscious farewell between mother and myself? It is an agony which can never be exhausted until the last day of my life. When the memory comes back to me, I feel like a deserted, lonely child, calling in vain for "mother." My whole soul cries out for her in whom I lost not merely the best and most loving of mothers, but everything in the world, everything indefinite and unmeasurable.

In this death there lay for me such terrible misery as, I believe, few beings have ever had to undergo. But my pen is unequal to the task of picturing it. Can I convey my thought when I say that from the moment of her death I understood the custom of the ancients, who in the intensity of their grief rent their garments and tore their hair? I, too, have this feeling, and as the remembrance comes back to me I have an overmastering desire to throw myself upon the ground and rend everything upon me.

But I may not do such things; and, instead, the ever-burning anguish must remain pent up in my soul, invisible to all the world — in which there is, happily for himself, no man who could comprehend it to the full.

CHAPTER XXV

THE HAND OF FATE

IN the first half of August, 1898, I went with Frau von Friese to Pörtschach, in Karinthia, to stay with the Kaisers. Mother did not wish to keep me with her at the moment lest she should appear to the Emperor to be acting out of mere stubbornness. Her own immediate return to Austria would have been too abrupt, while if I had remained at Nauheim it would have looked like flouting the Emperor's desires. So with a heavy heart she let me go.

Frau von Friese stopped at Pörtschach several days. Then, on August 23rd, she left for Denmark. She had originally intended to go there later on. But, as mother wrote that she wanted us to join her in Switzerland about the middle of September, she decided to go away now and return in good time to make preparations for our journey to Switzerland. Pirker and my maid remained in special charge of me, and with them I was to travel in a few weeks' time to Innsbrück to rejoin Frau von Friese.

Mr. and Mrs. Kaiser had leased the villa No. 1 attached to the hotel to which they had applied for rooms, the "Etablissement Wahliss." We took our meals at the restaurant of the establishment itself. It was the height of the season when I arrived at Pörtschach. I never had any great liking for the place from the first, and to-day its memory is detestable to me. It was at the time of which I am writing neither a cosy little summer resort, like Veldes for instance; nor an elegant spot, like Gmunden in particular; nor yet a gay and luxurious watering-place, such as people flock to in the summer. It was nothing special, but set up to be grand. The people there dressed themselves much with no reason for doing so. The amusements were forced and hollow. Everybody in the place knew everybody else, but they were of such different social ranks that no one really was on intimate terms with his neighbour. The principal distraction was the lake, which was certainly delightful for swimming and boating. Then there was bicycling, which was at that time much in vogue. I learnt to ride there, and we used to spend the mornings in the water and the afternoons on the bicycle — a vehicle which I loathed from the moment I first mounted it. I loved horse-riding too much ever to have any sympathy for this mechanical sport.

And now I have arrived at the most terrible and tragic moment of my life. My mother, my darling, adored mother, went from me for ever!

It was a cool, grey day in September — that is to say, I cannot be certain if the weather was grey and the sky overcast or not; but it is grey and gloomy in my memory.

Nor can I say how we spent the day. My foster-father was in Vienna, and I was alone with his wife and daughter. We were going home to the villa after supper. It was, I suppose, getting on for nine o'clock. On the way back we met one of the servants of the establishment, who cried out to us, "Have the ladies heard the dreadful news?"

"No; what has happened?" we all asked.

"The Empress has been assassinated!"

Had he at that instant plunged a dagger into my heart,

the agony could not have been worse than what I experienced then. My throat felt as though someone were strangling me. My temples roared, and the ground under my feet rocked like the waves of the sea. I remembered no more until I found myself in my bedroom. Laura told me afterwards that with a great effort I managed to walk to the villa. I myself recall that when I entered my room it seemed to me dimly lighted; and then I lost consciousness. Oh, why had I to wake again — to wake with an awful awakening, which has ever since that moment been like a ghastly nightmare to me?

So all was over. This was the last act of my happy, sunny youth. My mother had gone from me for ever. My darling one, farewell!

It requires an almost superhuman effort to describe this period of my life. To do so I have to re-live every minute of it, and that is a martyrdom which no one can realise.

Only after several hours did I recover from my swoon; that is to say, I opened my eyes, but I was unable to move. My head was burning as with red-hot irons. The doctor was fetched, and bags of ice were applied. After this I must have fallen asleep. It was the next morning that the real awakening came. I remember I unclosed my eyes and found myself alone. The dreadful truth flashed upon my mind again. My darling mother had gone from me for ever. Not knowing what I did, I screamed out "Mother!" Then, breaking into pitiful sobs, I buried my face in my pillows.

Laura, who was in the adjoining room, heard my cry and hurried to my bedside. She was very kind, and threw her arms about me, and I, without the strength to resist, let her do as she wished.

Everyone in the place tried to comfort me and to bring

a little calm to me. But their words almost drove me mad, and in order to rid myself of them I would not answer at all, and remained motionless in the bed. In fact, I felt quite unable to weep in any person's presence. It seemed to me like a profanation to share my grief with anyone else. This obstinate silence on my part had at last the effect of making those about me fear for my reason. Dr. Fischer, who was attending me, ordered them to let me stay in bed some little time, as he was afraid of brain fever. So I remained thus for several days, almost without moving.

One morning, however, they brought me a letter from Frau von Friese, after having debated for a time whether they ought to give it to me or not. They had finally decided to do so, in the hope that it might have a good effect and also help to put life into me.

"My poor, dear child," Frau von Friese wrote. "A dreadful misfortune has befallen you, my poor child. But you must know that, at this moment of the utmost anguish and suffering, you will show the most respect for the memory of your dear dead mother if you exhibit courage, patience, and dignity in bearing the heaviest blow that Fate could possibly deal you. Remember always what she used to expect of you. Remember that you are her daughter, and that you must show yourself worthy of her. Remember, too, the nobility with which she bore all her sorrows, and remembering this it will be easier for you also to bear up against all the miseries of this life.

"How dreadful it is for me to be prevented, even for a short time, from coming to you, it is unnecessary for me to say. But it will not be long now, only a few days more, my poor child, before I shall be able to hold you once again in my arms. I am the only person (may I say?)

who can be to you a little of that one who has been torn away from you so cruelly. Great changes may soon come to you; but in all circumstances of life you will remember where you can find the heart that bears for you the most motherly love in this lonely world.

"Courage, my brave girl! Think of the one who now looks down from heaven upon you, and who is so much happier than we."

Until the time when I read this letter I had not even made an effort to take in ideas. A terrible gloom had reigned over me, robbing me of all my strength. Now, for the first time since my blow, I had another feeling than that of anguish alone. Unconsciously I had been waiting for Frau von Friese, and I was disappointed that she had not come. But in spite of this her kind words aroused me a little. I could not read between the lines, or else I should have known that what she was saying to me was in reality her own eternal farewell.

For a moment I could see quite vividly the dear sad eyes of my mother, and she was saying again to me that which she had so often said to me before: "Babe, be reasonable."

At this remembrance, for the last time I burst into tears. But as soon as that was over, forcing myself to activity, I rose from my bed. When those about me wished to prevent it, I said: "Let me go into the open air. It will do me good."

Then I begged Laura to row me over to the other shore of the lake, to Maria Wörth. This is a quaint little place, with a very old church standing at the back, and on an adjoining hill is the churchyard, overlooking the quiet blue lake. Several times before I had been there and had thought how beautiful it would be to be laid there one day for my last eternal rest. Now I was standing here again, not to be buried myself, but to bury the golden time of my youth.

One never has the consciousness of one's life as a single and complete whole. At first one develops vigorously and pushes on to the height of one's physical and mental powers; but before ever that is reached one begins slowly to die. This day in the churchyard my death began.

My struggles, however, were only just at their commencement. Above all I wished to hurry back to Vienna. I wanted to see Her once more, for the very last time. But this could not be allowed. For one thing, I had not the physical strength to travel to Vienna. And besides how could I go, like some mere stranger, to her bier? On the other hand, it was impossible at that moment to make any special arrangements for me. The dreadful truth almost drove me mad. All my pride rebelled at the idea that I was not able at once to communicate with my relatives.

At this time my foster-father, who had arrived in Pörtschach again a few days after the tragedy, came closer to my heart than any of them, and his presence did the most to calm me. With deep gratitude I look back on the memory of this old man — he was very old then, about seventy, and quite broken down with grief too — as, with the utmost earnestness he could command, he tried to make me reason properly.

"For the sake of your mother, my dear child, you must endure it. You cannot make any trouble at this time."

These words of his were the wisest thing he could have said. Yes, for mother's sake I must endure it.

And yet what more cruel and inhuman Calvary can be conceived than is conveyed in this sentence, The child may not weep out her grief for the loss of her mother, nor bid her a last farewell?

Amid all this of which I have been telling, it could not remain hidden from me that my foster-parents were really placed in a very awkward position. At first it was given out that I had met with an accident, that I had taken an overdose of morphine, intended to relieve a cough I had. But, afterwards, what excuse could be found for my extraordinary grief? Why should I suddenly have become a hater of the world? Yet it would have been absolutely impossible for me to meet anybody.

When the first week had passed by, I began to be better able to understand the position. The last thing I wished was to be the slightest burden to anyone. My soul revolted at such a thought, and so I begged Laura to talk as much as possible to me, that I might have practice in learning to dissemble my feelings. With my own feet I wished to trample upon my heart. And little by little I succeeded.

I think I must actually have gone off my head for a time. In the presence of strangers I had never been as highspirited as then; for, of course, it was impossible to hold the balance properly. To those about me this state of mind seemed a happy deliverance. Had they not been — how shall I express myself properly? — so inexperienced in matters of grief, they would not have accepted the sacrifice.

After all was over we went back to Vienna. Vienna! how terrible, how awful it was! I really did not live then. It was a sort of evil dream; otherwise it would have killed me.

Naturally I resided with Mr. and Mrs. Kaiser, but this in itself mattered nothing, it had happened so often before. The household in the Strohgasse was kept on for a time. I had insisted upon that. Was I not waiting for Frau von Friese, who would then take steps with me for securing my recognition? No one spoke about this matter, nor did I speak to anyone. I preferred that none but she should interfere in these affairs.

About a week after our return to Vienna I was told that Frau von Friese had suddenly become so ill that she could not come back at once. A short letter was shown to me from her relatives, giving the bad news and saying that she was not even able to write herself. What could I do? This was one blow upon another. My darling mother had gone from me for ever. Was my guardian, too, going for ever? It seemed as if some dreadful fate held me fast in its grip. With perverse, almost fiendish cruelty to myself, I laughed at my misfortunes.

The weeks went slowly dragging on. From time to time letters came from Denmark, saying that the physicians believed that Frau von Friese had cancer. One morning in December I was sitting at the piano, playing with the same lack of interest that I now showed in everything else. Purposely I had devoted myself to music, because every tone of it almost was as a new wound to my heart. Music was always to me the most sublime influence that there is in the world. Every melody conveys its own story; and now the sadder it made me the more I loved it.

As I have said, it was one morning in December. Mrs. Kaiser came into the room, but I paid no attention to her, as she often used to come and go. So she had to speak to me to attract my notice.

"Lily," she began, "I have had some very sad news, especially for you."

I stopped playing, and looked at her. It was needless for her to say any more. I knew she was bringing me intelligence of Frau von Friese's death. But as I remained silent she continued: "Poor Frau von Friese is dead."

It may seem incredible, but I said nothing. I only stared at Mrs. Kaiser for a moment and then, as if nothing had happened, I went on playing.

Mrs. Kaiser had expected a violent outburst. She gazed at me in amazement. Next, thinking what she had so often thought before, that I had gone mad, she asked in a low voice: "Lily, did you hear me?"

"Yes," I replied. It was all I had the energy to say; but I continued at the piano. Shaking her head, she left the room. For a few minutes I played on convulsively, and only when I knew that I was alone again did my hands drop slowly from the instrument to my knees.

I had lost the last thing that was dear to me on this earth.

As when at night, on some lonely road, the last light suddenly goes out and plunges the belated wanderer in profound darkness, so it was with me now.

My poor beloved Aya, not one tear did I shed for you. My tears were exhausted; I could cry no more.

CHAPTER XXVI

ALONE IN THE WORLD

AFTER the shock of the news of my dear Frau von Friese's death, I seemed suddenly to enter upon a totally new life. So long as my two loved ones lived I had no right to dispose of my future; but now it was different. I had no right to stand still. I had but existed until now, henceforward I must act.

So finally one day, as I was sitting with Mrs. Kaiser in her room, I said to her, "I really think that it is time for me to do something."

"What do you mean by doing something?" she inquired.

"What do I mean? Why, to get in touch with my relatives, to remind them that I am in the world."

"But why this hurry?" asked Mrs. Kaiser. "Is there anything more you want here? Have you anything to complain of?"

"I am not complaining," I answered, somewhat annoyed, "but I do not think anything you can do is sufficient to compensate me for the loss of what I am expecting."

"You are a fool!" cried Mrs. Kaiser, all of a sudden growing angry. "Go, then, and make a scandal. They will soon know how to shut your mouth. They will put you into an asylum or a convent. Please leave me alone, and don't bother me with your complaints."

Though inwardly I rebelled at her tone, I kept silence; for I knew that when she lost her temper it was useless to argue with her. But that did not prevent me from taking advantage of the first opportunity to reopen the subject. This time Mrs. Kaiser seemed better prepared. She maintained her calm, and said that she had spoken about the matter to her husband, and that they were both of the opinion that, so long as my relatives took no steps, it would be dangerous for me to do so on my part. Then she asked, quite gently, "Don't we do all we can to make you happy?"

When she spoke like this, my mood grew softer, and I began really to think myself ungrateful. I recognised that the Kaisers did their best for me, and were exceedingly kind. In fact, they made little difference between Laura and myself. An outsider might merely have supposed that Laura was rather the favourite of two sisters. This means much, for it showed at any rate that they treated me as a daughter whom they loved.

At first, then, Mrs. Kaiser's attitude impressed me. Yet, after a short period of reflection, the old longing came back upon me, and I went again for the third time to speak to her on the subject.

"So you won't leave me in peace?" she exclaimed. "I must explain matters more clearly, it seems." And now, though perhaps unintentionally, she struck the death-blow to all my hopes.

"I will tell you the truth bluntly," she continued. "You are old enough to understand now, and perhaps I shall have some peace when you have heard what I have to say."

My heart beat faster and faster, and I felt my head

beginning to swim. I knew that she was going to tell me something dreadful. I have said before that she was a woman who took no pains to soften her words.

"You know very well," she now said abruptly, "that your mother and the Emperor never agreed. Is it any wonder, then, that they went separate ways, and as far as possible sought consolation elsewhere?"

At these words of hers I started as if bitten by a snake. But immediately she overwhelmed me with her speech.

"Now, don't try to play any comedy upon me. What is the use of mincing matters? We are by ourselves. I should never speak like this in the presence of others. But I must make you understand now that you must keep quiet for your mother's sake, if you don't want the story to be in everybody's mouth."

And hereupon she laughed, as though to throw me some grains of comfort by giving an air of frivolity to the whole affair.

But I was unable to bear any more, and rushed out of the room, feeling that I could dash my head against the first wall. Oh, it was intolerable! Running to my own room, I locked the door to prevent anyone from intruding upon my grief. I threw myself on the bed, where so often before I had lain gazing into space. For hours I lay there now, trying to unravel the confused tangle of my thoughts. My head was aching and burning furiously, my breast was heaving in a suffocation of dry sobs. And then at last, after so many months, the tears began to roll down my cheeks again; at first slowly, then in floods. Taking from under my pillow the pictures of my two dear dead ones, I whispered to them: "If only once more I might talk to you, I could bear it all!"

ALONE IN THE WORLD

From this day onward no one ever heard me speak of them again. They were my two patron saints, to whom I addressed my prayers, to whom I unburdened my whole heart. Yes, my saints — for suddenly I realised that they had both lost their lives for my sake, that my presentiment had been justified, that a trap had been laid for them, a trap into which they both had fallen; that the Anarchist who had killed my mother had only been a tool in the hands of more skilful murderers,[1] and that my Aya had also to disappear because she was a second mother to me.

Nobody, I resolved, should ever have the chance to speak to me of them until I could justify them. I forbade the members of the household to speak to me of my mother, and I endeavoured, as far as possible, not to hear the banal remarks which strangers made about the late Empress.

To those who did not know me it might easily seem that I harboured a feeling of resentment and blamed her for my misfortune. But it was not so. Never for a moment did I find the slightest stain in her. Yet, young and inexperienced as I was, I knew enough of the meanness and wickedness of mankind, and I knew that at this time I was too weak to fight; that if I wished to fight I had to live, and if I wished to live I had to be dumb until the hour of my deliverance had come.

[1] A curious fact in connection with Luccheni, my mother's assassin, deserves mention. In the year 1910 a commissioner from the United States, making a tour of prisons in Europe, paid a visit to Luccheni at Geneva and found him in a pleasant room overlooking the lake, passing his life in an agreeable manner, working at his prison-trade of bookbinding no more than he desired, and allowed a pint of wine and plenty of cigarettes every day. His room was furnished with a number of pictures, including those of the Emperor and Empress of Austria! In consequence of the commissioner's visit, all this became publicly known. A few weeks later — in October, 1910 — it was officially reported that Luccheni had gone totally insane, and had hanged himself in his cell. But there were many who believed that he had been secretly released.

I had almost forgotten to mention an old friend of mine — poor dear old Pirker.

After all was over, I had finally to consent to break up my home in the Strohgasse. Pirker until then had watched over it. Can it be realised what this meant to the old man, this destruction of all his golden hopes, one after another, this entire disappearance of a home where every little object, every little corner, was a cherished remembrance? And what of the manner in which the break-up of the establishment was carried out — the lack of respect for the dead to whom it really belonged; the lack of pity for the child whose rightful home it was; and, last but not least, the lack of consideration for the faithful servant whose heart was almost broken?

One day in January, 1899, a maid who had shortly before entered Mrs. Kaiser's service called me into the drawing-room. An old gentleman wished to speak to me, she said. I entered the room apprehensively. Who could it be?

Pirker! He had finished his task, and had come, so to speak, to receive his dismissal from me personally.

Poor old man! He could not utter a word. He, who all his life long had understood so well how to banish every expression of emotion from his sphinx-like features, now lost all control over himself.

I can picture him still standing there in front of me, both his hands encased in brown kid gloves, helplessly holding on to his hat and fingering the brim, while he desperately fought with himself to avoid taking out his handkerchief. But he fought in vain; for at last the tears were not to be kept back any more and came rolling down his poor old withered cheeks.

As for me, what recollections the poor old man was

ALONE IN THE WORLD

awaking in me! I could imagine, for a moment, that I was awaiting with him *her* return from a long journey, when he always had a cheerful greeting from her. But this time she was not coming back, and as I awoke to a realisation of this fact my eyes too ran over with tears. So we both cried together like two wretched shipwrecked beings — as we really were.

Then the old man, looking about him as if the very walls had ears and eyes, took out of his pocket a little book.

"A prayer-book," he stammered; "a little remembrance from a faithful servant," and, lowering his voice still more: "You must hide it at once carefully. Trust nobody. Some valuable documents are hidden in it."

Almost kneeling, he caught my hand and pressed upon it a fervent kiss before he whispered: "Farewell, Imperial Highness, farewell!"

Dragging his feet slowly one after the other, he left me. I stood gazing after him for a time. He, too, had gone away from me; and I felt that soon this faithful old friend would be out of my life for ever.

EPILOGUE

THE chief interest of this book for the reader perhaps ceased when the story reached the point of my mother's death. I do not, therefore, propose to prolong the detailed account of my life beyond that terrible period, and for the completion of my story shall content myself simply with telling briefly what happened to me thereafter. But it seems to me that I am bound to narrate the principal events which happened to me between that time and the present day, in order to explain why I have waited so long as sixteen years before revealing my secret.

As I have said in the last chapter, after Mrs. Kaiser's awful revelation of how the world looks on such situations, my courage gave place to the deepest despair. Dearly as it cost me, I forced myself to hold my peace. I had been placed, with diabolical skill, in a position from which escape was impossible.

How could I — the child loved beyond belief by a mother as good as she was noble — how could I speak out and proclaim to the world the truth which was choking me, when the world, in its pitiless malice, would soil with the worst suspicions the story that I had to tell of a life of inconceivable tenderness and self-sacrifice, built upon the ruins of a shattered youth? No, I must necessarily bow to the law of silence which had been imposed upon me, and bury my secret in the depths of my soul, perhaps to the very day of my death. I must not breathe a word, my mouth being closed by respect for the memory of my dear dead one, who had been followed to the grave by the veneration of the whole world. For me it was necessary to forget who I truly was, to renounce my own individuality as it were, to sacrifice myself entirely, without bitterness and without regret. At the thought that it was for her that I was abandoning all my hopes, I felt myself rewarded by the sensation of a new and closer approach to her.

As I did not deign to confide my resolutions to those about me, the new direction of my ideas remained unknown. Very little attention was paid to me apparently, and to outward seeming I was left quite free; but in reality I was a prisoner under the strictest control. I never went out alone. There was nothing unnatural about this, of course, for a young girl in the society in which I lived. But also I was prevented from speaking to anyone, whoever it might be, without being under close observation. Mr. Kaiser, or else his wife, opened all my letters before passing them on to me. I did not have a single drawer which I could lock up and keep to myself. Wherever I went, the Police-commissioner Windt haunted me. Just at first I attached very little importance to his presence; but when I found out that he was everywhere on my tracks, and that he followed me even on a journey, I was forced to realise the significance of this perpetual shadowing, and I knew that I was less forgotten in high places than I had supposed.

Although this perpetual supervision was in many ways very irksome to me, it failed to provoke me to rebellion. On the contrary, I was absolutely resigned to remain in the eyes of the world a Miss Kaiser. This captivity of mine was to me only a continuation of my existence of old. I found in it, as it were, a consoling proof of the bond which could not be broken between my past and my present life. And, besides, there is nothing in the way of misfortunes which cannot be borne by those who have firmly resolved to be patient. Had I not been through all my childhood kneeling in contemplation of the most noble example of patience which the world had ever seen?

So two long years passed, outwardly full of calm, interrupted only by the foolish distractions of the life of Society. At rare intervals I abandoned myself to a profound melancholy, especially on the morrow of some big social function, when it was borne in on me with bitterness how day by day I travelled farther from the happy time when I had a mother of my own, and how now I became day by day more completely the daughter of Mr. and Mrs. Kaiser. No one can imagine what a terrible struggle I had then to prevent my own personality coming to the surface.

"I must, I must," I would say to myself; and it was with a never failing determination that I strove to punish myself for my weaknesses by forcing myself harder than ever to keep up the fiction which was so hateful to me. My efforts, however, received not the slightest encouragement from those with whom I lived.

Mr. Kaiser was growing very old. He was beginning to be wearied out by the perpetual efforts which he had to make to keep his wife within the bounds of simplicity and economy, upon which he had always insisted. As a matter of fact, up to now there had been a certain strictness about the household of Mr. Kaiser. He demanded that we should dress ourselves very simply. Our distractions were kept within rigid limits. But as Laura grew towards womanhood she got more and more influence over her mother, and through her over Mr. Kaiser also. The appearance of their drawing-room gradually altered. Every fortnight there was a big party. Young people, of the idle class whose members are found in all the drawing-rooms of Society, came in numbers to their house. There would be about forty people at a time. It did not take me long to know them, and the knowledge engendered a profound dislike for their company. From this time onwards there grew up a discord of a lasting kind between Laura and myself. She, quite unlike me, took great delight in this society. While I sought rather the friendship of quiet and serious girls, Laura was carried away by her sympathy with those who loved to plunge wildly into the social whirl. It seemed to me that our good name might suffer through such companions, and this was a matter to which I was not indifferent. We squabbled continually on this point.

Mr. Kaiser died suddenly on May 30, 1901. He was found that morning in his bed, apparently still asleep; but they could not wake him, and, in fact, he had ceased to breathe.

This was a more serious loss for me than I was able to conceive at first. If he had not tried — or, I should rather say, if he had not been able — to do anything on behalf of my claims, at least he had been a real protector to me against the daily perils of life. His death, therefore, was bound to bring about considerable changes in the conditions of my existence. Mrs. Kaiser and her daughter were not slow to change their attitude toward me. In spite of all my efforts to conform myself to their constantly changing conduct, I clearly felt that my presence in their circle had the effect of a killjoy, and that decidedly I was a nuisance to them.

I had already foreseen how Laura's reputation would be affected, and constantly asked myself how I should act in defence of my own. For sooner or later, passing as I did for Laura's sister, and seen in her company all the time, I could not escape being involved in the unfavourable opinion which she must arouse against herself in the end.

I could not think of getting permission to go on some trip with a lady to accompany me, nor even of going away to some finishing-school. There was no way out of this false situation for me except marriage. But since my affair with Ferdinand Fellner I had an invincible distaste for all men.

Besides, it seemed to me impossible after this to fall in love again; this feeling disposed of the only possible solution. And then the majority of the young men who paid any attention to me inspired me with no esteem. One among them, however, managed to arouse in me some interest. This was the son of the Court Councillor Kühnelt, Richard Kühnelt, Doctor of Laws, who was at this period a lieutenant in the cavalry. He was a well-educated young man, and seemed to be of a thoroughly serious character. He had lost his father the same summer that I lost my mother, and the blow seemed also one which he could not get over. His state of mind, so like my own, made him very sympathetic to me — although, of course, he did not know in the slightest that I was mourning a beloved mother, and thought me really a Miss Kaiser.

Laura felt toward him a strong aversion, which did not fail to commend him still more to me. Mrs. Kaiser, although she detested him, did her best to encourage our meetings. I was far from dreaming that he would one day be my husband. If Mr. Kaiser had lived but a few years longer, this young man would have passed through my life, like many others who were indifferent to me, without leaving a single trace behind him. But, as it was, hardly had Mr. Kaiser gone when Mrs. Kaiser began to think how she might get rid of me. What I am about to tell may perhaps seem extraordinary, but it is the simple truth, the narration of which could only surprise those who were still ignorant of the history of my life.

Scarcely two weeks after the death of Mr. Kaiser, some foolish quarrel having broken out between Laura and myself, Mrs. Kaiser said to me: "This life is going to be simply unendurable. Things can't go on like this. You had better try to make some arrangement for your future; for you must understand that you can never get on with us, that you will never really be one of us."

The same afternoon she took me, to my great surprise, to pay a visit to Mrs. Kühnelt, the mother of Richard.

There, without having given me the slightest warning of her intentions, she said to her pointblank: "I believe, Madame, that your son is in love with my daughter Lily. Would it not be a good thing to fall in with their wishes at once and agree to their engagement?"

I must confess that my astonishment was nothing compared with that of Mrs. Kühnelt.

As for the son, who was there, as if by accident, I had a vague notion that he was perhaps in league with Mrs. Kaiser, and that in any case he had been warned of her untimely and uncalled-for behaviour. He took hold of my hand and turned upon me a look which conveyed entreaty quite as much as embarrassment, stammering out a few words which I could not understand.

A profound feeling of pity came over me. I knew that his mother was a woman of very difficult character, and I had not the courage to oppose a scheme upon which all his happiness seemed to depend. I do not believe that I uttered a single word during the course of this extraordinary visit.

My amazement had been so great that I remained for long hours plunged in a curious state of mind, without any definite thought or any particular wish. It was not until the next day that I became mistress of myself again. And then I thought that all that had happened was no doubt for the best. I felt that it was perfectly useless to rebel against the force of circumstances. Nevertheless it was not without a terrible aching of my heart that I determined to let myself drift. In agreeing to become the wife of Richard Kühnelt, must I not renounce for ever my hope of establishing the rights of my birth and realising my mother's dearest wish? It was not without difficulty that I succeeded in repressing the instinctive revolt of my soul against this irremediable calamity. Certainly if my poor mother had still lived I should never have dreamt for an instant of uniting my lot with that of him who was about to become my husband. But, of course, he believed simply that he was marrying a Miss Kaiser, whose social position was equal to his own. Therefore, in marrying under this assumed name of Miss Kaiser, I was going to bury all my hopes and all my rights. This was the absolute end of a great ambition and of the ardent desire which I had always cherished of dissipating the heavy mystery which had surrounded my childhood.

I must look forward to the final sacrifice of my true self; for it was clear that I could not possibly reveal to Richard Kühnelt, before our marriage, who I really was. I must hide within the depths of my heart the anguish of a renunciation which no one else could understand.

A few days after my engagement Mrs. Kaiser's lawyer, Dr. Werner, who was also Mr. Kaiser's executor, informed me that I possessed a fortune of four million crowns (£160,000), which my mother had left me. Up to this moment I had not troubled my head at all about the money questions which are involved in nearly all marriages, and although I was totally ignorant of the value of money such a discovery could not find me indifferent. All my ideas were upset, life appearing less gloomy to me, and the future holding out fair promise. My fiancé was very well educated, and while his talents were bound to be helped greatly by his father's high reputation on the one hand, on the other my fortune would aid him to make more quickly a brilliant career. He would enter upon diplomacy, and some day perhaps the secret of my origin might even be revealed. On the whole, therefore, my lot was not such a bad one.

Although I was not greatly attracted to my betrothed, still I thought him well worthy of being loved, and this in itself drew me to him. I wanted to make him happy, and the wish, it seemed to me, should suffice to bring me happiness also. For is it not the principal object of life to live for someone else and not for oneself?

Nevertheless, as time went on, I began to discover that Richard Kühnelt was far from being of so easy-going a character as I had imagined at the beginning. I confessed to myself that I had little understood his true nature, and I was many times on the point of breaking off the engagement and refusing to hear any more about it. But how could that be done? If only Mrs. Kaiser's home had really been mine, I should not have hesitated for a moment. But it was impossible for me to stay any longer with her and Laura.

I begged her not to hurry the wedding on, to wait a little longer before deciding my future absolutely. She replied that she was in a hurry to have done with it, that I was in the way, and finally that she had resolved to go to spend the winter in Paris, where she would on no account take me with her. Her daughter encouraged her to the utmost of her power. Both of them treated me with such harshness that I was forced to recognise that the cause of this unkind behaviour was the weariness and exasperation to which they had been reduced by the constant police supervision involved by my presence with them. There is indeed no doubt that this perpetual trouble had finished by becoming a regular torture to them, and had decided them to try to get rid of me at all hazards, so that they might lead their lives for the future in peace.

I did not feel that I could condemn them completely. On the contrary, I was inclined to make every possible excuse for them when I considered that they had never really suffered and were in consequence unable to realise my sufferings.

The worst of all my sorrows was that I had not near me a single friend whose advice I might take. Only one vague hope remained in my heart, that my fiancé, after we had been married, would alter in character. Laura's tiresome caprices furnished an explanation and an excuse for his ill-humour. They would not trouble him any more after our marriage, and as soon as he should have learned of my sorrows he might become my best adviser and a true friend to me.

The date of our wedding was fixed for January 26, 1902. But matters did not go quite smoothly yet. In coming to the preliminary formalities I must furnish the authorities with particulars about myself. For a time I really thought that my marriage was impossible; and it even seemed to me that the secret designs of Provi-

EPILOGUE

dence had only placed me in so false a situation in order to make me understand beyond all question the error which I was about to make. But this idea was soon banished, for no sooner did the difficulty arise than a way was found of surmounting it. As a matter of fact I had not sufficiently taken into consideration the secret supervision over every step I took. I had not reflected that those who had succeeded in appropriating the authentic documents concerning my origin had also the power of fabricating others, without fear, to furnish me with a false identity.

However, it was not very easy to manufacture on the spur of a moment a satisfactory certificate of baptism whose date went back some twenty years — to 1882, to be precise. But this was not too difficult for the astute ingenuity of my persecutors.

Mrs. Kaiser, being a Dutch or English sectarian (I do not know which), was forced to decide to become a convert to Catholicism, and I, in the rôle of her supposed daughter, must be converted at the same time, so as to be able to marry a Catholic. Then, on the date of my conversion, a register of baptism could be produced to take the place of the papers necessary for my marriage. It was Mrs. Kaiser again who was entrusted with the whole affair, with the aid of the Rev. Josef Pfob, the head in Vienna of the order of St. Charles Boromeus; he was a person very well known in the capital and popularly credited with being engaged in numerous intrigues.

An indescribable scene took place. Although every nerve in my body throbbed with indignation, I succeeded at first in maintaining an appearance of calm. I refused pointblank to lend myself to such a farce, declaring that I was a Catholic already, and that I could not go through a pretence of conversion. It was true that I might be one who made little outward profession, but my soul was too full of genuine religion to insult thus by a sacrilegious imposture the worship in which I had been brought up. I had been baptised a Catholic on coming into the world, and no force should induce me to pretend a conversion from Protestantism to Catholicism.

Now once more I was overwhelmed with threats of the convent or the madhouse. But these terrible words no longer frightened me. At last in my exasperation, I answered curtly that they could put me where they wished, even in hell itself, for nowhere, I was sure, should I have so many miseries to suffer as were mine here.

This outbreak let loose upon my head a tempest of sarcasm, and in her anger (I admit, very much provoked) Mrs. Kaiser forgot herself so far as to strike me. As for me, my persecutions had had such an effect upon me that I was quite willing to contemplate the convent, and even the lunatic asylum, as a haven of refuge.

But they understood perfectly that they dare not dream for a moment of creating such a scandal just now. We were so well known in Vienna society that my sudden disappearance, on the eve of a wedding ceremony which was looked forward to as a social event, would have aroused a great sensation and furnished matter for never-ending talk, and talk, too, of a malicious kind. It was therefore necessary at all costs to escape from so dangerous a situation. A few days after the scene which I have just described, I received a fresh visit from the priest. But this time he was alone, and our conversation lasted for more than an hour. He tried, by every possible means, to make me abandon my first resolution. He employed every resource which he had, was amiability and kindness itself, but in vain. I remained immovable. Indeed, as his benevolence toward me appeared to me sincere, I confessed to him that, as far as I was concerned, I was delighted with all that had happened; for if I listened only to my personal wishes, I was in no haste whatever to marry. Upon these words, the old priest stopped short, asserting that my marriage was a question which could not be debated, and that the means would certainly be found of establishing the necessary evidence. Before taking his leave of me, he extracted from me a promise that I would come to see him next day in the vestry of his church. When the moment arrived, as I was attacked by scruples against keeping the appointment made so much against my will, Mrs. Kaiser found a way of overcoming any repugnance. I let her take me to the priest, thinking of course that such a step was one of no importance. In spite of this, the interview was interpreted by Josef Pfob as an actual ceremony of baptism, and consequently he obtained, unknown to me, the indispensable document which gave me an entirely false civil status, but a civil status nevertheless. It was only a few days later, when I saw matters rapidly advancing, that I understood the abominable trickery which had been employed against me. I refrain from any further comments upon this affair, and leave it to my readers to pass upon it the judgment which it deserved.

In the first days of my married life I came to realise that I had not yet found happiness, and that my presentiments, alas! had only been too true. It was not merely the feeble glimmer of my last hopes which went out now, it was all that remained of the sentimental illusions of my youth that came to final and utter ruin.

Although, in accordance with the custom on the Continent, I had seen my betrothed but rarely alone, still I had imagined I could see that his mind and heart had not remained total strangers to me. I knew him to be silent and melancholy, but at least I imagined him sincere and loyal.

Alas! how tremendous was the shock to my heart when I discovered my fatal error. On the day after the wedding I thought to perform the most sacred of duties by telling my husband my true story. But he stopped me at the very beginning and asked me, in a haughty, ironical tone, whether I was really so simple as to imagine that he was unaware of my identity, and to suppose that he had consented to marry a mere Miss Kaiser. He assured me that he was sharper than that.

What a sentimental fool I had been! I had thought that in marrying me he had but followed his own inclinations. Suddenly I perceived, with great clearness, the true reason for my instinctive hesitation to confide my secret to him before marriage.

I had been continually held back by the apprehension that our union might be prevented at the last moment. The apprehension, I have said; but should I not rather say, the faint hope?

And now I knew how little confidence I had in him to maintain a reserve that was certainly prudent, but equally as certainly uncalculated. This knowledge, coming late in the day, at once assumed a capital importance in my eyes. I saw what a mistake I had made in yielding to any hopes of conjugal affection. I understood how blind I had been, when, to excuse him, I attributed his sudden outbreaks of ill-humour to the ungracious welcome given him by Laura, my supposed sister, and interpreted his taciturnity as the natural outcome of the wretched life he led with his mother and the genuine grief which he felt over his father's loss. I had fancied that I appeared to him in the light of a young and thoughtless girl, unshadowed as yet by the black wing of sorrow. How I had erred when I tried to persuade myself that all would be changed after our marriage, when he would know all, would be sincerely sorry for the pain he had caused me by his cross and disagreeable ways, and would become the consoler, protector, and friend of whom I had so much need.

These reflections brought to me the clear conviction that I had only persisted in my resolve to marry him because of my certainty, as absolute as it was groundless, that my revelation would bring about a radical change in his attitude, a complete revolution in his ideas and affections.

So far from being realised, my fair dreams had only lured me on to ruin. I had not been saved, but betrayed. My husband suddenly appeared in my eyes as a monster of egoism. What confidence could I have in him henceforth? Was he not the agent of my enemies, the executor of the wishes of that invisible power which laboured incessantly not only to keep from me my just rights, but also to take away from me in this world all hope, however modest, of joy and happiness?

I must admit that he did his best to conquer his sullen humour and was successful at first. Perhaps the satisfaction which his face seemed to express was sincere; for, after all, had he not succeeded in his designs? He told me, indeed, that henceforward his career was assured, if only I renounced my schemes and so avoided all scandal. This confession, however, did but confirm my cruel certainty. It was perfectly clear that my marriage had been cleverly planned to reduce me to impotence. The husband chosen for me was from one of those official families, every generation of which is brought up systematically on respect for the established order of things, and educated in an atmosphere of traditional acquiescence; a man ready to obey in all that was demanded of him, and promising by the natural feebleness of his character that he would say and do nothing that would give trouble; a man, in fact, the very reverse of the *chevalier sans peur,* who is always ready to risk his life for the weak and oppressed.

Had it not been for the dreadful gulf between my husband and myself, my existence might have been happy enough. I was surrounded by material luxuries and comforts, and as I appeared to be ready to agree to a life of self-suppression things were made as easy as possible for me.

A great consolation came to me when I found that I was about to become a mother. On November 17, 1902, my son, Antony-Francis, was born. This event gave a new value to my life, creating a bond between my husband and myself. We sat long, side by side, watching the pretty pink, fair-haired baby on the white pillows of his cot. We made magnificent plans together for his happy future.

After all, at that period I had not much of which to complain. I was pampered and spoilt. I had all that a young society woman could desire, horses, carriages, servants, jewellery, clothes, etc. I began to entertain largely, and my at-homes promised to become among the most popular in Vienna. Not without intention, I chose my new acquaintances principally among the families of the members of Parliament belonging to the Polish party.

EPILOGUE

Among my friends I numbered Mr. and Mrs. Bilinski, and, above all, Mr. and Mrs. Abrahamovicz, who were pre-eminent in that party.

The success of my entertainments was exceptional, considering how young a woman I was. But, if I myself made new friends every day, the same was not true of my husband. He gave himself too important airs for his twenty-five years, and his sullen humour was taken for arrogance and vanity.

So two years passed. This pleasant existence, peaceful in spite of all its distractions, was not destined to last long. Soon a new catastrophe was to cast me upon a sea of troubles to which I had hitherto been a stranger.

On the eve of my wedding, Dr. Werner, who on Mr. Kaiser's death had been appointed my guardian, told me that the control of my fortune would be in my husband's hands, as I was still a minor. At the period I knew little about business — so little, indeed, that I considered it bad taste for a girl to think of money matters.

I have been asked frequently since whether there was not a marriage-contract between my husband and myself. There was none; but at that time I had no idea how its absence could affect my interests, nor even that such things existed.

I therefore gave my husband full powers. I knew that the proceeds of my fortune would suffice amply for our needs, and that was all I asked. I admit that this aloofness from the practical side of life indicated in me a certain tendency toward frivolity, for which my youth (I was scarcely more than twenty) was but a poor excuse. The blow was all the more brutally cruel when my husband confessed to me, one fine day, that he had been speculating for several months past and had lost almost all that we possessed. His fault was all the more unpardonable because our income was fully sufficient. For the moment I could not see the consequences of so grave a mistake; but they were brought home to me vividly when I was compelled to give up our expensive social activities, and even to go without necessities.

Later I came to understand, although the truth only dawned upon me gradually, that this new blow was dealt me by the same pitiless enemies to whom I owed so much. My relations with the Polish party had aroused the suspicions of the Court. No doubt it was feared that I might create for myself a party in Austria, and that the weakness of my husband might enable me so to dominate him that, instead of thwarting my plans, he would range himself on my side. So little wisdom had he, alas! that he had no idea that a trap was laid for him. Unfortunately, he even thought himself a clever diplomatist, and often his vain desire of making an effect led him to pass the bounds of prudence in his speech. Perhaps, with the intention of securing some tactical advantage, as it appeared to him, he let slip something of which the echo speedily reached our enemies and threw them into a state of alarm. So it was decided at Court that I must be completely crushed; the Austrian Court has exceedingly few scruples in such matters.

They knew that if I were ruined and penniless I should at once lose all support. They were perfectly well acquainted with my husband's character. His vanity, which made him consider himself more intelligent and stronger than anyone else, was cleverly played upon to lead him toward the temptation of speculation. He was given to understand that by speculation he might gain for himself a fortune sufficient to render him independent of his wife's. I have never been able to discover the names of the people who enticed him along the dangerous road. My husband was one of the least expansive of men; he never spoke open-heartedly to me, and on this subject above all others he pretended to wish to avoid tedious explanations.

A short while before the catastrophe my husband had bought a farm in the neighbourhood of Vienna, called Kleinhart. This was now almost the only property which was left to us. He had not, however, told me about the purchase until the bargain had been completed, and it had been made in his name, not mine. The whole property was in a lamentable state of disrepair. Still it offered us a last refuge, and as it was in close proximity to Vienna, we could live there all the year round, while my husband could at the same time go to his office every day.

At the first start, therefore, our situation did not seem entirely desperate. But we were not allowed to cherish such illusions long. Of course we had had no preparation for country life, and to put this tumble-down place in a proper state would have needed hard work on the part of a skilful and practical professional. My husband again thought, in the new circumstances, that he had the necessary ability; and, as by law the property belonged to him, I found myself perfectly helpless to correct by any good sense that I had the wild ideas he held about the restoration of a country estate. I must add that I was scarcely in a condition to enforce my views, for I was in a delicate state of health.

On December 6, 1904, my little daughter Elisabeth-Marie-Christine saw the light of day. Poor child, she was not welcomed with cries of joy like her brother. No one congratulated us upon her entry into the world. Not a single mark of sympathy or attention came to us from the brilliant society which so soon forgets those who have ceased to shine. My maternal love, however, was all the greater through my pity and indignation at this neglect.

Our position daily grew worse. For a whole year we struggled in vain to recover ourselves. My husband made blunder after blunder. Such gross stupidity and such inability to learn might seem beyond belief; but they were, nevertheless, the causes of our final ruin. Any small peasant could get the better of him, and he rapidly earned over the countryside the reputation of a man whom anyone could take in. Soon he was loaded with debts. Not having the courage and energy to face the situation, he pretended to be ill and went to spend the winter at Abbazzia, on the Adriatic coast, leaving me alone with our troubles. The task was beyond my strength, and every day I had to put up with cruel humiliations. At length it became impossible for us to stay in Austria. Besides, my husband was neglecting his official duties, and must now give up all hopes of a brilliant career. Nothing remained for us, therefore, but to quit our native land — to quit that land which for so many years had been for me a vale of tears, to escape from which was my sole desire.

In May, 1906, we left for Canada with our two children, and their nurse, Fanny Latzlsperger.

I allowed myself to cherish the fond hope that there, in totally new surroundings, escaping from the worry of our debts and shaking off the conventions which in Austria forced us to continue ruinous expenses in order to keep up appearances to the end, my husband might summon back his courage and with renewed energy might provide for his family, in however modest a way. As for myself, I would not shrink from the necessity of working

EPILOGUE

if this were to be the price of regaining ease and happiness in our home.

So as to avoid useless waste of money, we settled down in the neighbourhood of Montreal, at Sault-au-Recollet, where living was cheaper than in the midst of a city. But before long affairs moved in a way that looked ill for the revolution in Fortune's wheel for which I hoped. My husband, who had obtained a post as interpreter with the Canadian Pacific Railway Company sufficing for our modest needs, left it at the end of a few months to embark upon the precarious career of a company promoter. He dreamt of vast speculations, and wanted to float powerful companies, in which he never succeeded because he never had the smallest capital to start them on. All the while I saw gradually melting away our last poor reserve of money.

This went on for a year. Thanks to my never-ceasing efforts, and by making sacrifices which were most painful to me, I had for six years maintained appearances between us; for I wished above all, as a mother, that my children might have peace at home if they had no other joys. But now I saw myself faced by incalculable miseries if I did not take some step at once. My love of my children drove me no longer to preserve their father for them, but to save them from his hateful treatment. He had, in fact, grown brutal towards them, showing so little feeling for them that at last he could not bear to have them near him. As for me, he would have treated me as a total stranger in the end, had he not seen the advantage of looking on me rather as a faithful servant.

His outrageous attitude became so manifest that I understood that he had taken it up intentionally to drive me to the point of seeking a separation. Or did he, perhaps, look forward to some more tragic solution? Whatever his idea, he fell in at once with a suggestion which I made to him, that we should each go our own way. He was to pursue fortune on his own account, I must look after my children's welfare with my own.

He left for New York on March 25, 1908. As for me, in the company of the faithful Fanny Latzlsperger, who refused to leave the children, I went to British Columbia, and settled in Vancouver, a city then only in its infancy as regards time, but already in the full tide of prosperity.

At this supreme crisis of my fate, when it appeared as if I must have touched the very bedrock of misery, a new harvest of young hopes sprang up within me. For the first time after so many years of moral oppression, I felt myself delivered from the fetters of wretchedness and falsehood which had crushed my soul, and before me there seemed about to open a future bright with happiness.

It was at first, however, a very difficult task to provide for the material support of the four of us. It required, if I may say so without unduly praising myself, an energy rare in women, and a courage hard for anyone to muster. In America, it is true, and especially out West, it is thought no shame to be obliged to work for a livelihood after having been accustomed to ease. Misery does not exist for those who have the will to work. The first months were painful, I admit. Many were the times when I called back to mind that sewing-school, when amid all the poor little daughters of the people I seemed to myself to be merely diverting myself with their toil, just as one plays at soldiers. But nevertheless it was that little game of soldiers which had taught me the way to extricate myself now from what was in reality a terrible battle. It was truly some miraculous force which increased my strength. I had a comforting assurance that I was preparing the way for my decisive triumph, and that fate had only been so harsh to me to make certain the path of my future.

To-day, when the picture of my trials comes back to my memory, it has lost much of its cruel vividness, and to realise it I should be forced to live again in the same atmosphere which was then about me. In that country, seven years ago especially, it was impossible for a woman to earn her bread by sewing. On the other hand, at this time of the year — it was spring — it was no good to think of teaching. So it was by no means easy to see what to do. I had thought of hiring a house and sub-letting the rooms; but I soon had to renounce this idea, for I could not find a house and was glad to get rooms for myself. I therefore resigned myself to taking a situation as cook at the Yale Hotel, so as not to have to spend more of the little money still left to me. After a short time, when I felt myself more secure, I opened a small shop for the sale of Viennese confectionery. Even in the Far West the epicures can appreciate confectionery of this kind.

In my circumstances my faithful Fanny was a very great help to me, and I can honestly say that but for her my life would have been infinitely harder. As it was, our affairs went on better and better, and at the end of a few months I was able to sell my little business at a good price, which was all pure gain to me. This money was the starting-point of the new fortune which I built up during these years, thanks to lucky speculations in land, while I provided for the daily needs of the household by giving lessons in languages and the piano.

This was certainly a time of hard toil. But it is the period of my life upon which I look back with the greatest satisfaction, not to say pride. It was then that I learnt to have confidence in myself. It was then that I came in closest contact with the realities of life, of which I knew little up to then, and few women in my sphere can ever know. And it was then, perhaps, that I developed those fighting qualities which, helped by the serious instruction which was given to me in childhood, will make of me one day, I hope, a fearless champion of the rights of the poor oppressed, the counsellor of those who have need of help.

My husband went back to Vienna a few months after our separation. As he had quitted his post under government at the moment of our departure for America without taking leave of his superior, his name had been crossed off the official list. Nevertheless, on his return he was at once reinstated, and a very short time afterwards he came in for a promotion which, to say the least of it, was unexpected.

In conformity with the rules of military discipline, my husband should have asked for permission to leave his regiment. This he failed to do, and, having made no reply to the reiterated demands of the Austrian consul at Montreal, he had been proclaimed a deserter. In spite of this, on his return, instead of being visited with some punishment as anyone else would have been, he was immediately restored to his regiment with the rank of lieutenant, and even had the rare privilege of being received in audience by the Emperor. How can I help being confirmed, by this paradoxical treatment of my husband, in the certainty that his conduct, though apparently as free as it was blameworthy, was in reality but the result of his blind obedience to orders received from those over him, and that he was in some measure no more than the docile instrument of a concerted plan to ruin me? Was he therefore rewarded for having executed his task so well? However that may be, he certainly never again troubled himself about my children or me.

Months passed by. I made in Vancouver some excellent acquaintances, who gradually extended my circle. As Vancouver was at this time a town of not more than eighty thousand inhabitants, the better people in society there were not so numerous that an addition to their ranks ran any risk of being overlooked. In this *milieu* I received general consideration — although, of course, my true identity was unknown. It was now that I met him who was destined to become my second husband, the Count Zanardi Landi, who from the first moment showed himself a most devoted friend to me. He was truly the personification of the good fortune of my life. As brave as he was energetic, he came to be for me the sure counsellor whom I had always wanted. It was he who first made it plain to me that since I had children I was not entitled to renounce my rights, for one day when it would be too late, they would be justified in reproaching me bitterly for my neglect of my claims.

Besides, he argued, would my mother have wished me to act thus? Had she dreamed for me of such a life as I was leading, in obscurity and almost in unhappiness? Surely respect for her memory must inspire me with firmer resolution. I must try to inform my nearest relatives of my existence and acquaint them to what a level I had been reduced. I must enlighten the ignorance in which they had been kept concerning me.

Consequently I decided first of all to write to the Emperor. I addressed to him a letter dated October, 1908, sending it under care of his private cabinet, and accompanying it with a portrait of myself. I took the precaution of requesting the private cabinet to put my letter before the Emperor himself.

I received no reply — as indeed I had anticipated. Another urgent letter written by Count Zanardi Landi in the December of the same year was equally left unanswered; as was one which I sent in March, 1909, to my sister the Archduchess Marie-Valerie. As it was reported that any letter addressed to the German Emperor was bound to reach him, I took on myself to write to him in the following September. I was not unaware, I may say, that all these attempts at correspondence would be without result. What could I hope with such feeble resources as I had at my command? I was only too well acquainted with the ways of Courts; but I wished, in acting as I did, to salve my conscience, so that it might not be said against me that I had failed to take the necessary steps.

I could not yet dream of proceeding to more drastic and vigorous action. My lawyer, one of the best known in Canada, advised me to avoid all scandal before obtaining a divorce which should give me the custody of my children. I could indeed easily be reduced to silence by the mere threat of taking them away from me. Canadian law being the same as English, and very strict as regards divorce, I had recourse to the United States. But the divorce, which secured to me the custody of the children, could not guarantee that this would remain mine in Canada or in Austria. I had now, however, the right to take Count Zanardi Landi as my second husband. I spent over a year on these proceedings without obtaining my great object, which was to give me absolutely and irrevocably the possession of my children, who alone made my life of any value. There remained but one way open to me. Since in Austria recognition would be refused to the divorce obtained in the United States, I could only demand of the Austrian authorities that they should arrange a divorce in what manner they might think fitting. But after a year of negotiation through the medium of correspondence, we were convinced that I should get nothing so long as I did not go to Austria myself. At first this step was very distasteful to me. I found myself on the horns of a painful dilemma. Either I must part from my children during my visit to Europe, or I must expose them to great dangers if I took them to Austria with me.

I therefore made up my mind to go without them, my dear, good Fanny assuring me that they should be as well looked after as if I stayed with them myself.

On July 15, 1911, I started on my journey, accompanied by my second husband, whose protection inspired me with abundance of courage. Yet what grief I felt at the moment of departure! Since my little ones had come into the world there had never been a separation between them and me — and now I was going so far and for so long. Only a mother can really understand the pang. But anyone who realises that for years I had consecrated my life to providing for them, and that my sole thought was their future happiness, can perhaps form some idea of the state of my mind when I left them to go to the other end of the world in pursuance of my duty as a mother.

We reached London on August 1st, and made a stay of three weeks there, because there was nothing useful to be done in Vienna at a time of general holiday. From London we went on to Paris, and from there to Munich, where we arrived on August 28th.

We proposed to stay for some time in Munich, whence we might make excursions round the Lake of Starnberg. On the very day after our arrival we went to Feldafing. I was eager to see the place where my poor mother had spent so many of her summers, where she had experienced such deep joy and had also suffered so terribly. We had only meant to stay one day at Feldafing, but an unforeseen circumstance kept us there longer. By a coincidence which we had not had the slightest reason for anticipating, at the hotel to which we went, the Hotel Kaiserin Elisabeth, there was staying Queen Maria-Sophia of Naples, my mother's sister. I felt that it was incumbent on me to take full advantage of so favourable an opportunity. Wishing to act with perfect correctness, I thought that I must write in the first place to her secretary, M. Barcelona. I begged him to come and see me, wishing to have an interview with him. He replied to me as follows:—

Feldafing, 6, 9, 11.

Madam,

I have just received your letter, and I hasten to present my excuses if I cannot pay you a visit.

Her Majesty lives in great privacy, and is here incognita, and I too, in consequence, am unable to visit anyone.

Please accept the assurance of my profound respect.

Your devoted servant,

Barcelona.

This answer showed me that I had done wrong not to indicate the reason of my overture. It seemed to me, therefore, to involve no loss of dignity if I explained to him in a second letter that I had only desired to see him because I wished to ask of Her Majesty, through him, the favour of being received by her, being the daughter of a great friend of hers. This was his reply to my second letter:—

MADAM,

I duly submitted to Her Majesty your request, but the illustrious lady receives nobody whom she does not know and can make no exception to this rule. I regret, Madam, that I cannot render you this service and beg you to believe that I am
Your devoted servant,
BARCELONA.

This M. Barcelona was a man of no extraction, who gave himself airs nevertheless. He took upon himself, as I discovered later, to refuse my request without even submitting it to his sovereign.

I might easily have approached my aunt in the course of one of the many walks which she took all alone; but my pride prevented me. I therefore decided to write to her direct. On the morning of September 8th, while she was engaged on the finishing touches of her toilet, I gave my letter to her second valet, Marsala. Slipping a twenty-mark piece into his hand, I begged him to take the letter at once to its destination, which he did, under my eyes. I watched him enter straight into the bedroom of the Queen, who was seated in front of her toilet-table.

I waited all day long and the following day without receiving an answer. I imagined that my fond relative might be afraid that I was in distressed circumstances and that my approach to her was made with the object of begging for pecuniary assistance from her. In my very brief note I had simply asked her whether she was aware of my existence and whether she would allow me to speak to her. I wrote her a new letter, in which after assuring her of my absolute disinterestedness I requested no other favour than to be allowed to kiss the hand of the sister of my much lamented mother.

I sent this second letter to her through the same medium as the first. The date was September 10th. On the previous evening I had been to see the parish priest of Feldafing to ask him to have a *Requiem* mass sung on the anniversary of the death of the Empress of Austria. He stated that the 10th being a Sunday, he could not have the *Requiem* mass before the 11th; and he added that in deference to the sister of the deceased he must discover whether she had not herself the intention of taking this pious step.

On the night of the 10th, about nine o'clock, my aunt sent for me to come to her rooms. I had been so much on the watch all the day long that I was not particularly surprised when Marsala the valet knocked at my door to ask me to come at so late an hour.

As my bedroom was quite near the Queen's — she being in No. 8 and I in No. 9 — it was perfectly easy for me to slip into hers without being seen.

The first few minutes of the interview were marked by an embarrassment which can be readily understood. I strove to repress my deep emotion, while the Queen, to hide hers, was extremely reserved in her manner. Nevertheless there was something about her which strangely recalled my poor mother. My aunt's behaviour, appearing to me a true family characteristic, instead of upsetting me, had quite the opposite effect, and even attracted me. Still I hid my real feelings, not wishing to be the first to abandon my reserve. In my opinion there is nothing in the world more tiresome than that somebody, who is quite ignorant of your sentiments, should overwhelm you with professions of friendship and urge upon you the claims of relationship. So I waited for my aunt to address the first word to me.

Soon she said, refraining from either using my name or calling me simply Madam: "I have received your letters, which, I must confess, have disconcerted me, for the person you claim to be is supposed to be no longer alive."

Her remarks, though they indicated in so brief a compass so strong a distrust in me, failed to abash me. Did they not show, after all, that she had been aware of my existence? The sudden profound satisfaction caused by this sent a rush of blood to my head.

"If your Majesty will only deign to listen to me," I answered calmly, "I believe it will not be difficult to prove my identity and to convince your Majesty thoroughly that they deceived you when they said that the Empress Elisabeth's daughter was dead."

With a gesture of her hand she pointed out a chair to me.

I began by asking whether she knew any details of my life, since she seemed to know that I existed. She answered with an affirmative nod of her head. Then, to discover down to what point she had been able to follow me, I asked whether she knew that I was married and had two children.

She gave another nod of her head, accompanied by a benevolent smile, which she could not repress. From that moment the ice was broken. I plucked up my courage and told her all.

She was soon convinced that it would have been impossible for me, unless I were really her niece, to recall to her so many minute details and mention so many circumstances that only her sister's daughter could know.

She knew that my husband had caused my ruin and that we had left with our children for Canada. But there her knowledge of my history ceased, for she had been told that out there I had soon succumbed to a dangerous disease of the throat. It must be confessed that while she knew me to be alive she had never manifested much interest in me; but I was perfectly well aware how difficult it was for her to do anything against the express desire of the Court, and on behalf of a niece with whom she was, after all, unacquainted.

I had my children's pictures upon me, and I showed them to her. She was struck by my little girl's resemblance to my poor mother, and by the Habsburg expression on my little boy's face.

I told her finally about my second marriage, and what a faithful friend, what a brave champion I had gained by it.

Before taking my leave of her I spoke to her about the *Requiem* service for the next day, and she promised to be present at it or at least to come to the church immediately after it. Then as I was about to depart she stretched out her hands to me, and, with a smile full of amiability, drew me towards her to embrace me. " Until to-morrow! " she murmured as she led me to the door, making a great effort to restrain the emotion which she was evidently feeling.

Next day, just at the moment when, in despair of seeing her, we were going toward the holy water basin, a few minutes after the end of the service, she entered the church. Holding out her hand to me she requested me to present to her Count Zanardi Landi, who had remained a little distance away. She spoke to him in Italian, having a marked preference for this language, it seemed. She thanked him for all he had done for her niece and bade us adieu, like a good Catholic, with the words: " May God bless you, and grant that you may soon be united in His sight too! "

On the evenings that followed I went to see her again in her room. She did not for the present wish our meetings to be observed, so that it was like a charming renewal of the long hours I used to spend in secret with my mother in the hotels where we stopped, when, after all her suite had retired, I had crept into her bedroom.

The Queen slept very little, not going to bed before one o'clock, and getting up again at six.

Several days passed thus. Every night we made an appointment for the next day. I need not tell that this sweet friendship was a delight to me. The Queen told me after the second evening to drop the formal " Your Majesty," and call her simply " Aunt," and she always addressed me affectionately by my name. Without my asking her to do so, she informed me that she had at once taken steps to have my position regularised; and she said she hoped for a prompt result, for she could not believe that the Imperial family would refuse to do anything for one of its own members when it knew the circumstances of the case.

On the morning of September 15th there was brought to me the visiting-card of the parish priest of Feldafing, on which was written: " The Rev. Karl Kolb, while returning his best thanks for the forty marks, begs to request Madame to call and see him to-day, if possible, at two in the afternoon, to receive an important communication."

That same morning the proprietor of the hotel informed me that Her Majesty's secretary begged me not to insist on being received by her as she could see no one at all. As the secretary was totally ignorant, like the rest of my aunt's suite (with the exception of Marsala), of our secret interviews, I could only suppose that he had sent this message, in its discourteous form, in order to increase his own importance. In any case it was not permitted to me to discover his real motive, as I never saw my aunt again.

In the afternoon I went to the Abbé Kolb's and found that what he wished to communicate to me was this. The Queen had charged him to beg me to leave Feldafing as soon as possible, if I wished to spare her grave annoyance. She had received the answer to the effort which she had made on my behalf; and this in laconic fashion ordered her not to interfere in matters with which she had no concern. He had been asked to express the very profound regret which such an ending to the affair had caused her; but I must know how dependent she was upon the persons whose help she had solicited on my behalf, and how powerless she was without this help. She gave me her blessing and prayed earnestly that I might succeed in spite of all opposition.

Once more my hopes faded away. I must state that, notwithstanding this great disappointment, I never dreamt for a single instant of blaming my old aunt or of entertaining the least resentment against her. I was absolutely sure that in the circumstances in which she was placed she had acted with the best intentions possible. Yet I was none the less brought to despair, I confess.

EPILOGUE

During those few days I had been living again in the atmosphere of my past existence, to which I had not even had the wish to return. What had spurred me on to act was the thought of establishing my children's rights, for personally I had long abandoned all ideas of re-establishing my rights and only wished for peace. It would not have been without a certain pride, indeed, that I should have enjoyed a freedom won by my own strength and resolution, after having had such great difficulty in overcoming the weaknesses of my heart. But there had been a reawakening in me of lawful ambitions. My interviews with my aunt had taken me back to the world in which I had been born and for which I had been trained. I had been treated for some days with the consideration to which my origin gave me a right.

And now suddenly I realized the inflexible laws governing the fate of all, against which no human will can fight. I saw with the utmost clearness that the independence which I had so fondly imagined that I had secured for myself would never actually be mine. How like a human being is to a plant, which one may tear up from the soil that bears and nourishes it, but, transplanting it to some foreign soil, finds that it cannot become acclimatised. Just so an imperial princess, bearing in the cradle the burden of her rank, is bound by all the fibres of her being to the traditions of centuries, which not even the most democratic education can efface. It is in her blood, her whole soul is steeped in it. It is a useless struggle to try to become merely the same as the rest of the world. At a crisis there will always be some little weakness which will overmaster her, from which there is no possible escape.

I knew now for how little counted my desire for independence and calm resignation. I understood that it would never be possible for me to renounce all finally, and the revelation affected me considerably — though, of course, I could not altogether complain of my lot, having a faithful companion to console and protect me, a husband who cherished me tenderly and was attentive to the least of my wishes.

On the day after my interview with the priest, September 16th, we left Feldafing. My pride rightly prevented me from making any attempt to see my aunt again.

My divorce in Austria was fixed for the month of October. With an anguish impossible to realize I set out for Vienna. Was I not putting my head in the lion's mouth? I was playing a game in which my own person was at stake, and my children were the prize. The journey across Austria was a prolonged agony. I saw a spy in every fellow-passenger, and every glance thrown my way made me suspect that I was specially watched. Then in Vienna, at the law-courts, when I had to give my name and address, my heart was wrung. But there was not the slightest hitch. On October 21st the divorce was decreed, leaving the children entirely mine.

I stayed ten days longer in Vienna. I now felt more at ease. After all that had passed, the letters I had written, and the adventure at Feldafing, I had come to the conclusion that no attempt would be made against my person for fear of a scandal. I met some good friends of old times, to whom I had not ventured to confide my troubles, but who now told me that they had been quite aware of them, and had even guessed the secret of the mystery which enveloped me during the Empress's lifetime. Belonging to Court society, they had felt bound by prudence to hold their peace. Now they protested their absolute devotion to my cause, and undertook to form a party at Court to uphold me.

I must be allowed to make an exception, in the case of these friends, to the rule which I have hitherto followed, and to withhold their names, as otherwise I should ruin them irretrievably. The gratitude and the admiration which I feel for their noble spirit of justice are so keen that, in spite of any personal benefit which I might get by naming them, I must be silent for their sakes.

All the while they were making their brave endeavours they were under the greatest apprehensions about my safety. Yielding to their urgent entreaties, I resolved to leave Vienna, and took my departure on November 2nd. As they thought my husband's assistance absolutely indispensable for some time still, and, on the other hand, did not consider it prudent to let me travel in the sole company of a maid, they arranged that I should be escorted by a young couple, an officer and his wife, who agreed to be responsible for me, though the cost to them might be nothing less than the impossibility of ever going back to Austria again. I stopped for a short while at Tann, in Bavaria, at the house of my good Fanny's mother. Here at least, in Europe, I had a home. Naturally, I wished to avoid all hotels.

While I was at Tann my friends were not sleeping. After careful deliberation they arrived at the conclusion that, above all, we must have the opinion of a good Viennese lawyer if we would be safe. The man selected was Dr. Walther Rode, who declared that nothing could be done without a personal interview with me. It was therefore settled that we should meet on November 7, 1911, at the Park Hotel, Munich.

The lawyer put me through a thorough cross-examination, which was only briefly interrupted for lunch. I was "in the box" for nine hours, answering all his questions. He made no secret of the fact that his original attitude towards me was one of distrust. But at the end of our interview he rose, and, kissing my hand, he said to me: "Madam, I beg you to consider me henceforward one of your most devoted supporters. I have no doubt whatever of the absolute truth of your statements and the complete justice of your cause."

On his return to Vienna, Dr. Rode began operations. On November 11th, he wrote to me that my friends had submitted my case to the military as well as the civil departments of His Majesty's private cabinet; that consequently Prince Montenuovo, Grand Chamberlain to the Court, Baron Bolfrass, head of the military, and Baron Schiessl, head of the civil department, knew all; and that he thought that steps should be taken immediately, so that on Monday, the 13th, he was going to apply to the courts for permission to inspect the Empress's will. The authorities could not evade giving an answer of some kind to this request, without much delay, and would therefore be compelled to consider officially the question of my birth.

In accordance with this programme Dr. Rode on Monday, the 13th, made his application in the proper quarter. The document consisted of seventeen typewritten pages, and set forth briefly the whole of my history. A week passed without any visible result. Dr. Rode wrote to me on the 15th that on the day after the application Prince Montenuovo and Baron Bolfrass went together to an audience with the Emperor, undoubtedly in connection with my affairs, as these two officials could not, of course, settle so grave a question and take on them-

EPILOGUE

selves the responsibility for the consequences which must inevitably follow.

In a second letter, dated November 18th, Dr. Rode informed me that he had made another application to the Minister of the Imperial Household,[1] claiming a civil status for me as a member of the Imperial family. One paragraph of this letter deserves quotation: —

"I have no doubt that, since the Court is now acquainted with this affair which had been thought buried for ever, everyone is in a state of utter perplexity. Besides, it is easy to understand that the head of the Imperial Family, were he to recognise you, would come up against all kinds of obstacles; and unless he succeeded in overcoming his objections, no force on earth could make him depart from his attitude of non-recognition towards you. However, it should not be forgotten that his age is such that thoughts of the hereafter must always be present to his mind, and consequently one must be prepared for unforeseen results."

Another letter from Dr. Rode, also dated the 18th, told me that it had been impossible for him, up to now, to trace my birth-certificate, although he had even gone so far as to search the Jewish registers in order to satisfy himself that I was not mentioned in them.

So finished a week of waiting. On November 20th I first of all received a letter from my lawyer begging me to give him a second interview at Passau on the Austro-Bavarian frontier; and then, in the afternoon, a telegram saying: —

"Matters apparently taking good turn. Appointment postponed. Letter follows."

[1] In Austria the Minister for Foreign Affairs also fills this post.

Next day came two letters from Dr. Rode. One, sent by express messenger, was very short, and informed me that he had had an interview with Councillor von Seidel. The second was more detailed, and told me how he had been summoned to the Chancellor's office, where he had been received with the utmost amiability. He had talked with Herr von Seidel for more than an hour, and had been promised by him that he would get the Grand Marshal, Count Zichy, to receive him very shortly. "I think I may say," concluded Dr. Rode, "that I succeeded, with my application, in hitting the bull's-eye."

It was easy to see in these letters my lawyer's enthusiasm about my affairs. Noticeable also was the benevolent attitude taken up toward him by the Court, where it was tacitly conceded that I had a perfect right to act as I was doing and no one disputed my claims.

On November 23rd, Dr. Rode was due to be received by Count Zichy. From this date his conduct suddenly changed. After having written to me almost every day, and sometimes twice in one day, he left me now forty-eight hours without any news whatever — and that when he knew that we were waiting most anxiously for the result of his interview with Count Zichy. At last, at midnight on the 24th, we received a telegram: —

"Shall be at Passau, Bayrischer Hof Hotel, Saturday night, 25th."

Next day we set out early so as to be punctual at the appointed spot. Dr. Rode told us that he had succeeded in having his interview with Count Zichy, who had begged him above all to maintain absolute secrecy about the affair. He himself, he had stated, had no power to give an official answer. This was Prince Montenuovo's duty,

EPILOGUE

although he certainly had the right of making unofficial propositions.

Count Zichy added that the Emperor was too advanced in age, and in too precarious health, to listen to matters which might grieve him seriously. But the Court — always this anonymous, indefinable " Court " — was not altogether hostile to me, and, having certain funds available, made me the offer, through my lawyer, of a million crowns.

Hearing this, I felt instinctively that Dr. Rode no longer was actuated by my interests alone. I answered at once that what I claimed was not money, but my birthright; that, thanks to my husband, I had no need whatever of the former; and that what I ardently desired was to meet my family and be received by them, if only in private and unseen by the rest of the world. Their money was nothing to me.

Dr. Rode at once raised his offer to a million and a half; and, impressed with the certainty that he would obtain my consent in the long run, he began to describe minutely the plan which must be followed to bring about, indirectly, a conclusion of the affair with the Court.

My husband here gave me a secret sign to let Dr. Rode proceed to the end of his argument. The doctor explained to me the solution which the Court suggested. I must call upon Mrs. Kaiser as a witness and demand from her circumstantial details about my birth, and her relations with the Empress of Austria. Mrs. Kaiser, in order to avoid a great scandal, would offer me the cash, which the Court would refund to her.

I was careful not to express my opinion with regard to such a proposal. I simply told Dr. Rode that a decision of such importance required more than an hour's reflection, and that I would send my answer in writing in a few days' time. We parted, therefore, on Sunday, the 26th, Dr. Rode under the impression that I was about to fall blindly into the pit that had been dug for me, and I only too sure that he was no longer acting frankly and that I must be on my guard. Still, I did not wish to make an enemy of him. I wrote to him on the 27th, explaining to him that my husband and I, seeing the affair growing more and more complicated, had decided after mature thought to avail ourselves of the help of a lawyer of non-Austrian nationality to second his efforts. We supposed that he would not take offence at this, because he himself, when he had first taken up the case, had pressed us to adopt such a course. Then, when we should have discussed matters with the lawyer whom we might select in Italy, we would communicate to Dr. Rode our intention of proceeding or otherwise.

By return of post I received an answer which betrayed the writer's extreme uneasiness. This time the letter was not typed, but written entirely in Dr. Rode's own hand.

"I am not at all offended at the idea of an Italian lawyer," he said; "but if you engage one, I must ask you kindly to dispense with my services — especially as I am persuaded that I am powerless. The parties in question will do absolutely nothing, and I should be wasting my time and my life in a vain and futile struggle."

We went immediately to Italy, where I consulted several lawyers. All expressed identically the same opinion, that Dr. Rode had been constrained by the Imperial Court to back out of his task; but, as the object which I had in view was not to make money, the only advice they could give me was to publish the book which I now pre-

EPILOGUE 337

sent to the world, so that my claims might at least come before the bar of public opinion.

I proceeded at once to make arrangements for the issue of an Italian version of my story. A prominent publisher, who had brought out books for the members of the Italian royal family, undertook the task, agreeing to secure publication in France also. The affair seemed well on its way, when, in February, 1913, only a few days before the printers had completed their work, the Italian government stepped in and confiscated the plates, proofs, and all.

I had meanwhile gone to London again, and had settled in a house there. When I discovered that my speedy return to Canada would be impossible, I had sent over for my faithful Fanny to bring the two children to me in London, where they arrived in August, 1912.[1] It was in London, in the following February, that the news of the Italian government's action reached me. Immediately afterwards I learnt that the French publication had also fallen through. The serial and book rights had both been placed with the same firm in Paris, which now, though the French version had been made and set up by the printers, decided not to publish it. I know the sum — forty thousand francs — which was paid to secure the book's suppression in France. With regard to what happened in Italy, my husband in the previous November had seen Cardinal Rampolla, with whom he had discussed matters for two whole hours; and we heard through the publisher that it was the Vatican which made the first

[1] I may mention that in London Fanny was approached by Austrian agents, who endeavoured to induce her to purloin documents from me or to betray my confidence in other ways; but all in vain. The poor woman was killed on February 27, 1913, near the Marble Arch, being run over by a motor-car while out with the two children, who escaped as though by a miracle. Some of my readers will no doubt remember seeing the incident recorded in the newspapers at the time.

move for the suppression of the Italian version, acting no doubt on behalf of the Austrian government.

The Italian publisher, owing to his business connection with members of the royal family, could not say much in the way of protest. The newspapers did not fail to report the affair and to remark on the illegality of the suppression; but somehow they were induced to let the matter drop.

I was therefore foiled in my attempt to make my story known to the world either in Italian or in French. I knew that German publication was impossible, except through the medium of some Swiss publisher, when exportation of the work across the frontier could be stopped. I decided to make my appeal in the English language, being anxious, moreover, to reach the great public of England and America.

Thanks to my own exertions, thanks to the assistance of disinterested friends, and thanks to the man who has grown to be a fond father to my son and daughter, I have at last come to see the day when my book will be in the hands of the reading public, which will be, I am sure, an impartial judge towards me and a generous protector to my children.

THE END

INDEX

INDEX

Abrahamovicz, Mr. and Mrs., 311.
Alexandra, Empress, 158.
Antony-Francis, birth of, 310.
Auersperg, Princess Aglae, and Rudolf of Austria, 217.
Augusta of Bavaria, 136.

Bartholme, Miss, 71.
Bayerl, Commissioner Georg, 252, 255, 259.
Bilinski, Mr. and Mrs., 311.
Billroth, Theodore, 62.
Bismarck and Ludwig II of Bavaria, 141.
Bolfrass, Baron, 231, 233, 332.
Bombelles, Count Charles, 214.
Brahms, Johannes, 62.
Bratfisch, 228.

Carito, Rafael, 44.
Chotek, Countess Sophie (Duchess of Hohenberg), 240;
assassination of, 245;
marriage of, 240;
political influence of, 138, 241.
Christomanos, Dr., and Elisabeth of Austria, 41.
Conrad of Bavaria, 136.
Court of Vienna, life at, 175, 207, et seq.
Crombé, Madame, lessons from, 8.
Crown Prince of Austria. See Rudolf.

Dancing classes, 261.
Dürckheim-Montmartin, Count Alfred von, 147.

Elisabeth-Marie-Christine, birth of, 313.
Elisabeth of Austria, Empress, —
and Bertha Habrda, 203;
and Court life, 39;
and Dr. Christomanos, 41;
and Ludwig II of Bavaria, 173;
and Professor Kraus, 105;
assassination of, 282;
at the Riviera, 83;

attempts to secure recognition of Countess Zanardi Landi, 274 et seq.;
birth of, 28;
childhood of, 32;
courtship of, 33;
"eccentricity" of, 43, 61;
explains her secret, 25, 126;
her habits of study, 40;
in mourning for Crown Prince, 9;
letters to Countess Zanardi Landi, 182, 186, 259, 277;
letters to Frau von Friese, 59, 64, 116, 168, 257;
public appearance in Vienna, 157;
relations with her family, 276;
sympathy with Ludwig II of Bavaria, 145;
telegram from Ludwig II of Bavaria, 147;
wedding of, 35.
Elisabeth of Bavaria, marriage of, 135.
Ersie, 223.
Eschenbach, Baroness Ebner von, 62.
Etlinger, Mina, 54.

Feldafing, 322.
Fellner, Ferdinand, 164, 185, 188, 262, 268
Ferdinand-Karl, Archduke, 244.
Ferdinand-Max, Archduke, 68.
Fernwald, Prof. Karl Braun von, 1.
Francis-Joseph, Emperor, —
affection for Countess Zanardi Landi, vi;
courtship of, 33;
interview with Rudolf, 225;
promises protection to Ludwig II, 147;
takes steps for recognition of daughter, 279;
tragedy of his life, vi;
visits Empress at birth of Countess Zanardi Landi, 1.
Francis-Salvator of Tuscany, Archduke, 138.

342 INDEX

Franz-Ferdinand, Archduke, assassination of, 245;
at Territet, 171;
history of, 239.
Franz-Joseph-Otto, 248.
Frauenerwerbverein, the, Countess Zanardi Landi at, 159.
Friese, Frau von, —
assumes charge of Countess Zanardi Landi, 47;
death of, 289;
history of, 48;
illness of, 180;
letter from, to Countess Zanardi Landi on death of Empress, 284;
rule of, 201;
spies of, 251.

Geneva, visit to, 174.
George of Bavaria, marriage of, 136.
Gisela, 135;
birth of, 25.
Gmunden, 93.
Gödöllö, 69.
Goëss, Countess, 2;
death of, 161.
Goldmark, Karl, 62.
Gudden, Dr. von, 146, 150, 151, 153.

Habrda, Bertha, at sewing-school, 203, 249.
Habrda, Johann, 203, 218, 230, 237, 253.
Hain, Fräulein, 53.
Hanauseck, Fräulein, 98, 101.
Hélène, Princess of Thurn and Taxis, 29, n., 32 et seq.
Hoffmann, Frau Louise, 15.
Hohenberg, Duchess of. See Chotek, Countess.
Hold, Herr Hans, 15.
Holnstein, Count, and Ludwig II of Bavaria, 143.
Hungarian Millennium, 109, 115.

Insanity of Wittelsbachs denied, 29.
Isabella, Archduchess, 241, 244.
Ischl, Countess Zanardi Landi at, 115 et seq.
Ives, Miss, 12 et seq., 27.

Joseph II of Austria and the Church, 212.

Kaiser, Laura, 12, 51, 94, 202, 298.
Kaiser, Mr., death of, 299.
Kaiser, Mr. and Mrs., agree to bring up Countess Zanardi Landi, 2;
at Pörtschach, 281;
Countess Zanardi Landi leaves, 51;
holiday with, 61;
silver wedding of, 115.
Kaiser, Mrs., illnesses of, 78, 96.
Karl-Franz-Joseph, Archduke, 242, 246.
Karl-Ludwig, Archduke, and Prince Rudolf, 213.
Karl-Theodor, Duke, 29, n., 32.
Karrersee, 191 et seq.
Kinsky, Countess, 138.
Kleinhart farm, 313.
Kolb, Abbé Karl, 327.
Kraus, Professor, as tutor of Countess Zanardi Landi, 101;
at Ischl, 116;
diary of, at Ischl, 117;
introduced to Elisabeth of Austria, 105;
recognises Countess Zanardi Landi, 103.
Krieau at Vienna, 183;
Kühnelt, Dr. Richard, early meetings with, 300;
goes to Canada, 314;
marriage of, 307;
returns to Austria, 318.
Kundman, Karl, 62.

Lainz, Countess Zanardi Landi's home at, 12.
Lambertus, Father, 15, 52, 57.
Langbath Lakes, 64.
Larisch, Countess, 220.
Latzlsperger, Fanny, 314;
death of, 337, n.
Leopold, 56.
Letters and extracts from letters, —
from M. Barcelona to Countess Zanardi Landi, Sept. 6, 1911, 322, 323;
from Elisabeth of Austria
to Countess Zanardi Landi, 182, 186, 259; July 18, 1898, 277;
to Frau von Friese, May 10, 1893, 59; 64; July 4, 1896, 116; 168; Dec. 18, 1897, 257; Dec. 26, 1897, 257;
from Fellner, Ferdinand, to Countess Zanardi Landi, 269;

INDEX 343

from Friese, Frau von, to Countess Zanardi Landi, 284;
from Rode, Dr. Walther, to Countess Zanardi Landi, Nov. 18, 1911, 333; Nov. 27, 1911, 336.
Levinsky, Joseph, 137.
Liechtenstein, Prince, 231.
Loschegg, 228.
Luccheni, Empress of Austria's assassin, 293 n.
Ludovica, Duchess, 31.
Ludwig II of Bavaria, 28, n., 29, 66, 67;
and Bismarck, 143;
and Elisabeth of Austria, 140, 173;
and money, 143;
and Richard Wagner, 173;
death of, 153;
history of, 141;
plot for escape of, 151;
plots against, 145 et seq.;
sepulchre of, 76;
taken to Berg, 150;
Luitpold, Prince, 142, 143.

Maria-Josepha, Archduchess, 244.
Maria-Sophia, Queen of Naples, 29, n.; 322.
Marie of Bavaria, Queen, 30.
Marie-Valerie, Archduchess, 244.
Marie Vetsera, Baroness, and Rudolf of Austria, 220;
assassination of, 234.
Marschall, Gottfried, 224, 237.
Max-Emmanuel, Duke, of Bavaria, 29, n., 61.
Maximilian, Duke, of Bavaria, 31;
children of, 28, n.
Maximilian II, 30.
Mayer, Clarisse, 162.
Mayer, Father, 100.
Mayerling, 218;
riddle of, 207.
Montenuovo, Prince, and Countess Zanardi Landi's claim, 332;
history of, 16, n.

Name-day in Austria, 160, n.
Nopsca, Baron, 81.

Osterholzer, 145, 149.
Otto, King of Bavaria, insanity of, 30.

Paoli, detective, and Elisabeth of Austria, 43.
Pfob, Rev. Josef, 305.
Philip of Coburg, Duke, 224.
Pidon, Mademoiselle, 12 et seq., 27.
Pirker, Aloïs, 2, 12, 54, 256, 294.
Pörtschach, 281.

Riviera, visit to the, 83.
Rode, Dr. Walther, 331.
Rothschild, Baroness Adolphe, 174.
Roumania, King and Queen of, at Ischl, 94.
Rudolf, Crown Prince of Austria, —
amusements of, 209;
and army, 213;
and Baroness Marie Vetsera, 220;
assassination of, 8, 234;
birth of, 25;
childhood of, 209;
Empress Elisabeth's love for, 134;
freemason, 211;
funeral of, 10;
interview with Emperor of Austria, 225;
marries Princess Stephanie, 216;
relations with Emperor of Austria, 222;
religious training of, 211.

St. Charles's Day, 160.
St. Gilgen, 61.
Sarajevo crime, the, 245.
Schedivi, Theresa, 2.
Schiessl, Baron, 332.
Sewing-schools, 159, 202, 249.
Sonntag, 146.
Sophia, Archduchess, 31;
and Elisabeth of Austria, 37.
Sophie-Charlotte, Duchess of Alençon, death of, 178.
Stephanie, Princess, 216.
Szilghy, President von, 115.
Sztaray, Countess, 197.

Territet, visit to, 168.
Thyr, Elsa von, 72.
Thyr, Frau von, 74, 261.

Valerie, Archduchess, 136;
birth of, 26;
marriage of, 138;
political ambitions of, 138.

INDEX

Veldes, 188.
Venice, 68.
Vienna in May, 182.

Wagner, Richard, and Ludwig II of Bavaria, 173.
Washington, Baron, and Ludwig II of Bavaria, 146.
Windt, Commissioner Camillo, 252, 255, 259, 297.
Wittelsbachs, history of, 29.

Zanardi Landi, Count, first meeting with, 319;
marriage to, 321.
Zanardi Landi, Countess, accident to, 79;
and Frau von Friese, 47;
and servants, 53;
at dancing classes, 261;
at the Frauenerwerbverein, 159;
at Frau von Thyr's dance, 165;
at the Riviera, 83;
birth of, 1;
birth of her daughter, 313;
birth of her son, 310;
claims birthright, 331;
decides to publish book, 337;
discovers her mother, 20;
divorce granted, 320, 330;
early home of, 12;
Empress's plans for, 176;
falls in love, 166;
first marriage of, 307;
goes to Canada, 314;
goes to school, 71;
goes to Vancouver, 316;
illness of, 94;
meets Ferdinand Fellner, 164;
meets Maria-Sophia, Queen of Naples 324;
punishment of, 14, 23;
recognised at Gmunden, 99;
recognised by Professor Kraus, 103;
religious training of, 52, 57;
second marriage of, 321;
settles in London, 337.
Zanders, 148, 151.
Zita, Archduchess, 247.

www.ingramcontent.com/pod-product-compliance
Lightning Source LLC
Chambersburg PA
CBHW030216170426
43201CB00006B/101